When News Lies

Media Complicity and the Iraq War

Other Books by Danny Schechter

Embedded: Weapons of Mass Deception—How the Media Failed to Cover the War on Iraq (Prometheus Books, 2003; ebook version: coldtype.net, August 2003)

Media Wars: News at a Time of Terror (Rowman & Littlefield, 2003)

News Dissector: Passions Pieces and Polemics (Akashic Books, 2001; ebook version: electronpress.com, 2001)

Hail to the Thief—How the Media "Stole" the 2000 Presidential Election, Ed. with Roland Schatz (Inovatio Books, Bonn, Germany, 2000; ebook version: electron-press.com, 2000)

Falun Gong's Challenge to China (Akashic Books, 1999, 2000)

The More You Watch The Less You Know (Seven Stories Press, 1997, 1999)

For other works by Danny Schechter,
visit www.newsdissector.org/Dissectorville

When News Lies

Media Complicity and the Iraq War

DANNY SCHECHTER

Including the complete DVD and Script of the Film
WMD (Weapons of Mass Deception)

SelectBooks, Inc.

When News Lies: Media Complicity and the Iraq War

Copyright © 2006 by Danny Schechter

This edition published by SelectBooks, Inc. For information address SelectBooks, Inc., New York, New York.

Library of Congress Cataloging-in-Publication Data
Schechter, Danny.
When news lies : media complicity and the Iraq War / Danny Schechter ; featuring the DVD and script of the film WMD (Weapons of Mass Deception)
p. cm.
Includes bibliographical references and index.
ISBN 1-59079-073-1 (pbk. : alk. paper)
1. Iraq War, 2003–Mass media and the war. 2. Mass media–Political aspects.
3. Journalism–Political aspects. I. Title.
DS79.76.S334 2005
070.4'4995670443–dc22

Manufactured in the United States of America

10 9 8 7 6 5 4 3 2

For a Journalism of Truth and Courage

Contents

Acknowledgments

My thanks to Mediachannel.org for carrying my reports and blogs, to the team at Globalvision who aided and abetted on the film, especially Kozo Okumura, Kristine Cardoso, and David DeGraw; to our investors who helped fund *Weapons of Mass Deception (WMD);* to Tony Sutton for posting an earlier ebook edition of this volume and my book *Embedded: Weapons of Mass Deception* on his Canadian-based website, www.coldtype.net; to Kenzi Sugihara of SelectBooks for publishing this far more ambitious version; to Lynne Glasner for editing; and to my daughter Sarah for encouragement; and to so many others in whose debt I remain.

See: http://www.wmdthefilm.com for more information on the film and my daily blog for daily updates to the story as it unfolds at: http://www.mediachannel.org/weblog

And as always, your feedback is welcome.
Write: Dissector@mediachannel.org

Foreword

Michael Wolff

On a hot summer day in 2003—not long back from covering the invasion of Iraq from the information-deprivation tank that was Centcom's headquarters in the Persian Gulf—I helped organize with Britain's Guardian newspaper a conference at the New School University in New York City to discuss the media's performance in the war.

It was a hot summer day because, frankly, I thought if we waited until cooler weather and a bigger audience in September, nobody would be all that interested in the war anymore. The story would certainly have peaked by then.

That's why I was a little taken aback when, just before the conference, Danny Schechter called me and asked if he could film the event for a documentary he was doing.

But then, I have always thought that documentaries were bizarre in that way. How can you spend months and months or more on a topic of immediate interest and possibly hope it will be relevant when it finally—and often by a circuitous route—gets to its audience?

In a way, the answer to why Danny was at my conference with his film crew goes to the heart of both the documentary form and the Iraq War.

Documentaries reflect a certain sort of obsessiveness—certainly made by obsessives. This compulsion to record every detail, this need to tell the whole story, this myopic focus on solving a puzzle—why these events happened as they happened, and what do they mean—can vividly recreate the fascination of the train wreck. Even in a peaceful world, I realized when I first saw it, Danny's film would be riveting–divorced from the event itself, Danny's portrait of hacks at war (or not at war, as the case may be) approaches high comedy. It's Evelyn Waugh in *Scoop*–that most famous novel of journalism's bracing incompetence.

But the other point is about the war itself and what Danny understood. While I was seeing the Iraq War as just another grievous example of media incompetence and mendacity which would shortly pass, upstaged–perhaps as soon as autumn came around–by some other unimagined example of grievous incompetence and mendacity, Danny, more accurately, saw Iraq as, in itself, an epic story.

Not only would the story still be around when the weather got cooler, it would grow ever larger, increasingly complex, more disturbing and tragic–Abu Ghraib was still months away–and would show no signs of doing anything but continuing to become more dangerous and corrupting and incompetent as I write this two summers later.

At the time of our conference, fewer than 200 American soldiers had died in Iraq. Now, 1740 are dead. By the time you read this ... well, the math is running at about three soldiers a day.

In some sense, I think Danny's early and instinctive understanding that Iraq was on its way to becoming a disaster of epic proportions–the signal disaster of our time–comes from his long acquaintance with what happens when the media punts.

At the center of Danny's film lurks the unsettling–and one might hope, guilt-ridden–issue of what might have happened if the U.S. media had been more skeptical of the Bush White House's stated reasons for going to war and of its cheerful forecasts of how *doable* it would be to wage such a war.

The largely unasked questions are haunting:

–How was it possible that a nation under draconian economic sanctions could have developed and maintained a sophisticated, technologically demanding, advanced weapons program? (Answer: it wasn't possible.)

–What was the plan if Iraqis fought back? If, in fact, we were not greeted with flowers? (Indeed, on what basis was everybody thinking we would be greeted with flowers?)

—Beyond getting rid of Saddam Hussein himself, what then? What was the larger goal—and, by the way, how would we accomplish it?

—Once in, if it all went wrong, how would we get out?

The perfect obviousness of these questions, the clear necessity of having to ask these questions, and the failure of the media to make them a central part of the story, demonstrates, rather painfully, that the American media was either hopelessly asleep at the switch, or so conflicted in its desires (to curry favor with the Bush Administration, to please the managers of the media corporations that owned the news outlets, not to disturb the shareholders of these corporations, not to look foolish when, if as the administration was promising, the war got over fast) that it was unable to do its job.

The fact that the media eschewed almost every bit of basic skepticism—decorating its coverage with flag graphics, patriotic icons, and grandiose rubrics—had two literally mortal effects:

The first was that we went to war at all. A reasonable amount of doubt, some serious questioning of the underlying assumptions, and some dutiful reporting on the basic situation would surely have made the Bush case for war much harder to make.

The second was that once we were there, the media had to continue to support the effort—in many ways they continue to support it still—because it was, in effect, defending itself. Even now, with the WMD canard wholly destroyed—with the press shown up to be fools and dupes—the best you get from the media poobahs are lots of tortured and circumlocutory explanations which ultimately add up to the conclusion that while the media was absolutely wrong about everything, it was ultimately right anyhow. And, obviously you can see *our intentions were surely good.*

Danny, not least because he has been covering the media longer and more consistently than anybody else, understood that this what-me-worry, see-no-evil, let's-get-on-with-the-show countenance on the part of the American media was a sure-fire recipe for the epic disaster that we now have on our hands.

There is something else to add here about the fact that Danny, doing his job as long as he has been doing it, has become something like the 2000-year-old media critic—he's one of the few guys who can be counted on to consistently know the real score.

Virtually everybody who writes about the media nowadays is in the thrall of the media. Media reporters tend to be like political reporters—we're in the Beltway, and deeply impressed with ourselves for being here. Indeed, this is who we want to be (media people) and where we want to work (in the center of the media business). So don't do anything or say anything to get us into trouble.

Danny (a.k.a. "Danny Schechter the News Dissector" back at WBCN, in Boston, in the 1970s) got over this a long time ago. Danny Schechter in *Weapons of Mass Deception* is to the news media what Joseph Heller in *Catch-22* is to the American military and the Second World War.

Our "news dissector" finds the media to be not only mendacious and incompetent, but absurd. It's absurd because it doesn't even know that it is mendacious or incompetent. Or, even that mendacity and incompetence has become so woven into the fabric of its function, that mendacity and incompetence has become the standard of a job well done.

Danny, by the way, is always laughing. It invariably puts me in a good mood to see him. The reason he's always laughing, I believe, has to do with his 2000 years of experience as a media critic. Unlike most of our fellow media critics, Danny is long past trying to come up with a strangled rationale for the world we live and work in. He sees clearly through to the ridiculousness; the cravenness; the pretensions; the corporate phobias; the small-time, pathetic, yellow-dog cowardliness that can only but get us into loads of trouble.

You can't help but laugh before you weep.

Michael Wolff is probably America's most provocative media writer. He is a columnist and contributing editor at *Vanity Fair* magazine and former columnist at *New York* magazine. His books include: *Burn Rate: How I Survived the Gold*

Rush Years on the Internet (Simon & Schuster, 1998) and *Autumn of the Moguls: My Misadventures with the Titans, Poseurs, and Money Guys Who Mastered and Messed Up Big Media* (HarperCollins, 2003). He is the 2002 winner of the National Magazine Award for columns and commentary.

Prologue

Journalism is more than a job; it is a calling that sometimes demands a call to action. As the son of a published poet, writing was in my bloodstream from an early age. But my heroes were Edward R. Murrow, I.F. Stone, and other writers, commentators, and muckrakers who fused a mission to their craft.

I have been a media maven all my life: From the summer camp newsletter I co-edited as a teen with CNN's Jeff Greenfield, in which we set out to give an alternative voice to community issues, to investigative reporting for *Ramparts*, THE muckraking magazine of the 1960s, my instinct was always to ask questions and probe for the truth. In 1970 I started working in broadcast journalism as an on-air newscaster at Boston's pioneering WBCN, where my moniker "news dissector" started and has stuck ever since. I set out to bring a more critical sensibility to reporting. I was later told it was a way of "branding" my work.

Some of my "news dissector" critiques in the late '70s were directed at mainstream and TV news, which was even then, becoming more entertainment than news. Those were the years of Vietnam, where government deception known as "the credibility gap" was already well advanced. That experience showed me how government spin and misinformation works, forever souring me on trusting official sources.

It was also the Watergate era, when investigative reporters helped bring down a President. These formative years as a media watcher helped me develop the skills of reading between the lines and challenging skewed news. I had no idea then that my career path would take me from writing to radio to the world of TV. I quickly graduated from local TV news to producing programs at CNN and ABC News, environments that did not value my outlook or share my proclivity for asking deeper questions. I detailed those experiences with all their contradictions in a mediaography. The title tells the story: *The More You Watch, the Less you Know* (1999).

Despite going against the grain, I also wanted to try to effect change on the inside; while I didn't fundamentally change any of the mainstream companies and/or programs I worked for, I didn't leave them the same either. Working inside what I now consider the "media beast" was a way to see who called the shots and how certain ideas were given prominence while others were sanitized or marginalized. Along the way, I learned some skills and came to respect the professionalism of many colleagues who didn't always agree with me even as I grew increasingly disaffected. I wanted to align the media I was making with my values and play some role in changing a media system that wasn't in sync with those values.

I am proud of a great deal of my work but I also know what could have been much better had I had freer rein and had I not been under-resourced and constrained by the pressures to conform to the homogenized, look-alike and feel-alike templates used to disseminate the news. These experiences allowed me to cite chapter and verse when I later began to speak out against media practices, including the coverage of war.

Some of this work did achieve recognition which is often cited to give me "legitimacy" as a journalist. Yes, I won a Nieman Fellowship in Journalism at Harvard and Emmys and a George Polk Award and the like. I appreciated it all, but I also saw how cynically the "award culture" is regarded by the media industry, where every TV station showcases its statues for excellence while continuing to churn out drivel. It is not uncommon for programs to win awards one day and be canceled the next. It happened to me.

Just look at all the heavily hyped awards shows on TV and ask yourself if they really mean anything except more celebrity pandering and cheap programming. When I was awarded my first Emmy in a ceremony presided over by then-Governor of Massachusetts Michael Dukakis, I explained how a week earlier in a radio commentary, I had denounced the Emmys as a self-indulgent exercise by stations that used their few awards to deflect attention from wall-to-wall shoddy shows. The audience gasped before I quickly changed my tune, winked and said, "I now feel these Emmys are the best way mankind has found to honor excellence." The audience laughed nervously. If surveyed today, most of the people in that audience back in 1979 would probably agree that TV is worse today, not better, despite all the awards and technical innovation.

After my network years, I defected from the mainstream media in 1988 to become a "network refugee," co-founding Globalvision, an independent media company where I co-created TV series and produced and directed more than 15 documentaries, often probing issues that the media had relegated to the back pages or were missing completely. I was later labeled a "hero of downward mobility" for doing socially conscious shows on budgets that gave new meaning to the term "low overhead."

I had joined the media with a desire to showcase the problems of the world and came to see that the media was often times THE problem. I decided to do something about it by co-founding Mediachannel.org in 2000, which has become the world's largest online media issues network. I write a 3000-word daily "dissection" on the news and views of the day through my blog at Mediachannel. I have written six books since 1997, including *Media Wars* and *News Dissector,* with two more on tap. My most recent book is *Embedded: Weapons of Mass Deception—How the Media Failed to Cover the War on Iraq* (2003).

My film, *WMD: Weapons of Mass Deception,* is a follow-up and response to what I saw in writing that last book, "embedding" myself in front of my TV and comparing and contrasting coverage across the spectrum of print and television, both here and abroad. Making the film offered an opportunity to fight fire with fire, to show what I was talking about as only a visual medium can do. The film is an exercise in investigative reporting and personal filmmaking.

When News Lies gets into the politics of the film and the deeper issues it raises with more detail and elaborated argument, as only a book can do. This is not just an examination of the coverage of the war in Iraq but also of my own attempt, however imperfect, to scrutinize and challenge it. Together, this unique multimedia "package" adds ammunition to the media war I am still fighting against the ongoing deceptive coverage of the Iraq War. *When News Lies* is an appeal for a broader engagement with our media as an issue. I have answered my call and now hope readers will as well. This work is one journalist's cry for truth and media responsibility.

In the end, in this "faith-based" era, works like this are gestures of hope, hope that they will touch a chord or awaken a conscience somewhere, or move someone more eloquent than I to speak up and speak out and help move these dark times as they so need to be moved.

In writing these words, I am reminded of a joke from the "new South Africa" where some journalists couldn't find anyone who ever supported the apartheid system. That is likely to be the case eventually with this war as the casualties mount, as things continue to go badly in Iraq, and as public opinion turns.

In the summer of 2005, polls found only 38% still backing the "war for Iraqi freedom." Even Bush-supporting conservatives were becoming more skeptical as the costs of the war became undeniable and the Pentagon less confident of victory.

This frustration began to increasingly percolate into the opinion pages, finding expression in a media that can no longer cling to its patriotic correctness and collective certainty. When the Global War on Terror (GWOT) was ultimately repackaged as a "global struggle against violent extremism," policy makers finally acknowledged that this war is no "cakewalk" and not even a real war because there can be no simplistic solution to a deep political problem. Noted George Packer in *The New Yorker,* "The Administration is admitting that its strategy since September 11 has failed, without really admitting it."

And then, just as this book was off to press, an unexpected media implosion with important admissions, this time that our most venerable media institution the *New York Times* had become a vessel of misinformation and deception.

Judith Miller, the *New York Times* reporter who had become a lightening rod for war criticism, and who had nominally gone to prison after refusing to reveal her source in the Valerie Plame affair, suddenly recanted: "WMD– I got it totally wrong. The analysts, the experts and the journalists who covered them–we were all wrong. If your sources are wrong, you are wrong."

Was it all some honest mistake? I don't think so. This way of framing the issue narrowed her culpability, blaming it all on her "sources," but having her admission–"I got it wrong"–did not do much to explain why the *New York Times'* self-described "Little Miss Run Amok" got it wrong and for so long, or how her stories went unchallenged internally, and why her behavior was defended by the paper's top executives.

As I write, there is still much we don't know about Miller's role. She says she was also given a top security clearance and intimates even deeper collusion between our elite corporate media and the government. We don't have all the details of these questionable practices, but we do have an important confirmation of malfeasance on the record.

Jeff Cohen, founder of Fairness & Accuracy In Reporting (FAIR), spoke for many media critics in saying in an article published in October 2005 on Commondreams.org:

> There's a special reason this scandal is so personally satisfying to me as a media critic. It's because elite journalism is on trial. Powerful journalists are playing the role usually played in these scandals by besieged White House operatives. They're in the witness dock. It's a *New York Times* reporter who is failing to recall key facts ... mysteriously locating misplaced documents ... being leaned on to synchronize alibis. Elite journalism is at the center of Weaponsgate, and it can't extricate itself from the scandal.

Times editor Bill Keller offered a waffling apologia of his own inaction in an internal memo posted on the newspaper's website:

> By waiting a year to own up to our mistakes, I allowed the anger inside and outside the paper to fester. Worse, I fear I fostered an impression that the *Times* put

a higher premium on protecting its reporters than on coming clean with its readers. If I had lanced the WMD boil earlier, I suspect our critics—at least the honest ones—might have been less inclined to suspect that, THIS time, the paper was putting the defense of a reporter above the duty to its readers.

Would he consider journalists like me among his "honest critics"? I doubt it, and I am not sure if that reference just masks a deeper desire to determine who has the legitimacy to stand in judgment. What seems clear is that the *New York Times* had believed its own distorted coverage, protected the distorters and is still incapable of investigating its own role and the role played by other media outlets.

Juan Cole, a University of Michigan professor and the country's leading blogger on Iraq, points toward a deeper probe about the unholy alliance between right-wing money and ideology writing:

> The wider context is that Rupert Murdoch, and Richard Mellon Scaife, and other far rightwing billionaires have deeply corrupted our information environment. They are in part responsible for what happened at the *New York Times*. Miller attempts to excuse her shoddy reporting on Iraq's imaginary weapons of mass destruction by saying that "everyone" got that story wrong. But the State Department Intelligence and Research Division did not get it wrong. The department of energy analysts were correct that the aluminum tubes couldn't be used to construct centrifuges. ElBaradei of the International Atomic Energy Agency was not wrong. Imad Khadduri, former Iraqi nuclear scientist, was not wrong. "Everybody" got it wrong only in the sense that "everybody" had been brainwashed by Rupert Murdoch.

You can't blame one man. As critical as I am of Rupert Murdoch for this failure, a system of corporate-run media is involved. Was the *Washington Post* or CNN or CBS much better? In the end, this is not a story implicating just one reporter or one mogul or one news outlet. It indicts a myriad of institutions and the industry they are part of with some notable exceptions including the hard-hitting team at *Editor & Publisher* that has stuck to the story like a dog on a very juicy bone.

There is more rot to expose; more revelations to come.

As the government changes its tune, the media tends to change, too. Hopefully this small book will contribute to the growing realization that our journalistic community has more admitting to do. We still have a critical and independent watchdog role to play.

The voices in this book need to be heard, but it will not be easy. After all, Bob Dylan's famous refrain, "something is happening but you don't know what it is, do you. Mr. Jones?" was written about a journalist at *Time* magazine.

Another singer and poet, Leonard Cohen, understood the power and the limits of the critical word in his anthem *Hallelujah:*

"I did my best, it wasn't much
I couldn't feel, so I learned to touch
I've told the truth, I didn't come to fool you. …

Danny Schechter
New York City

"If you are looking at a map of the world and wondering where the United States is, you can find it over there, trapped between Iraq and a hard place."

–John Bell Smithback
Author, *Idiom-Magic*
www.Idiom-Magic.com, July 2005

Preface

Unembedded and Uncensored Reporting
Dahr Jamail
Iraq War Correspondent

In these times of corporate-controlled media, the job of monitoring what the public is being fed in terms of news has become more critical than ever. Perhaps never before has a society had such access to both independent and foreign news sources via the internet; yet the sad fact remains that most Americans rely on the mainstream news sources available on their televisions. Most of these news sources have now made it clear that their interests are in serving the bottom line rather than honest journalism.

Thus the need to constantly monitor what these outlets produce is greater than ever in order to combat the lies—yes, that's what they are—that most Americans are being inundated with on a daily basis.

I first met Danny Schechter at the World Tribunal on Iraq in Rome, Italy in February, 2005.

He testified in front of a panel of experts. His thesis was simple:

There were two wars going on in Iraq—one was fought with armies of soldiers, bombs and a fearsome military force. The other was fought alongside it with cameras, satellites, armies of journalists and propaganda techniques. One war was rationalized as an effort to find and disarm WMDS—Weapons of Mass Destruction; the other was carried out by even more powerful WMDS, Weapons of Mass Deception.

To me, this statement, along with the rest of his excellent presentation sums up what I have witnessed first-hand during my eight months of reporting from occupied Iraq. For without the corporate media sell-job of this illegal invasion and ongoing occupation of Iraq, over 100,000 murdered Iraqis would still be alive today, along with over 1600 U.S. soldiers [as of May 2005], and U.S. taxpayers would not have been fleeced for over $300 billion of their hard-earned currency.

But Schechter's expert testimony was just the tip of the iceberg of the work he has been doing for years as the "news dissector." A one-man watchdog of our corporate media, his work has consistently highlighted the importance of his ongoing job of working to keep the corporate media in check.

While he was working each day to provide the facts about the "news" that corporate media outlets were streaming into the homes of Americans, I spent most of 2004 reporting on the daily atrocities occurring in Iraq.

Working in Iraq as one of a handful of independent journalists, I can personally attest to the myriad difficulties encountered there. Kidnapping, bombs, fighting, rampant crime, lawlessness and constant power outages are the daily reality for those of us who ventured into the streets to get the news first-hand. Interviewing Iraqis at the scene of bombings, talking with soldiers at checkpoints, documenting testimonies of detainees after they'd been released from Abu Ghraib are the fruits of labor for those of us who refuse to embed with the military.

The risk is great, but worth it in order to work as a true journalist, rather than succumb to "hotel journalism," as Robert Fisk accurately terms the method most corporate media journalists now use in Iraq. While it is much easier to act as a stenographer for the military in Iraq, repeating their military press releases from the safety of a hotel room or military base, getting the facts means talking to U.S. soldiers without embedding, and to Iraqi civilians and doctors in order to accurately reflect the brutal nature of the failed occupation.

Thus, my coverage of Iraq differs greatly from that provided by corporate media because I work to show how the occupation has affected U.S. soldiers and the Iraqi people, showing their dignity alongside their suffering.

Proper coverage of Iraq should show daily the true cost of the occupation, both to the Iraqi people and U.S. soldiers, rather than affirm the daily military and government press releases that act as cheerleaders for the military commanders and U.S. Administration who continue to insist that things in Iraq are getting better. Proper coverage should show that next to no reconstruction is occurring in Iraq well over two years into the occupation; it should investigate the companies that have been awarded huge no-bid contracts in an effort to hold them accountable to U.S. taxpayers. Proper coverage should regularly scrutinize the responsible members of the Bush Administration for leading our country into an illegal war and occupation that has turned into the biggest disaster our country has known since Vietnam.

With the U.S. corporate media continuing to prove their inadequacy and irresponsibility on a daily basis regarding Iraq and just about every other important topic, the time for the public to utilize independent reporting is upon us.

Using the internet to read foreign media and independent journals is an easy method.

Just as important is taking advantage of sources like Schechter (www.mediachannel.org) and groups such as FAIR, to allow oneself access to the truth behind the lies propagated by most mainstream outlets.

Dahr Jamail is a widely-admired American freelance correspondent who bravely covers the Iraq War for internet outlets like the NewStandard and other news agencies. He has spoken widely about the war and its coverage across the United States.

Preface II

If You Don't Like This War, Wait for the Next One

Sam Gardiner
Colonel, U.S. Air Force (Ret.)

How could so many smart people have been so wrong about the rationale for the U.S. attack on Iraq? Why has our democracy failed us?

The Congress failed us: Our representatives assumed the role of cheerleaders without either balances or checks.

The intelligence professionals failed us: They dutifully followed the government storyline and assumed their role in marketing the product.

The military failed us: Somehow blinded by their own salesmanship, they weren't prepared for anything after the fall of Baghdad.

Finally, the media failed us: We needed good journalism, and it was not there.

During the first six weeks of the war, I was under contract with the "News Hour with Jim Lehrer" to appear regularly with an analysis of the fighting. That obligation forced me to probe very deeply into what was happening on the ground, what was being put out in the regular press briefings and how the media was covering the events.

As U.S. forces pushed on toward Baghdad, I became increasingly concerned with what I was hearing. At the time, my feelings began as just uneasiness. I have been around things military for over 30 years. I was hearing military press briefers talking about "terrorist death squads" rather than irregulars. Military people don't talk like that. What was happening?

My unease turned into somewhat of a compulsion. I spent four months following threads. What had been said by the Administration and the military? Where did the stories originate? What turned out to be the truth? Who was responsible?

By the end of my four months, I had a very comprehensive picture. There was so much fabrication. We had not just entered a war—we had entered a world of fiction. I had identified 50 stories that were fabricated in the course of the marketing effort before and during the war. I had done a detailed analysis of some of the press conferences by the Secretary of Defense and Chairman of the Joint Chiefs of Staff. Less than half of what they said was truth. The rest was either fabrication or spin.

The political operatives were doing what they do. I guess I could understand that a little. I was pained, literally pained, by military officers not telling the truth. General officers were behaving in a way that would have gotten them kicked out of a military academy had they been cadets. An officer's word is his bond. There is no footnote that says tell the truth "unless working to get support of a war for the political leadership."

My research was good. I had uncovered things no one else had seen. I was ready to break my news to the world. I discovered, however, the world did not care. The media was not interested in the story.

I went to the *Washington Post.* Four of their best reporters agreed to listen to me for 45 minutes. They were very impressed with what I had done but not interested in doing anything with my work. One of my examples was how the *Post* had been duped on the Jessica Lynch story. I don't know. Maybe they did not want to investigate themselves.

I talked to producers of "60 Minutes." I got a couple of very nice lunches in expensive restaurants, but no interest in the material. The whole story was just too complicated, I was told, and they wanted stuff that would be "more focused."

The editor of *The Atlantic* reviewed my work. Again, I got a nod for good research, but his email said that his "readers already knew they had been lied to."

The *Los Angeles Times* did show some interest, but they wanted more detail on ten of the stories I had identified as being fabrications. These were stories that had not previously been made public. One of their reporters went to Iraq and was looking into one of the stories. Unfortunately, he died of a heart attack and after that, the paper completely lost interest.

I even had some discussion with my friends at the "News Hour." Again, they were polite, but said they don't do investigative pieces.

By this time, I'd had enough. I had to get this monkey off my back. I had to move forward rather than to keep looking back. I had to have some closure. My solution was to publish my stories on the web.

That was when Danny Schechter and I became acquainted. We talked by phone. Exchanged emails. He came to Washington. We discovered a kinship. We shared a passion for truth. We shared a belief that the line had been crossed.

Danny Schechter's book is not a history book. Its importance is not in our understanding the past. More than anything, he is warning us to be prepared for the future.

In July 2003 as part of my research, I attended a conference in London on information warfare. I heard Administration PR consultants and military officers talk about the lessons they learned from the Iraq War. They were candid. They were pleased with what they had done.

In the next war, the message makers said they could do better. In some cases, they said they had lost control of the Iraq story. That won't happen again. In some cases, they did not counter negative stories quickly enough. That won't happen again.

They said in the next war they don't want to let retired military people take away the story context. Since I was one of those retired military people who did that on the "News Hour with Jim Lehrer," I took that statement personally.

Based upon what I heard at that conference and in other places, I would say that if you did not like what went on in the last war, wait until the next one. It will be much worse.

We have to take Danny Schechter's message seriously. The stakes are very high. His is a plea for making our democracy work.

Sam Gardiner is a retired U.S. Air Force colonel who has taught strategy and miliary operations at the National War College, Air War College and Naval War College. During the early part of the Iraq War, he appeared regularly on the "NewsHour with Jim Lehrer" (PBS) as well as on BBC radio and television and National Public Radio.

Note: Danny Schechter interviews Sam Gardiner in the film *WMD*.

"As journalists struggle to report on and understand their times, they cannot escape being part of their times. ... During the last several decades, American society has moved steadily to the right and so has the journalism that reflects that society. Too many reporters and editors seem to have become 'embedded.'"

–Ron Javers

Assistant managing editor, *Newsweek International*

Nieman Reports, Summer 2005

Opening Salvo

W*hen News Lies* details an examination of media coverage of the Iraq War through the war's second anniversary in the spring of 2005. This book and companion film, *WMD,* together tell a multi-layered story of the war itself and the way in which it was spun and miscovered by so many journalists and leading media outlets in the U.S.

My report on the role of the media in the Iraq War began with an earlier book, *Embedded: Weapons of Mass Deception,* in which I tracked the TV coverage that Americans were exposed to from the run-up of the war through the summer of 2003. *When News Lies* brings the story up-to-date, furthering the chronicle while trying to ferret out the shifting rationales given for engaging in the war in the first place. When *Embedded* was written, it was a rather lonely dissent because I focused on the media coverage while a large and feisty global anti-war movement put all the blame on the Bush Administration, largely ignoring the key support role played by TV news outlets.

There were a few journalists who complained that journalists were failing. In the *Independent* in London, Mary Dejevsky wrote under the heading "Let's be honest: journalists failed" (3/2/04):

> It is hard now to think back to September 2002 and January 2003 when the government issued its two dossiers on Iraq's weapons. To hazard that these [the WMDS] might not exist was to invite ridicule. ... Very few of us have anything like the specialist expertise needed to assess the technical information we were given [about the alleged existence of WMDS].

A few newspapers are finally legitimizing the issue even as TV news fails to acknowledge its role. Michael Ryan challenged his colleagues in the *Houston Chronicle* in August 2005:

> The news media are failing to acknowledge their own responsibility for the invasion of Iraq, even as they report with glee Cindy Sheehan's antiwar protest outside George W. Bush's ranch in Crawford …

> Coverage of the Administration's high-profile pitches to promote war was so blatantly unbalanced, the media sometimes looked like an arm of the Bush propaganda machine …

Earlier in 2005, a *New York Times* writer called the critics of the day "lonely people." "Lonely"? Had he missed the 30 million people in the street in the largest protest in the history of the world? In fact, there were critics on media outlets worldwide, and many in the U.S., especially in the independent media sector. The problem is they were largely ignored, and still are.

When News Lies revisits the media coverage of the ongoing war with a deeper indictment of the role of the media. The addition of the film, *WMD,* adds a visual dimension to the story I've been telling through *Embedded;* various essays, columns and articles that have appeared in print; and my daily blog at Mediachannel.org about the media war being fought alongside of the military conflict. In many ways I consider myself at war with the war and its coverage.

My concerns are, and for a long time have been, focused on the uses and convergence of media in an era, as Marshall McLuhan once put it, in which "the coverage is the war, … news men and media men around the world are the fighters, not the soldiers any more." *(Understanding Media,* 1964).

When News Lies offers a subjective assessment and a personal perspective of the subject because it is also about this journalist's own fight for larger truths. My battle is being fought not in some academic institution but in the media trenches, where my weaponry "deploys" the ammunition of words, online and off, through media appearances, lectures, panels and op-ed columns, along with the power of documentary cinema to expose and challenge a carefully constructed pro-war narrative disseminated by the U.S. media.

The film itself as a subject is included in *When News Lies* not as a self-promotional exercise; it's because I believe why and how our media is made (including my own) is a legitimate topic to examine. My first book, *The More You Watch, the Less You Know,* delved into the internal culture of media companies to try to explain their arcane decision-making processes. This is important not only to expose the intricacies of mainstream media but also to discuss the politics and impact of counter or alternative media in challenging a dominant media paradigm. In my view, it takes a media insider to best explain how it all works, and an outsider to evaluate what effect it has. *When News Lies* not only critiques the mainstream media but dissects my own work as well.

I am a believer in participatory journalism. I don't pretend, like so many of my colleagues, to be a detached "objective" observer. I don't deny I have a point of view or that I can make mistakes. At the same time, I try to be careful in my conclusions and to avoid simplistic media bashing. After all, I am a media maker, too, struggling to get my work read and seen in an environment of declining respect for fact-based journalism.

I often put myself into my work as a witness, explaining my motivations and rationale. It makes for more honesty. In *When News Lies,* I also speak personally, and sometimes humorously, about what a struggle the *WMD* film project has been without minimizing the obstacles that independent filmmakers face. The journalists who covered the war were well-equipped and well-compensated by big media companies. Those of us who challenge them are not.

When News Lies is based on my own close observations and monitoring of many media outlets from the run-up to the "shock and awe" campaign, to the devastation it created in the cradle of civilization, to the continuing occupation and the ongoing battle to engineer a partial exit strategy. It peers into the way our media system helped make the Iraq War palatable to a frightened public and therefore possible and also examines the media crisis inside a much larger political crisis.

When News Lies represents an attempt to probe below the surface of the issues and behind the scenes of the coverage. I recognize that I am only one media analyst in a sea of media folk with louder voices and larger followings. It was harder for me to get heard with only a low-budget megaphone and an online electronic media platform.

Our hyper-competitive media world today is an insecure one where journalists and media executives feel constant pressure and experience intense anxiety. It is no wonder that many mainstream journalists tend toward defensiveness or even outright hostility at unwelcome criticisms, especially from anyone whom they perceive to be on the margins. When you live through the coverage of a war, you don't always want to hear carping from someone who didn't. I remember how my own credibility as a Vietnam War critic was strengthened after I had gone there. In the case of Iraq, they were there. I wasn't. Yet the TV coverage did bring me closer to the action. My complaints are less about individual journalists, including the embeds, than the media companies that exploited the war for their own reasons.

When News Lies further explores an ongoing debate about the war that is perhaps more advanced in other countries than in our own. In February 2005, I testified in Rome before a citizens' World Tribunal on Iraq in a session that examined the role of the media and found its conduct highly immoral and perhaps illegal. It also examined media complicity in promoting the war. My testimony is included here to help open the forum to domestic debate as well.

As I write, there is still a great deal that we don't know about why the U.S. went to war or how the war is being fought. Many of these decisions and practices are still smothered in secrecy and laced with disinformation. Prominent experts and journalists still disagree not only on the whys but also on the whats. There is no definitive accepted history, even on the "facts."

I have focused on the problem of deception because the Iraq War was and is deceptive in all of its dimensions from its rationale to its method, from its military tactics to its reconstruction commitments. Not surprisingly, a deceptive war begat deceptive news coverage and the other way around. We now know thanks to recently released internal documents like the Downing Street Memo, a report on a leaked high-level intelligence briefing in London, that the U.S. and its allies were busy inventing and reinventing their rationales for the war, a process that included "fixing" the intelligence to bring it in line with government strategies. I believe the coverage was also "fixed."

This book is about "crossing the line," not by individual reporters but in a larger sense by media companies and our media system which was (and is) far more collusive with the war makers than is publicly understood. I am in no position to judge the specific choices and work of individual colleagues, but I can and do make judgments about the coverage overall. A World Tribunal on Iraq which did sit in symbolic judgment in February 2005 judged the coverage harshly.

And so *When News Lies* is not just an academic treatise but a call to action. It is more than a polemic because the issues it raises go to the heart of the future of democracy. The media companies who rallied the public to war were not just bad journalists but criminally complicit in an illegal and immoral undertaking. This is serious. They relinquished their constitutional duty, neglected professional standards and, as the World Tribunal found, violated international law.

The words of the late United States Supreme Court Justice Hugo Black on the "duty" of a free press must not be forgotten:

> Paramount among the responsibilities of a free press is the duty to prevent any part of the government from deceiving the people and sending them off to distant lands to die of foreign fevers and foreign shot and shell.

American democracy was invaded by the invasion of Iraq. A response and a counter-narrative are vital in the fight for a deeper understanding and more truth in media. My films and books are my contributions to this profound and ongoing challenge. I bring an insider's experience and an outsider's perspective to the task. I have done the best I can to be as accurate as I can, and of course am responsible for all errors and omissions.

The stakes in the fight for truth are high, as veteran PBS producer Bill Moyers made clear in a speech to a National Media Reform Conference in mid-May 2005:

> An unconscious people, an indoctrinated people, a people fed only partisan information and opinion that confirm their own bias, a people made morbidly obese in mind and spirit by the junk food of propaganda, is less inclined to put up a fight, ask questions and be skeptical. And just as a democracy can die of too many lies, that kind of orthodoxy can kill us, too.

It is my sincere hope that *When News Lies* will challenge our contemporary media-fed war dances and point to some of the answers we urgently need if we are to renew our media and save our democracies.

Postscript

What Katrina Showed Us

In the aftermath of the devastating impact of Hurricane Katrina, we saw how an outraged American media could, in some quarters, find the courage to challenge government officials in a way they have yet to do about the war in Iraq. Even though the Iraq connection to these events—the funds diverted from emergency planning to the war effort, the Louisiana National Guardsman defending the "new" Iraq instead of helping the people of New Orleans when help was needed the most and even the privatization of the initial disaster planning—was minimally covered, we did see skeptical and concerned journalists harshly cross-examining those nominally "in charge," while openly showing the suffering and deaths of civilians. We often saw them questioning policy failure in an aggressive manner. We heard them denouncing the shame and disgrace of it all.

It was encouraging in that it showed us that the American media can still act as a moral conscience and do the job it is there to do. Sadly, the catastrophe in the Gulf States knocked out coverage of the continuing catastrophe in the Gulf Region.

And it also, in contrast, underscored the reconstruction yet to be done in Iraq, left in the wake of Katrina's "shock and awe."

Labor Day, 2005

"Political documentaries are becoming very, very important. People will tell you that five or ten years ago, they never would have thought to go to a documentary in the theater, but because now they are so disenfranchised by what they see on TV in terms of news, they go to theaters to see a movie."

–Philippe Diaz
Founder, Cinema Libre Studio
www.HollywoodReporter.com, June 2004

Challenging the Mainstream

From Blogs to Books to Docs

Like most of my colleagues in the media world, I had been closely follow-ing what is now universally called the "run-up" to the war. You couldn't escape the shrill escalation of rhetoric in Washington about the danger posed by Mr. Hussein and his fearsome Weapons of Mass Destruction. You could-n't miss the Bush Administration's fanatical determination to kick Saddam's ass. Even before the war started, the Bush Administration launched a "decap-itation" air strike (i.e., assassination attempt by cruise missile) that turned out to be, perhaps along with the war itself, a costly and big bloody bust. This debacle was a sign of what was to come but we didn't know it then.

At the time, I was blogging every day, as I still do for Mediachannel.org, and trying to dissect the details of a rush to war that had been validated, legitimated, and reinforced hourly and daily by media outlets, all of which seemed to be following the same script and echoing the same narrative. They asked few questions, and as we know now, they told many lies. (As a word, *lies* seems strident but the excuse that we didn't know better or "were operating on the best available information" is a contrived rational-ization—weasely, wimpy and a cop out.)

Although blogs had become decidedly more popular, they were still nowhere near as widely read as the mainstream press or watched like network and cable TV news. I decided then to "embed" myself in front of my living room TV and at my computer as a disgusted witness to a media war that was then unfolding, and to catalogue what I saw. I compared and contrasted coverage across the spectrum of print and television both here and abroad. What I found was very disturbing. There was a patriotic correctness on the airwaves, and a uniformity in viewpoint that did more selling than telling about the war.

I heard only a few criticisms of the coverage, and they were mostly about reporting flaws by elite newspapers, even though 80 percent of the American people rely on TV for their news and the impressions gleaned from it. It seemed as if many anti-war activists focused their anger only on the reporting of the *New York Times* and *Times* reporter Judith Miller, as if she was single-handedly shaping coverage and was, in effect, responsible for the war. This personalized the problem and lacked a more systemic understanding. Focusing only on the *Times* gave its role too much prominence. The ongoing TV war was largely overlooked, perhaps because many on the left hate television news and don't watch it.

As the war drum grew louder, larger numbers of Americans and people around the world dissented, but their views were rarely seen and seldom heard. As I watched protesters rail at the government and pick at its rationalizations, it became clear that few in the big media-megaphone were listening.

It reminded me of the mascot seen on the old RCA Victor record labels, the little dog with its head in an old-fashioned speaker, listening to "His Master Voice." Despite our many channels and choices, there were few other voices. As I continued my immersion, digesting coverage from around the world, I saw many flaws in the media menu that the American public was being fed. It was apparent that American TV news was being driven by a clear political line posing as neutral information. It was as if a nominally competitive news system had transformed into organs of state media. Being continually tethered to the wall-to-wall coverage, it was hard to assess how any state-run system would have done it differently, if as well. A seamless on-air presentation is very effective at not calling attention to its techniques or behind-the-scenes influences.

Journalists all over the world commented on the way our war journalism (sic) was infected with jingoism. It was blatantly obvious to others, but many on the inside couldn't or wouldn't see it. News professionals seemed to be blindly inculcated inside a gung-ho news bubble that tended to automatically accept government claims as inherently true and unworthy of challenge.

In her book *Bushwacked,* Molly Ivins catalogued all the shifting official rationales that were duly reported on TV without anyone pointing out how surrealistic and contradictory they were: "First it was regime change, then disarmament, then he had a nuclear program, next he was suddenly in bed with al-Qaeda about to hand off anthrax to terrorists, then it was because Iraq was in violation of Resolution 1441 ... then it was dozens of UN resolutions, then it was weapons of mass destruction, then we couldn't back down because it would destroy our 'credibility' and then it was regime change again."

Around and around it went with media outlets acting like ad agencies marketing a new product.

The truth is that TV news loves war. It's an action-oriented, anything-can-happen, ratings-getting spectacle, not merely a boring replay of familiar news routines and the usual restrictive formats. Insiders consider it "great TV." As TV programmers know all too well, violence sells.

WMD includes a section on Vietnam, with the title "The Past Is Never Past." Before the war some Iraqi military leaders actually visited Vietnam seeking advice from the one country that had actually defeated the United States, according to a report in *Asia Times.* The Pentagon, in turn, wanted to avoid recurrence of the Vietnam press coverage that allowed journalists more access to the fighting that many military leaders still believe undermined their efforts in that war. Both sides looked for different lessons.

As leading anti-war organizer Leslie Cagan says in the film, such under-reporting was not the problem: "What there was not decent coverage of was the analysis. What we were trying to say about what was wrong with the war, why we never should've gone to war, why the war needed to end, what was driving–the motor force behind the war. That analysis never got into the mainstream media."

Orville Schell, the head of the journalism department at the University of California, Berkeley, explained that that's because media outlets "not only failed to seriously investigate administration rationales for war, but little took into account the myriad voices in the online, alternative, and world press that sought to do so."

The "group think" cited by the Senate as the reason for our "intelligence" failures was not confined to government agencies. This apt phrase could as easily be applied to the one institution charged with scrutinizing official failures: the media. I was pleased when former CBS correspondent Thomas Fenton agreed in his book *Bad News* (2005) that "our industry has too long suffered from a case of 'group think.'"

To the list of institutional failures that led to war, we can now add the failures of the powerful U.S. news industry, which gave the war its legitimacy and organized public support for it by a pattern of over-hyped and under-critical reporting.

In the post-9/11 news world, all too many editors, journalists and anchors nodded in agreement as President Bush urged the terrorists to "bring it on." When they finally did, they bemoaned the growing loss of American lives. Across the dial, "Count Us In" became the mantra as a macho military culture went on display and patriotic "America United" or "America Fights Back" slogans branded the programming. Dan Rather of CBS went on TV after 9/11 and said, "I am ready to do what my commander-in-chief orders." American flags sprung up on the lapels of just about every newscaster and infiltrated the TV graphics. TV news often resembled a USA #1 pep rally: Fox animations had eagles flying off to battle; MSNBC promos would later proclaim, "God Bless America."

As local police staged bio-war drills in the security-obsessed environment of post-9/11 America, government officials led by the W-in-chief stoked the threat warnings and beat the war drums, insisting there was only one choice: to side with him or the terrorists. Forget the evidence. Forget debate. "We" were going "in" and it was better to get in line and accede to the inevitability of it all than to question a narrative that had captured every TV channel and newspaper. It was a consensus. A *Washington Post* editor would later tell his colleagues who complained about their coverage that war was "inevitable" so why not just go along and get on top of the story.

Fear hyped by TV news became a political weapon, and polarization became its main effect. We were told that we either had to stop "them" in Iraq or we would have to fight "them" in our own cities and towns. Prime Minister Tony Blair's white paper claimed London was only 45 minutes away from impending doom by an Iraqi missile.

Condoleezza Rice, then national security advisor to the President, invoked the specter of a mushroom cloud. The oft-used White House "bully pulpit" now had a real bully in command. As President Bush saddled up to lead what he called a new "crusade" based on instructions from God and a cabal of neo-cons, the big guns of the American media moved into his amen corner.

The Pentagon rolled out a sophisticated new strategy of "information dominance." Media control was what it meant, involving the careful shaping of the information they disseminated to mould American and global public opinion. That strategy used a savvy PR message machine, embedded journalism and "perception management." It has remained in effect since 2001. There is no denying its success in winning support for the war and winning over most of the U.S. media from the early days of "the showdown with Saddam" through the Iraqi elections of 2005.

Embedding was designed to put more eyes on the ground to discredit the enemy. Explained Victoria Clarke, who ran the program, in a talk to the Brookings Institution in 2003:

> I knew with great certainty if we went to war, the Iraqi regime would be doing some terrible things and would be incredibly masterful with the lies and the deception. And I could stand up there at that podium and Secretary Rumsfeld could stand up there and say very truthfully: the Iraqi regime is putting its soldiers in civilian clothing so they can ambush our soldiers. Some people would believe us and some people wouldn't. But we had hundreds and hundreds of credible, independent journalists saying the Iraqi regime is putting their soldiers in civilian clothing.

There were many debates about embedding and related issues. Questions like these were raised by a panel at Washington's Brookings Institution, but were not picked up or pursued more widely in our media:

- Were reports from journalists embedded with various units overly-sympathetic toward their military companions?

  My Answer: Yes.

- Were non-embedded journalists who attempted to cover the war impeded by the Pentagon?

  My Answer: Yes.

- Did the Pentagon withhold bad news and exaggerate, or even create, good news?

  My Answer: Yes.

- Did the corps of retired military officers, hired as commentators by TV networks and cable channels, offer any real insights?

  My Answer: Not many.

- If media reports had shown more death and devastation, would public opinion have turned against the war?

  My Answer: It did in other countries.

- How will the experience in Iraq affect press coverage and Pentagon press policies in future wars?

  My Answer: It already has.

The U.S. government has invested millions of dollars not only in managing media but in creating and subsidizing media outlets to carry and echo its spin. It would be wrong to think that their propaganda efforts are always successful as the *Sunday Herald* in Scotland reported in December 2004:

> The Pentagon has admitted that the War on Terror and the invasion and occupation of Iraq have increased support for al-Qaeda, made ordinary Muslims hate the U.S., and caused a global backlash against America because of the "self-serving hypocrisy" of George W. Bush's administration over the Middle East.

> The *mea culpa* is contained in a shockingly frank "strategic communications" report, written in late 2004 by the Defense Science Board for Pentagon supre-

mo Donald Rumsfeld. On "the war of ideas or the struggle for hearts and minds," the report says, "American efforts have not only failed, they may also have achieved the opposite of what they intended."

So here we have a case of government media-making faulted by the same government that much of the media continued to rely on as a principal source of information even as it was increasingly clear that it lacked credibility—even by its own standards.

Bear in mind, that this was nothing new, just a far more elaborate effort than we have seen before. Veteran CBS correspondent Thomas Fenton admits in his book *Bad News,* "most of the time, in truth, most of the media take their cues *from the government* [emphasis his] in deciding which foreign news stories to cover." The group think that Fenton finds so pervasive has a consequence: it "reduces all the news into a homogenous repetitive gray sludge," he argues.

Many TV journalists reported being pressured, even "spooked." ABC's Peter Jennings told Fenton: "'World News Tonight' was regarded as the most critical of the networks, and it made some people in the shop a little bit nervous, because the vocalness of the conservatives in the country is very considerable and it spooks some people a little." ABC News was clearly spooked when government officials misled its producers as to when the war would begin and ABC was the only network without its anchorman on duty when the fireworks started. Network insiders told me they believed they had been deliberately embarrassed as payback for a critical program aired the week before the war began.

In its efforts to cultivate public opinion, the Bush Administration also relied on 24/7 support from several well-managed private and partisan media assets including Fox News, Sinclair Broadcasting's right-wing TV programs, websites, an echo chamber of talkradio hosts, bloggers and media organizations that served to reinforce its views and attack its enemies. The approach was strongly supported by formerly centrist mainstream media outlets that did not challenge the shift to the right. Those who did not go along sheepishly were baited as biased and denounced as "liberal" media. The mainstream media system soon became a willing servant for the President's War on Terror. A leading conservative media group would give CBS its top award for war coverage.

In the two plus years since the war began, there has been a continuity in media coverage. Even as the evidence used to make the case for going to war failed to materialize, even after the President himself acknowledged that there were no weapons of mass destruction (WMDS) in Iraq and no link between Osama bin Laden and Saddam Hussein, even as major media organizations admitted their coverage had been flawed, the daily drum beat of propaganda posing as news has allowed for more stories questioning how the war is being fought but has not deviated from the necessity of fighting it.

In the spring of 2005, studies surfaced reporting on blatant government censorship and media self-censorship. American University's School of Communications reported that "many media outlets self-censored their reporting on the Iraq invasion because of concerns about public reaction to graphic images and content, according to a survey of more than 200 journalists by university researchers."

The study also determined that "vigorous discussions" about what and where to publish information and images were conducted at media outlets and, in many cases, journalists posted material online that did not make it to print. One of the most significant findings was "the amount of editing that went into content after it was gathered but before it was published," the study stated.

> Of those who reported from Iraq, 15 percent said that on one or more occasions their organizations edited material for publication and they did not believe the final version accurately represented the story. Of those involved in war coverage who were in newsrooms and not in Iraq, 20 percent said material was edited for reasons other than basic style and length. Some 42 percent of those polled said they were discouraged from showing photographic images of dead Americans, while 17 percent said they were prohibited. Journalists were also discouraged from showing pictures of hostages, accord-

ing to 36 percent of respondents, while only 3 percent reported being prohibited from showing them.

Editor & Publisher, which has done an excellent job of monitoring media subservience, noted additional anonymous comments from those who took part in the survey:

> We went in with no ground rules except those of the military, which prohibited photos that would show the faces of captives, and also which discouraged photos that would ID wounded or dead U.S. troops. That said, I think we knew that HIGHLY explicit photos of gore were not likely to get published. The editors were eager for powerful photos though, and went further than many U.S. media outlets in that regard.

> Our rules are against anything which might offend our audience, i.e., we are in the realm of taste and decency, which is difficult to quantify. ... On the one hand, I don't want, say, my kids to turn on the TV after tea and see some of the things I have seen in the field. But on the other hand, the effect of this is to sanitize the coverage, and glamorize the conflict. ... We delayed or didn't even publish lots of information on which we had contradictory or incomplete reports.

Inside the Pentagon and White House, a sophisticated media monitoring operation was set up to assess the coverage worldwide. Media spin and management was a top priority for war commander General Tommy Franks and the Pentagon who were determined not to lose the media war. Franks was obsessed with how the media was covering the war; his information warfare operation monitored coverage so it could be corrected when perceived wrong and continuously influenced.

After the invasion of Iraq was pronounced a big success, John Keegan, the defense editor of the *Telegraph* and a leading military historian in Britain, sat down with Franks in a London hotel for a book he was doing on the Iraq War. Franks told him about how he managed "the intelligence front" by describing the way his personal command center was arranged at his headquarters at Qatar. In front of his desk, Franks said, "he had four screens which he viewed continuously. One displayed, at five second intervals, the different outputs of the main television news channels—CNN, Fox, BBC; he needed to know what each was broadcasting because public coverage of the war so closely affected strategy."

In addition, corporate PR firms helped with the "messaging" while Hollywood producers and even some journalists advised on media management. Press conferences gave the appearance of openness while new restrictions were placed on access to government documents. Networks like CNN consulted with the Pentagon on which military experts to use. Friendly journalists were carefully leaked information, like the top secret war plans developed by Franks, while others carried government leaks, like journalists who were leaked the identity of Valerie Plame, the CIA agent and wife of a former ambassador who became a cause célèbre.

The Administration sneered at its critics as too "fact based" as the government offered slogans meshed in story-telling to shape an "us versus them" narrative. The fact-based tradition of reporting soon found itself up against "faith-based" argumentation built around the use of well-crafted framing and advertising techniques sprinkled with selective "facts" and religiosity.

Government authorities usually behaved authoritatively, often citing secret information that only they had access to. (Some of this was leaked to media outlets that then attributed it to unnamed sources.) However, in March 2005, we would learn officially that most of this intelligence was bogus, "dead wrong," in the words of one member of the very same commission Bush himself had appointed a year earlier to investigate why no WMDs were found in Iraq. Less than two months later, the Downing Street Memo would surface in Britain, showing that the war planning was underway well before the public knew about it and that the intelligence and rationales were molded and massaged to align with the desired policy. Frequently repeated declarations like "you are with us or against us" polarized the debate and baited and demonized anyone who dared to oppose this view.

The governments were able to manage the media because most of the media bought into the assumptions and claims of government officials and experts they marshalled to buttress their case. American photojournalist Molly Bingham in a speech given at Western Kentucky University in 2005 described how American reporters identified with the war and abandoned all pretense of objectivity:

> Many journalists in Iraq could not, or would not, check their nationality or their own perspective at the door. One of the hardest things about working on [the story of the war in Iraq] for me personally, and as a journalist, was to set my "American self" and perspective aside. It was an ongoing challenge to listen open-mindedly to a group of people whose foundation of belief is significantly different from mine, and one I found I often strongly disagreed with.
>
> But going in to report a story with a pile of prejudices is no way to do a story justice, or to do it fairly, and that constant necessity to bite my tongue, wipe the smirk off my face or continue to listen through a racial or religious diatribe that I found appalling was a skill I had to practice. We would never walk in to cover a union problem or political event without seeking to understand the perspective from both, or the many sides of the story that exist. Why should we as journalists do it in Iraq?

Meanwhile back home most anti-war warriors would rather flail at Bush and his cohorts than take on a media system that has served as the main interface between the war and the public. Few could see that had the media not rolled over, and instead exposed government propaganda, the controversy could have slowed the rush to war. One proposal by activists to picket CNN was even derided by a bigger peace coalition on the grounds that it might "alienate" the mainstream journalists from covering their anti-war movements. No fear there–they weren't really doing so anyway.

In many ways examining the coverage of the war in Iraq confirms how the corporate world was as much involved in backing the war as the government. Sure there is big money to be made in fighting wars–there always is–but it is more than that. The corporate media is the marketing arm of the corporate world, supported by its advertising dollars and the platform for its ideology. Let us not forget how and why the Bush administration attracted so much corporate support. They share a world view in which private interests and U.S. supremacy are paramount. Their media reflects and propagates this view, especially at a time of war.

The way the war was promoted and then covered, the way it is still covered, speaks volumes about how a media system given constitutional protection to strengthen democracy has evolved into a threat to it; democracy is always at risk when the public is not fully and honestly informed. The absence of media independence and critical reporting enabled military planners to achieve their goal as enunciated in Tommy Franks' war plan to orchestrate media coverage as a "fourth front." So much for a vibrant and informative fourth estate.

This may not have been all that accidental. The infamous journalist Hunter S. Thompson whose coverage of the Vietnam War became a classic of the genre, and who took his life in February 2005, believed that our media is actually a part of an "oligarchy" that rules America.

"The oligarchy doesn't need an educated public. And maybe the nation does prefer tyranny," he was quoted as saying. "I think that's what worries me." Thompson's view of the Iraq War was that it was "manufactured" for political gain and the economic interests of the oligarchy. That belief may have deepened his despair about the future of our democracy.

U.S. reporting developed an "all about us" quality with the experience (and deaths) of our soldiers displacing most reporting on civilian casualties or the destruction of Iraqi society. But even here the coverage was tightly controlled with few pictures of the dead and injured being sent home and little follow-up with their families. (Please be wary of these numbers. There have been reports that soldiers who died on the way to hospitals or in hospitals are not counted.) In June 2005, the *Santa Maria Times* editorialized:

> The fact is, more than 30 U.S. soldiers have been killed in Iraq just since the first of this month. In all, more than 1,700 U.S. military personnel have lost their lives in Iraq since the March 2003 invasion, and close to 13,000 have been wounded.

> Do the numbers surprise you? They shouldn't. The combat toll has been widely reported in every U.S. newspaper—including this one—since the war began.

What readers and TV viewers aren't seeing a lot of is the actual loss of life. There are a host of reasons why you don't see the photos and video of combat fatalities and injuries, mostly because the Bush Administration and Pentagon officials would rather you not see them.

And when news outlets make the effort to put a real, horrifying face on the war, the outcome isn't always universally accepted. Editors at the *Star-Ledger* in Newark, NJ, learned that lesson the hard way last month when they ran a photo of a fatally wounded army private. After the photo appeared, the *Star-Ledger's* editors took a thorough tongue-lashing from readers, who accused the newspaper of being crass, insensitive and even unpatriotic.

Editors at the *Los Angeles Times* recently completed a survey of several major newspapers and two of the nation's largest news magazines to see how other editors were handling the reporting of the war. They found that although the death toll was being dutifully reported, there was scant photographic evidence that American men and women are being killed in a war that seems to have no end. Whatever purpose Americans found in the conflict at first has now all but disappeared. ...

This may be because the larger war discourse became framed around "Supporting Our Troops" rather than questioning the policies or interests that brought U.S. troops to Iraq and are keeping them there.

Few reporters were as honest as Molly Bingham about the way this narrative was internalized by many of those covering the war:

Our behavior as journalists has taught us very little. Just as in the lead-up to the war in Iraq, questioning our government's decisions and claims and what it seeks to achieve is criticized as unpatriotic. ...while I was out doing what I believe is solid journalism, there were many (journalists and normal folks alike) who would question my patriotism, or wonder how I could even think hearing and relating the perspective "from the other side" was important.

Certainly, over the last three years I've had to acquire the discipline of overriding my emotional attachment to my country, and remember my sense of human values that transcend frontiers and ethnicity. And with a sense of duty to history, I needed to just get on with reporting the story. My value of human life and rights don't fluctuate depending on which country I'm in.

Countdown to War

As war neared, as a countdown added drama, a news army was put in place, not only alongside the army of soldiers but embedded within it. The Pentagon trained journalists for "safety's sake." The media war was soon marching in lockstep with the Pentagon's war, and the mainstream media system became a volunteer army of its own in the War on Terror.

As I watched the war and wrote about it, it seemed apparent that the U.S. had moved into a post-journalism era where packaging and "militainment" prevailed over the facts on the ground. I concluded that our media organs were functioning as weapons systems themselves—weapons of mass deception that were targeting viewers, listeners and readers.

I soon realized that I was fighting a media war too. Only my "front" was in the media itself, using the tools of the trade and whatever airtime and media space I could find to confront and debate these issues with a wider audience as well as with my colleagues. I quickly found that the very institutions that were distorting the news were reluctant to debate their own practices. Overseas broadcasters seemed to have more interest in hearing from me than their American counterparts.

I did make occasional appearances on some TV programs as well as on Fox, CNN and even CBS networks. Media industry magazines published some of my articles, although the non-response to them from inside the media was pretty deafening. I guess the fact that editors published them at all signals that they agreed that the issue was important and that I had the credibility to write about it.

But it didn't change as I catalogued the collusion between the military and the media through my daily blogs and hundreds of columns and articles, both online and off. My book, *Embedded,* published first online in August 2003, and then in hardcover in November 2003, had no major impact. It was ignored by reviewers. But I couldn't give up. I believed I was right even as most major media remained tied to their uncritical formulas of presentation. I worried about becoming obsessive but was encouraged by some colleagues who shared my disgust with what was on the air.

It was then that I began making *WMD* as a film to fight image with image and offer a counter-narrative.

As a former CNN and ABC News producer, I made the subject of the film an investigation of how and why our media blew it—not just on missing weapons of mass destruction. Oddly, the response later from some critics was that the public already knows all this—even though it hasn't been covered.

Making the film was a problematic exercise from the get-go. Years ago a studio mogul famously said, "If you want to send a message, go to Western Union." Media-critical movies have been around for years and often do well, from *Citizen Kane* to *Wag the Dog*. But documentaries are a bigger challenge to make and distribute. Docs have traditionally offered an alternative voice to Hollywood. Although the box office receipts can't usually compete, docs are becoming more popular as a means to add critical voices about what the politicos don't want us to know and what the media can't/won't tell us. The problem is that in a media world with fewer and fewer companies in command, dissenting perspectives are often not welcome.

Luckily, independent media outlets have served to educate their audiences and counter the ongoing, insidious strategic planning by the Bush Administration. But as important as exposing it, is resisting it. Happily, a cultural resistance has been emerging. In a play called *A New War,* playwright Gip Hoppe ridiculed coverage of a war that "is being fought somewhere against an unknown enemy because the Pentagon has decided that to reveal whom and where American forces are fighting would be a security risk."

The play ran in New Haven, CT. A review in the *New York Times* described how the play "satirizes a television broadcast from a newsroom at a network very similar to CNN, [and] is a ridiculing send-up of the Bush Administration and a kowtowing news media. It owes a great deal to the Weekend Update feature on 'Saturday Night Live.'" It is significant that leading lights of popular culture are beginning to take on the war and war coverage. An earlier play, *Embedded,* written by and starring actor Tim Robbins, played in New York and London, challenged the neo-conservative policies that led to the war. An embedded journalist was one of the characters.

Perhaps because TV news often seems like it has become a satire on itself, many young people have been turning to the Comedy Channel and other satirical outlets for their news, finding them more credible. A version of "Crossfire," called "Crosshairs," appears on Jon Stewart's "news" show. (Later, when Stewart appeared as a guest on CNN's "Crossfire," he attacked the show so forcefully that CNN officials said they would take it off the air, but have yet to do so as of this writing.)

Criticizing the government had a lucrative market. Al Franken's satires of political and media organizations in his books and radio shows became best sellers, as were the spoofs in the weekly *Onion* news parody newspaper. Although Stewart is satire, his "news" often speaks more truth than mainstream media. With its credibility shattered, TV news is in danger of becoming a caricature. Other alternative venues provide comic relief to serious issues.

We are all living in the crosshairs of powerful media institutions that offer more spin than truth. Their fire is "incoming," into our living rooms, and then into our brains. We need more than self-defense. We need collective action to challenge mainstream media assumptions and push-back. We need to support independent media with our eyeballs, dollars and our marketing know-how. We need to encourage media literacy education in our schools. We need to challenge candidates to speak out on these issues, and media outlets to cover them.

Enter *WMD*

My hope is that activists will use all resources to become better informed and that *WMD* will play a part in encouraging more critical thinking and open the public debate on the media failure that is as problematic as the intelligence failure that led us into a bloody and still unresolved war.

Clearly there is a market for topical non-fiction served with an edge. The success of *Fahrenheit 9/11, Bush's Brain* and *Uncovered* was fanned by partisanship in an election cycle, while the attention paid to *Control Room* and *OutFoxed* demonstrated that media issues can attract audiences, especially when the focus is on Al Jazeera, a network the right rightly fears, and Fox, the anything but fair and balanced Newser the left loves to hate.

But much of the rah-rah over the popularity of documentaries missed the deeper reason: mounting disenchantment and disaffection with the uniformity and shallowness of TV news. This media story was not widely covered in the media because it indicts the media.

Today some of our most thoughtful journalists and filmmakers are bringing their experiences and points of view to movie theaters because there appears to be less censorship with fewer gatekeepers blocking access in this arena. The popularity of film festivals points to the public hunger for more creative and outspoken fare. Yet there are signs that business-as-usual-oriented theater owners may shut out political films believing the demand is over. Not true. The mass media crowned 2004 "the year of documentaries." Will the trend survive?

Going the indy route became my only route to making a film on the media coverage. As I began filming *WMD,* the war looked like a "cakewalk." Ratings went up when Saddam's statues came down. Not surprisingly, it was "hard" (to borrow a "Bushism") to find financing. Cable channels "passed" without seeing it. PBS was, as usual, risk-adverse and controversy-free and rejected it without any explanation. When I first began filming, I had no funding. I knew timing was important so I'd have to get it going myself, which I did. Fortunately, a few investors enabled us to continue and finish the film.

As a former network producer, I did my own investigation for the film, drawing on insider experience as a news packager at ABC and CNN and interviews with front-line reporters. First observation: the people I interviewed were not nearly as bullish as most of the embeds we saw on the nightly news. I put myself in the film to offer a personal witness from someone in the media trenches, not to "out Michael Moore Michael Moore" as *Vanity Fair* suggested. I knew that I had to establish my credentials with the audience in order to have my criticism taken seriously. Once I did that, I clearly labeled *WMD* a "personal film."

The film shows how the Hollywood narrative story-telling techniques constructed a form of "militainment," fusing news biz and show biz. It exposes media coverage that was clearly based on misinformation and deception. Although newspapers and networks later admitted some of their errors, as Senator Robert Byrd observed, the networks bought it and sold it, "hook, line and sinker."

While some documentaries (like *Supersize Me* or sexsational films like *Capturing the Friedmans)* generally have an easier time in the commercial arena than serious investigative efforts, it is particularly difficult to get funding, distribution and exposure when taking on the media system itself. Bashing Bush or Enron is one thing; slamming the media is something else.

Even as top film festivals honored *WMD,* top distributors declined it. (Moore's payday didn't sway them.) No surprise. I later learned that most of them are now part of the corporate media cartel I critique in the film.

As the Iraq War implodes and public opinion turns, isn't it time for more of us in the industry to join the challenge to the disgraceful media failures that helped get us into the bloody mess in what Jon Stewart calls "Messopotamia"? *WMD* is one such attempt at doing so. Fortunately, you can watch it before or after reading this text.

"Our once-noble news media—and network TV news in particular—have abdicated their responsibility to the American people, and endangered us in the process. ... We need more and better news. Our lives depend on it."

—Thomas Fenton

Foreign correspondent, CBS News, 2005

→2←

Media on Trial

Are Media Mistakes Accidental or Criminal?

During the run-up to the war in Iraq and through the U.S. invasion, it was obvious that our media system had signed up as an unofficial megaphone for war. There was a uniformity of perspective, a reliance on the same sources and "facts," alongside a dismissal of critics and dissenters.

As the war wound on, some in the media began to take a second look at what had been reported. Some were horrified. Journalists outside America had problems distinguishing between what our government was saying and what our TV networks were reporting. The focus was the same.

From time to time, media scandals forced the larger issues of journalistic ethics and practices into the limelight. There was the case of Jayson Blair, the young reporter who invented his stories at the *New York Times* or the *USA Today* journalist Jack Kelly, also accused of fabrications. Then there was the Dan Rather document flap at CBS where an investigation he reported on was denounced as partisan and based on questionable source material. However when it came to war coverage, the media response was more tepid. No one was fired for false reporting or abandoning journalistic standards. (No one except some war critics, that is.)

Soon there were some *mea culpas* in print, but for the most part war reporting and distorting engendered only mild criticism. Partly that was a function of a political climate that had been shifted to the right by the Bush Administration and its media allies. No one, however centrist, was above being attacked for questioning any aspect of the war.

ABC's "Nightline," which is known for in-depth news analysis, briefly became the epicenter of a media storm in the spring of 2004. All hell broke loose when it was announced that Koppel would devote a special edition of his program to read the names of the war dead on the eve of the anniversary of President Bush's appearance on the U.S. aircraft carrier, the image pressed in memory by the carefully placed banner announcing "Mission Accomplished." That program was also scheduled to air on the anniversary of the end of the Vietnam War, April 30, 1975, when the city of Saigon fell (or was "liberated," depending on your point of view) to the North Vietnamese and NLF forces.

Sinclair Broadcasting Group, the owner of a large group of television stations, including ABC affiliates, decided to preempt the broadcast explicitly on political grounds. In their decision to kill the program, Sinclair accused Koppel of having a "political agenda designed to undermine the efforts of the United States in Iraq." Some pundits then pounced on Koppel, even questioning his patriotism. Sinclair executives were hardly above politics themselves in that the bulk of their political donations in the 2004 election year went to Republicans. The broadcast went ahead even though some stations did not run it. It honored the war dead but steered clear of questioning the war itself.

A long-time Washington insider, Koppel has for years been criticized more by the left as being a crony of conservative policy wonks like Henry Kissinger with whom he has socialized for years. So it was ironic that he himself was targeted as some kind of radical during this episode.

It was unusual for Koppel to be in the limelight this way. The last time that he had so much media attention was when Disney, ABC's parent company, threatened to cancel "Nightline" to clear the time slot for David Letterman's show. At the time, all of the most credible names in American journalism rallied to defend "Nightline" and Disney backed down. Even Letterman supported "Nightline." In 2005, Koppel announced his plans to retire amidst speculation that "Nightline" would finally be canceled when he left and replaced with more profitable entertainment programming. It wasn't canceled but the approach will be decidedly softened; Koppel is going to HBO to do documentaries.

This time he got little support from either the right or left. The right claimed he was "anti-war" and unpatriotic while anti-war activists questioned Koppel's decision to focus only on the American war dead and not read the names of Iraqi civilians who died in the war without much media attention. "That would be more of a mini-series, even a telethon," wrote one MediaChannel reader who favored the idea of including under-covered civilian deaths in the reading. It can be done—and has. In the summer of 2005, I attended a Stop the War protest in Scotland where the names of dead British soldiers and Iraqi civilians were read together.

In many ways the Koppel broadcast resembled a famous Vietnam War edition of *Life* magazine, which in 1969 devoted a whole issue to the photos of the more than 200 soldiers who died in one week of combat in Vietnam. That issue signaled a turning point in media coverage of the war. Until then, much of the press was pro-war. After that widely commented upon issue, more anti-war coverage appeared. Perhaps that is what the Sinclairs and the opposition to the broadcast were worried about.

Many media outlets worldwide covered the controversy, thinking that the story might lead to more dissent. CBS, NPR and a leading newspaper in Japan called me for comment. My argument was that Koppel's move represented a media shift toward more independence in coverage. Coupled with the recent photos of the caskets of U.S. soldiers and a recent "60 Minutes II" report on abuses of Iraqis by U.S. soldiers, I thought it was likely to embolden more critical journalism in the timid but patriotically correct world of U.S. media. I was overly optimistic.

During the invasion, Ted Koppel himself had been an enthusiastic embed, joining his fellow journalists during the Iraq War. No grunt he. His status as an anchorman insured his being embedded with a high-ranking officer. He reported from the front lines in a straight-forward manner and rarely if ever criticized U.S. policy. He had traditionally tended to tilt toward the logic of whatever Washington establishment happens to be in power.

After Koppel returned from the battlefield, however, he grew more critical than he had been when he was there. "Watching war on TV from a distance," he insisted on C-SPAN, not ABC, "is pulse-pounding entertainment.

That's damn good entertainment. We need to show people the consequences of war. People die in war."

Koppel was interviewed by ex-network correspondent Marvin Kalb of Harvard's Joan Shorenstein Center on the Press, Politics, and Public Policy. In that conversation, he criticized "live journalism from a war zone" calling it "not good journalism." He has since probed the rationale for the Iraq War in interviews with Richard Clarke, the former Bush Administration terrorism-chief-turned-critic who's now an ABC News consultant. His views seemed to be changing both with time and distance from the battlefield. Perhaps there was a legacy issue at work, too. Everyone in broadcasting is aware of how Walter Cronkite's reporting from Vietnam helped shift public opinion and bolster his status. President Lyndon Johnson was reported to have said, "When we lost Cronkite, we lost the American people." Ted Koppel's reputation could only rise by the appearance of critical independence.

It is a comment on the times that Koppel had to re-position his broadcast as a tribute to U.S. soldiers in hopes of forestalling attacks from the right. Those attacks came anyway from inside the media.

We still do not have many TV programs willing to take on the Administration on the War on Terror and Iraq. As most journalists proved more reluctant (or more likely restrained) to actually investigate and probe government policy, non-profit organizations have started to fill the gap.

Among the bravest: The American Civil Liberties Union.

Since when did the American Civil Liberties Union become a media organization? Or put another way: why has so much of our press fallen down on the job of pushing the Bush Administration to disclose information about its war-related practices, ranging from how it provides for our troops to detailing military abuse of prisoners and detainees?

Documents pried from the government by the ACLU under the Freedom of Information Act, and disclosed in December 2004, suggest that the abuse of detainees was more systematic than we knew and was ordered from on high. One email even indicates that President Bush signed off on the policy. While the Administration disputes the document, that famous question raised during the Watergate investigation comes around again in a different form: What did the President know and when did he forget he knew it?

The ACLU's success at breaking news also raises the question of how aggressive our press has been in challenging military rationales and White House message points.

Even as the frame and focus of coverage changed from liberation to occupation, from invasion to insurgency, the essential news dynamic has remained the same. It's still AAU: All About U.S.

Compare the number of stories devoted to the impact the war has had on the people of Iraq with the number on body armor and troop deployments. The destruction of Fallujah has slipped not only off the front pages, but every page. Not only is there no continuing reporting on civilian casualties (estimates range from 20,000 to 100,000 or more) but also few on why so many average Iraqis oppose the occupation.

The destruction and savagery of the campaign to pacify Fallujah was poorly explained and followed up. The use of illegal weapons like cluster bombs and depleted uranium fortified anti-tank shells was rarely explored.

Ironically the best mainstream account of on-the-ground realities remains the one by Farnaz Fassihi, the Wall Street *Journal* reporter whose gripping account of massacres on the ground was sent out in a private email, not a published story.

One of our best war reporters, Chris Hedges of the *New York Times,* seems to find it easier to get his perspective out in books and magazines than in his own newspaper. In a piece he wrote for *Harper's* magazine (2004) he observed: "War is presented primarily through the distorted prism of the occupiers. The embedded reporters, dependent on the military for food and transportation as well as security, have a natural and understandable tendency, one I have myself felt, to protect those who are protecting them. And the reporting, even among those who struggle to keep some distance, usually descends into a shameful cheerleading."

Stories of abuse of detainees only became well-known after photographs appeared on TV and in *The New Yorker.* But even then, when CBS did its story on Abu Ghraib in April 2004, the major media was late to the story. CBS admits it held up its story for three weeks at the Pentagon's request in order to permit a response by a U.S. marine general who predictably blamed the abuse on grunts, not higher-ups.

This story was known about well before it was reported. We now have personal "trophy" photos of horrific abuse from service families dating back to May 2003. Amnesty International began campaigning on the story with videos in July 2003. And yet it only became a big deal in the late spring of 2004. In July 2005, more than a year after the CBS broadcast, the Pentagon refused to obey a judge's order to release more of the pictures and videos.

Then the major media filed it away again, until that famous news organization, the ACLU, gave them more fodder in December of 2004. And to this day, the focus has been on individuals who committed abuses, rather than those up the chain of command who ordered it, or knew about it and said nothing. To this day sanitized terms like "abuse" are frequently used to substitute for the more legally correct words like "torture" and "war crimes." By the spring of 2005, only a female general who claimed to be following orders was blamed, along with a few prison guards who were accused of wrongdoing. Two were convicted.

Investigations since that time have been extensive: 10 major Pentagon studies, 20 Senate hearings, and Freedom of Information Act findings by the media and human rights groups. But extensive does not equate with exhaustive. Holes remain, and so do questions. Other news outlets soon began their own investigations of abuses at Guantánamo Bay, Cuba.

Thanks to probing by the Pentagon and others, the public knows that Abu Ghraib did not represent a few isolated cases. The abuse has stretched in a global arc from the U.S. military prison in Guantánamo Bay, Cuba to Afghanistan. The cases of abuse number in the hundreds and include at least two dozen suspicious deaths.

As for punishment, the military has issued either criminal or administrative charges against 125 soldiers and officers related to 350 cases in Iraq and Afghanistan.

It was a different story with senior military officers, however. A study by the army inspector general reported in May 2005 exonerated all senior army officers in Iraq and elsewhere except the brigadier general in charge of U.S. prison facilities in Iraq.

If TV programs were slow to cover abuses, TV executives were even slower to acknowledge their network's complicity in misleading the public. Six months after the *New York Times* acknowledged its own flawed reporting—"an institutional failure" was what Public Editor Daniel Okrent called it—presidents of the Big Three network news divisions finally were forced to comment. In November 2004, they told a Stanford University seminar that their news shops uncritically conveyed deceptive information that convinced the public that an invasion of Iraq was the only option. They admitted that they reported inaccurately about the threat of weapons of mass destruction.

"Simply stated," confessed David Westin, president of ABC News, "we let the American people down."

Sadly, their partial *mea culpa* was not repeated on their broadcasts. (C-SPAN covered it.)

Veteran journalists are conscious that they have become part of the system and rarely stand apart from it or challenge it. That is the nature of today's corporate media.

Bill Plante, White House correspondent for CBS, spoke with the Echo Chamber Project that is investigating the network role in covering the run-up to the war. The conversation is instructive. Plante is asked, "What would you have changed in looking back on this time period, if anything at all? Would it have been the same?"

> PLANTE: You're basically asking me to suggest that the news media could have done something in this case, and I don't really think that the way we operate we could have. The news media in the United States are not generally argumentative about the processes of government. They may be skeptical, and generally are, but not argumentative. It's a whole different discussion on how we see our role.
>
> I mean, this is part of what we discussed going into this. But to look back and suggest that because of the UN resolution in November, because of the weight of international legal opinion, things might have been different—is to suggest that the news media themselves, that is the daily reporting, would have

brought this up. You're never going to see that in this country. If we're lucky, you will see specialists arguing this on the Op-Ed pages of the newspapers and on television documentaries. But it isn't the kind of thing that you see in regular news coverage, because argumentation is not part of our ethos.

ECP: Does that seem to be a big gaping hole that needs to be corrected though?

PLANTE: What needs to be corrected, in my view, is the lazy reliance on a stream of facts which are presented to the public every day. There needs to be some interpretation of those facts. There needs to be some checking of those facts—reality check if you will. But to turn around and make the argument that an opposition politician would make is not the function of the daily press. Those voices must be heard, but it is not the function of the daily press to bring them to the fore.

So much for the tradition of investigative reporting. Journalism, in this view often devolves into simple stenography.

The news presidents did not offer any explanation as to why network coverage of Iraq marched in lockstep with the Bush Administration or discuss how that approach would change going forward.

Toronto Star columnist Antonia Zerbisias, a Canadian, has been closely following American television coverage. Her conclusion: It has barely changed, even as the Administration wanted it to be even more "positive."

"It is all but impossible to know what is happening on the ground in and around Fallujah. It's a humanitarian disaster for sure," Zerbisias wrote. "But who knows how many civilians have been affected by the bombardment, not to mention the lack of food, water, and medical care? Even many who escaped the fighting are short of the necessities of life. The Americans are not counting the civilian dead. So there's no way to know their number."

Zerbisias is not alone in believing that the Comedy Channel gets closer to the truth than our news channels. To quote Jon Stewart, host of "The Daily Show": "There is some good news coming out of the hunt for WMDS, as coalition forces in Iraq have, in fact, uncovered and disarmed one of the most dangerous and destructive weapons known to man: the free press."

Our news media has covered "intelligence failures" and "policy failures," but it has yet to turn a probing eye on systemic "media failures"—its own role in the patriotically correct selling of war.

Ironically, many of the TV and print outlets cover and encourage whistleblowers in other industries. Their allegations are a staple on all the TV news magazines. When it comes to media whistleblowers, their ears tend to be sealed.

As I probed more deeply into the daily indifference to Iraqi suffering and the continuing orchestration of coverage, I came to see the problem not as continuously flawed reporting or even as a series of institutional failures, but in the same way as whistleblowers tend to view the practices they expose—as a crime. And given the number of lives lost and the amount of money wasted, these were the moral equivalents of serious felonies. When crimes take place in other settings, eventually government officials step in. As the scandals become public, there are exposés and then prosecutions. In this case, it is the government committing the crime!

Official scrutiny of media practices rarely happens, partly because of constitutional protections afforded to journalists and media outlets, and partly because the wronged parties usually have no recourse.

Even when the government is investigating its own leaks, as in the Valerie Plame affair in which the special prosecutor had a journalist jailed for refusing to disclose a source, the source of the leak remains unidentified and Robert Novak, a long-time Republican hack and the journalist responsible for first publishing the leak, remains unscathed. Although the evidence suggested a much more widespread deception over two years ago, that connection is largely ignored. As Senator John D. Rockefeller IV (D, WV) said in writing to FBI Director Robert Mueller asking for an investigation of the Niger letters (March 21, 2003), "There is a possibility that the fabrication of these [Niger] documents may be part of a larger deception campaign aimed at manipulating public opinion and foreign policy regarding Iraq."

It's hard to fight back against media irresponsibility except perhaps through lawsuits that can take years. Public shaming seems to be the only recourse, and that depends on whether critics can be heard in the so-called public square. Usually, judgments like this are left to historians.

The media failure here is not new—2005 marked the 60th anniversary of the liberation of Auschwitz, an occasion for media commemorations and "never again" reminders.

Today the world knows what happened in the Holocaust, although mostly after the fact when it was too late to do much about it. We also know that our own media was not overly aggressive in alerting the world about the Holocaust for fear of undermining the war effort. The BBC has admitted it had information that it sat on for fear of making it appear that the war was about the survival of the Jews. During that war censorship was widely practiced. *Life* magazine did not run a photograph of a dead American until 1943, and the director of the Office of Censorship was given a special Pulitzer Prize citation.

After the war, at the Nuremberg Tribunal, American prosecutors wanted to put the German media on trial for promoting Hitler's policies. State propagandists were indicted. More recently, hate radio was indicted by the Rwanda tribunal investigating the genocide there, while in the former Yugoslavia, Serbian and Croatian TV were criticized for inciting the war that divided that country.

The principle that media outlets can, for reasons of omission or commission, be held responsible for their role in inflaming conflicts and promoting jingoism, has been well established. Many remember William Randolf Hearst's famous yellow journalism dictum: "You give me the pictures, I will give you the war."

So the pubic continues to be misled by those who are supposed to inform them. Fully 50 percent of the Bush voters told pollsters before the election that they believed there were still WMDs in Iraq, even after the President himself said he no longer believed it.

If public opinion on the war has started to shift—with 56 percent by late 2004 saying the invasion was a bad idea—it can't be because of the media.

These issues do not belong to the past; they are still with us. In February 2005, Italy hosted the citizens-initiated World Tribunal on Iraq, which put the media in the dock for its role in doing more selling of the Iraq War than telling. The Tribunal was modeled on an earlier initiative during the Vietnam War by the then-leading international intellectuals. Led by Bertrand Russell, Jean-Paul

Sartre and Simone du Bouvoir, they held public sessions to condemn war crimes by U.S. forces in Southeast Asia. As a young journalist, I covered their sessions in Stockholm in 1968. I saw it as an act of conscience. Most of the U.S. media saw it as an exercise in propaganda. Most of the charges they made then about U.S. war crimes are largely corroborated by the historical record even though only a few were reported when they occurred.

I still remember watching CBS correspondent Morley Safer filming a stand-up in Stockholm, denouncing the Tribunal. Years later, his show "60 Minutes" returned to the scene of the My-Lai massacre with interviews with soldiers who were charging the U.S. military with the very war crimes Safer had dismissed when it mattered.

Critics today believe the media has covered up war crimes in Iraq, minimized civilian casualties, downplayed the destruction of cities like Fallujah, and misreported the reasons for going to war and how it was conducted. In early July 2005, I met a young officer and West Point graduate who was just back from Iraq. He had commanded units in Fallujah and told me that he felt the media got it wrong by focusing on U.S. casualties. "We killed 400 insurgents," he told me. "That's a big win." He justified the all-out U.S. offensive and acknowledged it was what critics say, a form of collective punishment and retaliation for the killing of U.S. contractors. He seemed shocked when I questioned the tactics. "Were you there?" he asked me dismissively. "Were you there?"

This young man speaks Arabic, is very bright and was undoubtedly sincere; he characterized himself as a "conservative." At a time of intense polarization, he clearly has bought into the Bush-led mission and seemed unwilling to consider alternative ways of thinking about it. In justifying the policy and military abuses in Fallujah, this soldier cited the uncritical media coverage of Fox News to bolster his case. For him, Fox reporting of the army's rationalization made it true.

Will anyone in TV news face any consequences for their actions? Unlikely. Has there been any outbreak of conscience in newsrooms or, more important, any commitment to cover Iraq in a less jingoistic manner? Not that I can see.

During the Vietnam War, the journalists who went there as gung-ho boosters often changed their views when they saw the impact of the pacification programs, and the use of napalm and Agent Orange. That doesn't seem to be happening in Iraq. Perhaps that's because the Vietnam War was so protracted and it relied on a draft of soldiers who didn't want to be there. Perhaps it's because the '60s was a time of questioning and protest. Whatever the differences, it's hard to understand why so many journalists have lost the capacity to be more challenging. Is it a function of the ultra-corporatization of the media or a news culture that neutralizes points of view that disagree with the official government line?

A decentralized World Tribunal on Iraq organized along similar lines to the one held during the Vietnam era has been holding hearings in cities throughout the world, largely uncovered in the U.S. media. When a bold international lawyer who worked in the Lelio Basso Foundation in Rome (Basso was a member of the original Bertrand Russell Tribunal) wanted to hold hearings on media crimes, he contacted me and asked me to testify.

As a journalist, author and filmmaker, I accepted their invitation. I saw it as another venue to blow my little whistle on how the media, whether intentionally or not, misled the American people into "buying" the Iraq War. After hearing from me and others, a panel of international "judges" voted to condemn the coverage as a crime.

Independent reporter Dahr Jamail, who also testified, reported on the Tribunal's conclusions in a report he filed with Inter Press Service (IPS):

> The informal panel of WTI judges accused the United States and the British governments of impeding journalists in performing their task and intentionally producing lies and misinformation.

> The panel accused western corporate media of filtering and suppressing information and of marginalizing and endangering independent journalists. More journalists were killed in a 14-month period in Iraq than in the entire Vietnam War.

> The Tribunal said mainstream media reportage on Iraq also violated article six of the Nuremberg Tribunal [set up to try Nazi crimes] which states: "Leaders,

organizers, instigators, and accomplices participating in the formulation or execution of a common plan or conspiracy to commit any of the foregoing crimes [crimes against peace, war crimes, and crimes against humanity] are responsible for all acts performed by any persons in execution of such a plan."

The final session of the World Tribunal on Iraq was held in Istanbul in June 2005. No major U.S. media outlet covered any of the sessions or the final judgment. David Cromwell of Britain's Media Lens reported: "At a press conference after the Tribunal, jury chairperson Arundathi Roy said, 'If there is one thing that has come out clearly in the last few days, it is not that the corporate media supports the global corporate project; it is the global corporate project.'"

Cromwell explained: "This is a perfect summation indicating why corporate crimes rarely surface in the corporate media. A newspaper database search on July 5 revealed that only one newspaper—the small-circulation *Morning Star* [London]—had reported on the Tribunal. There was nothing in the *Guardian*, the *Observer*, the *Independent*, the *Independent* on Sunday, the *Financial Times*, the *Times* or any of the other 'watchdogs of democracy.' There were also zero mentions at BBC news online."

My testimony at the Tribunal follows.

The Tribunal

THE TESTIMONY: *An American Journalist and Filmmaker Indicts Iraq Media Coverage*

TESTIMONY OF DANNY SCHECHTER TO THE WORLD TRIBUNAL ON IRAQ

Assessing Media Wrongs

It is complicated and problematic for a journalist to offer testimony at an international tribunal in another country. Most us tend to stay away from the appearance of advocacy or even activism. Testifying overseas—even to a citizen's panel like this—could be construed by some as presumptuous or even unpatriotic.

Yet I have come because I believe that our media, like other institutions, have a responsibility to be accountable, audit their own practices, and acknowledge their errors and omissions.

We are living in an age of a profound global media crisis that goes beyond borders and boundaries.

Journalists who are closest to our media system—really embedded in it—are often in the best position to understand media practices and recount experiences. We know how the industry works and are most aware of the pressures journalists face from government interference and corporate control. It is time we woke up and spoke up. It is time we told the truth about our own institutions. We need higher standards and deeper values.

I have been in journalism since my high school years. I have been an investigative magazine reporter, a radio news director, and worked in television at the local and national levels with a long stint at ABC News and a shorter one at CNN. I have reported from 49 countries.

I am a media critic with six books in print and a columnist/blogger with MediaChannel.org, the world's largest online media issues network. As an independent filmmaker with my company Globalvision, I have made fifteen social issue documentaries. The latest, *WMD (Weapons of Mass Deception)* is about the media coverage of the Iraq War and is based in part on a book called *Embedded* that I wrote on the subject.

I have come wearing all of these hats to discuss my findings in the belief that if we could agree on the existence of media crimes, we would agree that many have been committed during the Iraq War. Some through insensitivity and indifference; others with a more conscious intent.

This is not a partisan issue. It raises deeper issues about the integrity of our democracies.

In point of fact, in earlier wars, media outlets and personalities have been indicted for their role in instigating conflict and contributing to it. The special International Tribunal on Rwanda has pointed to the role of hate radio stations in inflaming a genocide. In the former Yugoslavia, TV stations in Serbia and Croatia became propaganda organs that incited ethnic cleansing and mass murder.

The post-World War II Nuremberg Trial established a precedent in this regard. I quote one article on what happened there:

> The prosecution case, argued by Drexel Sprecher, an American, placed considerable stress on the role of media propaganda in enabling the Hitler regime to prepare and carry out aggressive wars.

> The use made by the Nazi conspirators of psychological warfare is well-known. Before each major aggression, with some few exceptions based on expediency, they initiated a press campaign calculated to weaken their victims and to prepare the German people psychologically for the attack. They used the press, after their earlier conquests, as a means for further influencing foreign politics and in maneuvering for the following aggression.

Thus, the presentation of an illegal invasion of a foreign country as a 'preventative' or preemptive war did not originate with Bush, Cheney or Rumsfeld.

The prosecution raised an issue that is of the greatest relevance today: the role of Nazi media propaganda in inuring the German population to the sufferings of other peoples and, indeed, urging Germans to commit war crimes.

Historical parallels are never exact and I am not here to argue that because the Nazis distorted their media, the U.S. or British media are Nazis. That is specious reasoning. But a broader point also argued at Nuremberg does have resonance today:

The basic method of the Nazi propagandistic activity lay in the false presentation of facts. … The dissemination of provocative lies and the systematic deception of public opinion were as necessary to the Hitlerites for the realization of their plans as were the production of armaments and the drafting of military plans.

There Was a Media War

There were two wars going on in Iraq—one was fought with armies of soldiers, bombs and a fearsome military force. The other was fought alongside it with cameras, satellites, armies of journalists and propaganda techniques. One war was rationalized as an effort to find and disarm WMDS—Weapons of Mass Destruction; the other was carried out by even more powerful WMDs, Weapons of Mass Deception.

The TV networks in America considered their nonstop coverage their finest hour, pointing to the use of embedded journalists and new technologies that permitted viewers to see a war up close for the first time. But different countries saw different wars.

Why?

For those of us watching the coverage, the war was more of a spectacle, an around-the-clock global media marathon, pitting media outlets against each other in ways that distorted truth and raised as many questions about the methods of TV news as the armed intervention it was covering—and in some cases—promoting.

This is not just traditional censorship.

Censorship, self-censorship and spinning seem common in every war, as governments try to limit negative coverage and maximize reporting that will galvanize support on the home front. Every war inspires jingoism in sections of the media, and deceptive coverage.

Sun Tsu the great Chinese analyst of war said that deception is a tool in every war, by definition. Wars happen because of deception. They are fought with deception. But what was often discussed in the past as a tactic or a tool has become a well-deployed strategy with sophisticated high-tech information warfare doctrines guiding attempts to achieve strategic influence based on policies built on deception. This concept is deeply grounded in neo-conservative ideologies based on the work of the late University of Chicago philosopher Leo Strauss.

It is not accidental. It is deliberate.

Many in the Pentagon believe to this day that it was the media coverage that was responsible for the loss of the Vietnam War. We saw a media war within that war, too, as former *Washington Post* reporter William Prochna remembers before Vietnam:

We had already endured a century full of wars. Heavily-censored wars. So total was the government manipulation of public opinion in World War I that the chief U.S. propagandist charged with getting us into the fray later described his efforts as "the world's greatest adventure in advertising." Censorship was so uniformly accepted in World War II that *Life* magazine did not run a photograph of a dead American until 1943, and the director of the Office of Censorship was given a special Pulitzer Prize citation. The Cold War, with its threat of nuclear extinction, brought self-censorship to a new level.

In Vietnam, at first, Kennedy actually believed he could fight it as the communists fought theirs—in secret. How could you censor a war you weren't fighting? So Vietnam began uncensored and stayed uncensored. But Kennedy could not keep the war small and surely not secret.

Inevitably, Kennedy ran head-on into the beginning of the so-called generation gap that would haunt the '60s, and (or did Vietnam start both?) a massive sea change in American journalism. Wars are fought by the young. They are also reported by the young. And the young Vietnam reporters of the early '60s were neither constrained by censorship nor total-war certainties.

Shockingly, they began to report that the emperor wore no clothes. Americans were dying. The government was lying. Perhaps the unkindest of cuts, the United States was losing despite the rosy optimism of inflated body counts and politicized "victories" in non-battles fought by its South Vietnamese clients.

Some of the early correspondents—David Halberstam of the *New York Times;* Neil Sheehan of UPI; Malcolm Browne, Arnett, and Faas of AP—became legends and worked their way into history as surely as the policymakers. Sheehan, standing in an airport knot of reporters, once welcomed Defense Secretary Robert S. McNamara to Saigon with a loud, mocking stage whisper, "Ah, another foolish Westerner come to lose reputation to Ho Chi Minh." The sea change was not without its bruises among the reporters. Most of them still in their 20s, the reporters were attacked as too young and inexperienced by Kennedy's government and chased down as communist sympathizers by the South Vietnamese secret police. They also were assaulted, their patriotism questioned by the old guard in the press corps, veterans of the "last good war" against the Germans and Japanese.

With Vietnam over, the study groups, seminars, and lectures at the War College began the preparation for handling the media in the inevitable wars to come. If censorship couldn't be the rule, outflanking would—time has not narrowed the gulf.

Post-Vietnam Media Management

So what we have had are large amounts of money and manpower invested in controlling the media. At the same time, with mounting media consolidation, with the corporatization of the news biz and its integration into show biz, there was a sea change inside the media business. This is the context that is often missed with all the Bush bashing. One man did not organize this war.

It took powerful institutions: a military industrial MEDIA complex.

We have to put it in the context not just of U.S. foreign policy but of the way our modern media system works. Viewers in Italy have watched how your TV system—from RAI to private channels—has been Berlusconized. You know what I am talking about. Here you have an unholy alliance of media and government power. In the U.S., corporate media has become a handmaiden of special interests.

News managers who were not journalists took over and bottom-line pressures begat infotainment and more and more celebrity coverage. Pundits soon outnumbered journalists. Journalism schools started producing more PR experts than reporters.

The government took PR to a new level: It is called "perception management" and it treats war as a product to be "rolled out" and promoted. It is serious and systematic.

Twenty-four-hour cable news channels offered more news, not better news. They soon degenerated into a headline hit parade. Investigative reporting had long since given way to "breaking news" free of context and background. In-depth documentaries disappeared from the prime time environment. Reality-based programming replaced reports anchored in reality.

Anchormen complained that the media had gone from being a watchdog to a lap dog, but did nothing about it.

It was this transformation of the media system—implemented over twenty years with an assist by deregulation of public interest laws—that made the media a willing accomplice—especially in the post-9/11 environment of fear and patriotic correctness. When news anchors started emulating politicians by wearing American flags in their lapels, it became clear that the news media was being integrated into what amounted to a state-run media system.

Soon there were embedded reporters narrowly focusing their reports on the ground campaign while the air attacks, use of prohibited weapons, special covert operations teams and civilian casualties went uncovered. It was deliberate but occasioned little comment with news networks seeking Pentagon approval for their on-camera experts and former generals to offer sports-like play-by-play assessments. Reporters in the field began to identify with the soldiers, often saying "WE" when they began their reports, as if their news organizations were part of the war —as they were. Hollywood story-telling techniques replaced fact-based journalism with a master narrative and "message points" influencing media coverage. Hollywood producers and graphic artists were recruited to give war coverage high production values. It was like a movie shoot. *Time* magazine called it "militainment."

The U.S. military commander Tommy Franks created a "Secret Plan" which was quietly leaked to friendly journalists like those at Fox News. He spoke of the media as "the fourth front" of the war, not a separate and autonomous fourth estate. No wonder CNN's Christianne Amanpour would later admit: "It looks like this was disinformation at the highest levels."

It didn't just look that way. It was that way.

She charged that her own network was "muzzled" and blamed not just the government but the foot soldiers at Rupert Murdoch's Fox Network. In a hyper-competitive environment, no journalists or networks want to be accused of backing terrorists. When the President says repeatedly, you are "either with us or the terrorists" a clear signal is sent. Media companies that need favors, access to power and regulatory rule changes are unlikely to become a critical platform. It is not in their interest. In this environment, you get along by going along. That's what most did.

One result: out of 800 experts on all the U.S. channels from the run-up to the war until April 9, 2003, when the statues were brought down by the U.S. military and a carefully assembled crowd of U.S. supporters, only six opposed the war.

Only six!

The media environment was soon charged with a mix of seductive co-optation that gave selected journalists access to the front lines and military protection and intimation, attacks on critical reporting, denunciations of journalists who stepped out of line and even, some charge, the deliberate targeting and killing of journalists in incidents such as the one at the Palestine Hotel.

My film, *WMD: Weapons of Mass Deception,* reports on these incidents and quotes the distinguished historian of the media and war, Phillip Knightly, as saying that he now believes that the firing on media sites was deliberate. CNN's Eason Jordan told a panel at the World Economic Forum in January 2005, that journalists were targeted. When challenged, he seems to have backed away from his initial claim that 12 journalists had been killed by the U.S. military. There has yet to be an independent investigation.

Please understand, this does not add up to a critique of a few lapses or media mistakes. The Iraq War was not a catalogue of errors or flaws. It was planned and formatted, pre-produced and aired with high production values, and designed to persuade, not just inform.

Yes, some news organizations including the *Washington Post* and *New York Times* did limited *media culpas* and admitted they were not critical enough, especially on the WMD issue which turned out to be total hoax despite repeated assurances over months that they were there, had to be there, would be found, etc., etc. Once this fraud was unmasked, the Administration and the media shifted message points and asserted that the WMDs that were pictured as threat to the world were no longer terribly important. They were counting on the public's short attention span.

More recently we saw that the Iraqi election in which voters came out to demand an end to occupation was spun as vindication of the Administration's war policy. The focus was on their bravery, not their motivation. President Bush was clearly the winner with a rise in public opinion approval.

The template and routines of pro-war coverage continue even as the public turns against the war. Critics still have to fight for airtime while Administration officials and pro-war Democrats are constantly on the air.

What does all this mean?

That we live in a mediaocracy, not a democracy.

That our media which enjoys constitutional protections to act as a guardian of democracy is actively undermining it. Media intimidation made it impossible for our opposition party to even make the war an issue. John Kerry was viciously demonized for his opposition to the Vietnam War and his service record was distorted—for weeks. This is a pattern that has not changed.

That is why this issue is so relevant and timely.

What we are seeing is a crime against democracy and the public's right to know.

It is a crime against the people of Iraq who have suffered and died in large numbers in this war even though the extent of it is not reported. We have had coverage of torture incidents but no real investigation of the responsibility of decision-makers. Only a handful of journalists follow that story closely, including Seymour Hersh who exposed the My-Lai massacre in Vietnam. He publishes in a smaller magazine, not a big newspaper.

This is a crime against our soldiers whose grueling experience goes largely unreported as do their casualties and psychological traumas.

It is a crime against the profession of journalism that has been shamelessly distorted even as many conscientious reporters soldier on, often in an alternative media that reaches a smaller audience.

Crimes demand exposure and punishment.

That's why I have come all this way to Rome, to add the voice of an American journalist to the call for consequences for these crimes and more debate about them in the anti-war movement. This kind of media complicity has to be challenged, refuted, condemned and opposed.

This World Tribunal is doing it. That's why I am here.

Will this Tribunal be covered—or covered up?

The fight for a free and independent media is a global fight. We need to show solidarity with each other. Journalists in other countries need to appreciate the fact that many Americans are speaking out and to understand the pressures we are under.

We need to dialogue with each other and support media freedom.

I have come to stand up and be counted, to offer myself. That's all I can do. Grazie.

Danny Schechter
News Dissector
Feb. 8, 2005

"So far, there has been little unvarnished ground-level detail, let alone *Black Hawk Down* scenes of gritty action. Instead, the broadcast news channels spend the bulk of the day *oohing* and *aahing* about military hardware or serving as very expensive communications systems for soldiers to talk to their families back home ("Hi mom! I'm OK!").

"There's nothing wrong with this human-interest reporting on its own terms, but live TV has overemphasized novelty and sensation, such as an MSNBC reporter excitedly experiencing a sandstorm, which was transmitted at length in a fuzzy orange-pink haze on Tuesday morning."

—Meghan O'Rourke
Culture editor, *Slate* magazine, 2003

"…my going there is a giant fuck you to the insurgents. They know that I go. They all have cable TV. They know I bring this bravado. These concerns I'm expressing, I'm voicing to you—I don't express them on TV. So I am swaggering in there, 'Here I am—fuck with me if you can.' And the GI's get a tremendous kick out of it. I am going to pump them up at every place we stop. To do my best at any place I stop, and I will sign as many autographs as I can, say as many 'Hey Moms' as I can. In a sense it's my duty."

—Geraldo Rivera
Embedded reporter, Fox News Channel
Reporting on plans to return to Iraq, *The Atlantic,* June 2005

⇒3⇐

Media Cover-ups and Complicity

Crossing the Line

The ongoing Iraq War is a media war as well as a military conflict. It has been one of the most covered wars in history: 2700 members of the media were registered before the start of the war at U.S. military headquarters in Kuwait, 600 became embedded under the terms and conditions of the Pentagon program, another 2100 were so-called "unilaterals."

Each news organization brought along small armies of support staffs including armed security personnel. Some came to report the war and others ended up fighting it, as Bill Katovsky observed in another book called *embedded* (with a small *e*) (The Lyons Press, 2003). His volume features over 60 interviews with journalists and government officials who were there. It puts the lie to the idea that all the embedded journalists were tools of the Pentagon or security risks but also shows how limited their reporting was.

On the positive side as Katovsky writes, "From both the Pentagon and press's perspective, the embedding experiment was a gamble worth taking. On the surface, it was a demonstration of democratic values and freedom of speech and in action, in contrast to the dark tyranny and disinformation of Saddam's government."

That was on the surface, and it did produce some good reporting. But beneath the surface, as he also noted, "Those journalistic impulses to write the truth have almost always been warped and bent and twisted under the more powerful forces of national interest, force, propaganda and ideology."

53

No wonder Dick Cheney thanked reporters after the invasion phase ended and Donald Rumsfeld called U.S. coverage "helpful."

Katovsky explained how the press became embedded: "A few of these correspondents quietly admitted that they became attracted to the adrenaline rush of battle. Others confessed that they continue to be haunted by what they saw and heard. Some reporters crossed the line of sacred objectivity and grabbed hand grenades, pointed out snipers, wore guns or hired armed security."

The identification and excitement with what was happening "in the field" was mirrored at many network headquarters in New York where producers sought to maximize production values and get the most dramatic shots on the air. At NBC, according to the network's own book chronicling the war and their coverage (also packaged with a DVD), using the Administration's own campaign theme *Operation Iraqi Freedom* as its title, there was "pandemonium" in the control room when the statues of Saddam were brought down by U.S. troops, who later disclosed it was part of a PsyOps operation.

Moments later, after the Iraqis with sticks and hammers had attacked the statue's head, it was time for a replay of what had just happened. Senior producer Bob Epstein, connected by intercom to the tape-editing area, barked through his microphone, "Gimme smashing head, I need smashing head." Perhaps it was our heads—the viewers of all this—that were being "smashed"—smashed into accepting the war.

Why did we stage a preemptive war in the first place? What was the real agenda? And why aren't the media investigating THAT? On August 10, 2004 former war commander General Tommy Franks—in a talk only reported by the Jewish Telegraphic Agency and not picked up by major media—explained why the Pentagon rushed to war:

> The reason we could not afford to give up time is because we wanted the water infrastructure to remain in place. We wanted the oil infrastructure in Iraq to remain in place. We did not want to subject ourselves and Israel to the potential consequence of a long-range missile being fired into Tel Aviv or Jerusalem.

How much media time and energy was spent investigating the Israeli connection to the war? How much time on military preparedness or the "plan" that got us into Baghdad quickly and then stirred a hornet's nest of resistance? How many of our media experts, pundits, prognosticators and Mensa Men prepared us for what was to happen next? There was instead an over-current of triumphalism that ignored and minimized the reaction by Iraqis to the occupation of their country.

The coverage failed to anticipate—or even effectively criticize the looting of Iraq's historic treasures. By the time the U.S. media focused on the issue, it was too late. On April 8, 2003, Tony Blair and George Bush said: "We reaffirm our commitment to protect Iraq's natural resources, as the patrimony of the people of Iraq, which should be used only for their benefit." And so they did—by protecting the Oil Ministry while the country's museums and cultural treasures were looted. Some of that was covered—but the aftermath has been ignored as Tom Englehardt notes on his blog TomDispatch.com:

> Worse yet, the looting of antiquity, words and objects, not only never ended but seems to have accelerated. From well-organized gangs of grave robbers to American engineers building bases to American soldiers taking souvenirs, the ancient inheritance not just of Iraqis but of all of us has simply headed south. According to Reuters, more than 1,000 Iraqi objects of antiquity have been confiscated at American airports, priceless cylinder seals are evidently selling online at eBay for a few hundred dollars apiece. And this represents just the tiniest fraction of what's gone. The process is not only unending, but in the chaos that is America's Iraq, beyond counting or assessing accurately.

And what about the real conduct of the U.S. military operations? As the war began, NBC's Tom Brokaw assured viewers that the military would keep damage to a minimum because "we are going to own that country in a few days."

So how do we explain the less than "pinpoint" bombing that took out the infrastructure including electricity, the widespread civilian casualties, the use of cluster bombs, napalm-like fire bombs and weapons

hardened with radioactive depleted uranium? What about the privatization of the war and all the contractors making a fortune overcharging
for services in no-bid contracts? One subject that was undercovered:
Who got what and why?

And what about oil? When activists started chanting "No Blood for Oil,"
news programs and government officials dismissed the charge as conspir-
atorial and denied it. In early April 2005, Ian Routledge wrote to the
Financial Times:

> So when, according to the former head of ExxonMobil's Gulf operations, "Iraqi
> exiles approached us saying, you can have our oil if we can get back in there,"
> the Bush Administration decided to use its overwhelming military might to cre-
> ate a pliant—and dependable—oil protectorate in the Middle East and achieve
> that essential "opening" of the Gulf oilfields.

> But in the words of another U.S. oil company executive, "it all turned out a lot
> more complicated than anyone had expected." Instead of the anticipated post-
> invasion rapid expansion of Iraqi production, the continuing violence of the insur-
> gency has prevented Iraqi exports from even recovering to pre-invasion levels.

> In short, the U.S. appears to have fought a war for oil in the Middle East and
> lost it. The consequences of that defeat are now plain to see.

Why did most media outlets ignore all these issues? What about systematic war crimes and human rights abuses? The atrocities in Abu Ghraib prison
were known as early as June 2003 but only exposed in April 2004. How could
we justify the bombing of civilians in Fallujah and, a month later in Najaf?
How is it that media outlets in other countries can report on Iraqi protests
against U.S. military practices in Iraq and ours cannot? Why did Mr. Murdoch's
newspaper *The Australian* call U.S. military operations in Najaf a "slaughter"
while the U.S. media was focusing on a raid on a dissident cleric's home?
(Perhaps this is because a dollop of anti-Americanism sells well in Australia.)

Most of our media, with the exception, perhaps, of excellent reporting
by Knight Ridder and some exemplary dissenting journalists, have largely
supported the war including the government's rationalizations and narrative. ("Support" can be measured in what is covered and what is not, what

experts we hear from and which we do not, and how many thoughtful Iraqis themselves make it into our news.)

These larger media failures have still not been acknowledged, much less debated. That's why the term "weapons of mass deception" still applies to a media that are at war with their own uncomfortable truths.

Media coverage tends to lurch from event to event, and from spectacle to spectacle as a substance-deficit disorder hyperactively drives the news agenda. No sooner are we focused on one major story, than another intrudes to change the subject and insure that there is no time for follow-up, much less thoughtful processing. The pace of the coverage tends to insure that little will be remembered, much less understood.

One minute, we are still debating election returns in Ohio and Florida. And then, in a flash, the story largely disappears and the subject changes. In some cases, this is the natural disorder of news, but in many others, there are hidden hands shifting the agenda in a conscious effort not simply to influence what we think, but control what we think about. For example, the Administration wanted to refocus us on the elections in Iraq, not the reports of deep flaws in the American elections.

"News of the war in Iraq is treated as an inconvenient interruption of all the entertaining reports on movie stars getting married and pop stars going on trial," explained the indefatigable Studs Terkel. "As a result, it becomes too easy to forget that kids from this country are dying just about every day in some distant fight that, because of our media, is too easily forgotten." Quickly, we moved on as the news media converged on Fallujah to report on, and in the view of many, support what has been the bloodiest chapter to date of the Iraq War.

The coverage of the fight for Fallujah is a case in point; the U.S. military made clear that "information control" was its first priority. When U.S. troops seized a hospital there, the goal was said to insure that news about civilian casualties not infiltrate the news agenda.

The Guardian and the BBC managed to cover events that were barely discussed in the U.S. A film, *City of Ghosts,* aired in February 2005 on BBC in the U.K. Here's how the Beeb describes the film:

It [the battle of Fallujah] was billed as a resounding military success. Over 1200 insurgents were meant to have been killed and another 2000 trapped inside Fallujah. But now this version of events is being challenged. Far from being crushed, rebels claim they left the city in an organized withdrawal. "It was a tactical move," explains insurgent leader Alazaim Abuthe. "The fighters decided to redeploy to Amiriya." Before they left, fighters booby-trapped many bodies. People are too scared to move them so the corpses lie rotting all over the city. Rabid dogs feed off them and then attack returning residents. Far from stabilizing Iraq in preparation for this month's election, the assault on Fallujah has fanned the flames of civil war. Today Fallujahns are too busy trying to stay alive in freezing refugee camps to worry about ballot papers that haven't arrived for an election they have no intention of voting in. As one resident comments, "We're not interested in this sort of democracy."

Even though the British government backs the war, British media were able to get this gripping story on the air. The U.S. networks could have bought the rights to show the film had they wanted to. Neither the media nor the Pentagon, it seems, wanted to tell the story.

Firms like The Rendon Group, run by the shadowy PR svengali John Rendon, were used to map the world of news and figure out its vulnerabilities. They created channels of influence, people who would do their bidding. It was a form of infiltration—but infiltration with little resistance. Jerome Doolittle, a former White House speechwriter turned blogger writes about the work of Robert Baer, a former CIA officer who worked with Rendon starting at the end of the 1991 Gulf War, recounting the experiences of a staffer who understood how profitable this work could be:

... the company signed a secret contract with the CIA which guaranteed that it would receive a 10 percent "management fee" on top of whatever money it spent. The arrangement was an incentive to spend millions. "We tried to burn through $40 million dollars a year," a staffer said. "It was a very nice job."

From an office near Victoria Station, The Rendon Group set out to influence global political opinion against Saddam. Given Saddam's record of atrocities against his own people, it wasn't a hard sell. "It was a campaign environment, with a lot of young people, and no set hierarchy," he recalled. "It was great. We had a real competitive advantage. We knew something about the twenty-four-hour media cycle and how to manage a media campaign. CNN was new at that point. No one else knew how to do these things, but Rendon was great at issue campaigns." The group began offering information to British journalists, and many articles subsequently appeared in the London press.

"Occasionally," he said, "the company would be reprimanded by project managers in Washington when too many of those stories were picked up by the American press, thereby transgressing laws that prohibited domestic propaganda. But, for the most part, it was amazing how well it worked. It was like magic."

Preceding the war, months of demonization of Saddam Hussein played out in the media. A dictator in a sanctions-crippled society that the U.S. had put in power in the first place and had armed for years was pictured as prepared to attack the United States or the world—take your pick. He was compared to Adolph Hitler; *Time* magazine even redid a classic cover of the Führer, replacing his face with the "butcher of Baghdad." Virtually no media outlets challenged the parallel or the "intelligence" behind a comparison that was later exposed for its lack of intelligence.

The Hitler-Saddam comparison played well with neo-conservatives who compared Baathism to Nazism and designed a de-Baathization program for a post-Saddam Iraq modeled on post-World War II de-Nazification. It was this ideological construct that led to the firing of the whole Iraqi army as a Baathist-dominated institution, insuring the chaos to come.

The Bush Administration, which successfully mobilized the media and public opinion behind their military war, still uses the same techniques in their political war to control public perception. In many ways, the Bush Administration's obsession with Saddam's authoritarianism led to its imitation. They replaced Saddam's Ministry of Information, which had controlled Iraqi media, with their own system of media control. Saddam used the old Soviet commissar system to insure party control; the U.S. has since done almost the same thing—political officers were inserted into the military; campaign operatives ran the Doha media center.

The embedded reporters may be gone now, but the routines of political coverage and their deferential approach can be relied on to achieve the same results.

Ministry of Newsspeak

In their book *All the President's Spin,* authors Ben Fritz, Bryan Keefer and Brendan Nyhan analyze the White House spin machine and assesses why it is so successful. They explain:

> Bush's White House has broken new ground in its press relations strategy, exploiting the weaknesses and failings of the political media more systemati-cally than any of its predecessors. The Administration combines tight message discipline and image management—Reagan's trademarks—with the artful use of half- or partial truths and elaborate news management—Clinton's specialties—in a combination that is near-lethal for the press.

The authors cite four key weaknesses of the press that help a deter-mined media spin operation get its message—and none other—through. It is an aggressive strategy consciously fashioned against a media establish-ment wary of giving credence to charges of liberal bias and fearful of chal-lenging a self-described "war president" after September 11:

> First and foremost, reporters are constrained by the norm of objectivity, which frequently causes them to avoid evaluating the truth of politicians' statements. In addition, because reporters are dependent upon the White House for news, the Administration can shape the coverage it receives by restricting the flow of information to the press. The media are also vulnerable to political pressure and reprisal, which the Bush White House has aggressively dished out against critical journalists. Finally, the press' unending pursuit of scandal and enter-taining news often blinds it to serious issues of public policy.

University of California, Berkeley, linguistics professor George Lakoff analyzed the way the issues were carefully framed by speakers at the GOP convention in August 2004 to focus their messages. "Effective framing," he writes, "is equally about what's excluded from the frame. Frames, once established, are hermetically sealed. You can only think within the frame, only reason with what the frame allows."

Lakoff applied this analysis to the convention speeches given by John McCain and Rudy Giuliani:

> McCain's speech framed the Iraq War as an inseparable part of the Great War on Terror, a battle of Right versus Wrong, of Good versus Evil—a war of necessity, not choice. "We must fight; we must," he [McCain] said, calling the Iraq War a "rendezvous with destiny" [quoting FDR on World War II] and arguing "there was no status quo to be left alone."

The argument became that, although apparently Saddam Hussein didn't have weapons of mass destruction, he would have had them sooner or later. Exactly when isn't important, because as Giuliani said, Saddam "was a weapon of mass destruction himself." When the literal isn't there, the metaphorical will do.

For months in the run-up to the war, it was WMD this, and WMD that, even though in most of the world, and for most of the years in which that term was in use, it only referenced radioactive nuclear weapons such as the ones that took hundreds of thousands of lives in one blast in Hiroshima and Nagasaki. (That's real mass destruction.) The Bush Administration, for political reasons, took the term WMD and stretched, bent and spindled it to describe chemical and biological agents of every exotic design.

By the time Bush's reelection rolled around, the carefully managed and manipulated narrative had already become well propagandized. As many as 80 percent of Bush supporters told pollsters they believed that there still were WMDs in Iraq even after the President dropped the issue and when directly questioned said none had been found.

A study of Iraq's biological warfare program by Geoffrey Holland of the University of Sussex found that "the United States breached the Biological and Toxin Weapons Convention (BTWC) by supplying warfare-related biological materials to Iraq during the 1980s, at a time when that nation was at war with its neighbor." Holland also reports, "… that the anthrax threat from Iraq, a repeatedly cited reason for the 2003 invasion of that country, actually originated from a dead cow in South Oxfordshire."

And so the concept of WMDs was transformed for political reasons without any media challenge. This approach reflects a sophisticated understanding of how to use language to be persuasive. Concludes Lakoff, "People think in terms of frames. If this frame is accepted, all such 'rational' arguments will be beside the point. Negating the frame would just reinforce it. The facts alone won't do the job."

The careful framing of the issues by officials during the war still continues. The White House handles the press the way TV producers package programs: with careful preplanning, structured themes and packaged information. And so the "militainment" we saw during the war has given way to "electotainment," a carefully concocted blend of news business and show business. The dynamics of coverage remain largely the same: simplistic, superficial and uncritical.

Spinning and framing events invariably rely on deception as a key component of war fighting. There are five elements of this strategy currently in play:

1. Shape a Narrative

    In Fallujah, the U.S. narrative and key talking point was making Iraq "safe" for democracy and elections. To achieve this—or so the storyline goes—the U.S. must restore "local control," end the insurgency and kill or otherwise neutralize "foreign fighters" from whose ranks the U.S. forces exempt themselves and their "coalition" partners.

2. It's All About U.S.

    The U.S. media focuses on "our boys" and U.S. government agendas, not Iraqi civilians, religious leaders or political representatives. It is always all about us, not Iraq. In that context, Iraqis who are resisting U.S. forces are referred to as "insurgents" or "foreign fighters." In the case of Fallujah, for example, Iraq specialists argued that what the townspeople wanted was local control, but in their own hands. Much of what the U.S. refers to as the "insurgency," the locals call the resistance or *mujahideen.* Yet in the U.S., we rarely hear that this movement is home-grown, not foreign in origin or direction. But why let the facts get in the way of a misleading if marketable narrative?

We can see this in how we frame the death toll as well. The death toll is always rationalized afterwards as necessary and unintentional. This is a point made with eloquence by *The Guardian's* Madeleine Bunting, with a perspective conspicuous by its absence in most U.S. reporting:

> Assaults on cities serve symbolic purposes: they are set showpieces to demonstrate resolve and inculcate fear. To that end, large numbers of casualties are required: they are not an accidental byproduct but the aim. That was the thinking behind 9/11, and Fallujah risks becoming a horrible mirror-image of that atrocity. Only by the shores of that dusty lake in Dreamland would it be possible to believe that the ruination of this city will do anything to enhance the legitimacy of the U.S. occupation and of the Iraqi government it appointed.

Little attention is paid to the effect these actions may have in actually thwarting our stated goals. There were warnings by the UN's Kofi Annan and European leaders that this ferocious attack on Fallujah would make fair elections nationwide unlikely. As it turned out, Iraqi Sunnis did not vote, while most other voters said they were voting to get the Americans out, not for some abstract concept called "democracy."

3. Control Media Access

The U.S. military plays the press as a "fourth front," not a traditionally autonomous fourth estate. Suddenly, the embedding program is back in place, with journalists dependent on U.S. forces for their information and protection. As Madeleine Bunting explained further in *The Guardian,* "It's long since been too dangerous for journalists to move around unless they are embedded with the U.S. forces. There is almost no contact left with civilians still in Fallujah; the only information is from those who have left."

The result of this is largely one-sided coverage.

4. Spin the Theme of Iraqi Control

To undercut any suggestion of a foreign occupation running things, the official story line had it that it was the Iraqis under the Allawi government (actually, but rarely mentioned, was its status as a temporary, unelected and unstable entity), who are in charge, with the U.S. troops merely supporting them.

Julian Manion of Britain's ITV put the lie to this assertion on the first day of fighting, November 8, 2004, reporting, "We've had now, this morning, the formality—some would call it, I'm afraid, the fiction—that Iyad Allawi, the prime minister of Iraq, has given the official order to commence the operation against Fallujah. Of course in reality it is an American operation." On that same day, CNN was reporting that the Allawi government was calling the shots.

5. Avoid Historical Parallels

While media critics were invoking parallels to towns in Vietnam that were destroyed in order to be saved, there was little perspective offered on the realities of that parallel. AP reported: "Sgt. Maj. Carlton W. Kent told an assembled group of 2500 Marines in a 'pep-talk' on November 7 [2004], 'You're all in the process of making history. This is another Hue City in the making. I have no doubt, if we do get the word, that each and every one of you is going to do what you have always done—kick some butt.'"

Even when this parallel was invoked directly by U.S. soldiers, the media failed to offer the context and remind the public of the historical outcome of that military intervention. Only a few analysts reminded audiences that after U.S. soldiers reoccupied Hue after the Tet Offensive of 1968, then-Under Secretary of the Air Force Townsend Hoopes described the results as leaving "a devastated and prostrate city. Eighty percent of the buildings had been reduced to rubble, and in the smashed ruins lay 2000 dead civilians. ..."

While American media outlets have largely avoided any parallels between Iraq and Vietnam—with pundits insisting that none exist—overseas some see what many of us don't or won't. Unreported in the U.S. were reports of a protest in Hanoi against the bombing of Baghdad. I have seen the photo. A BBC story April 30, 2005, by Matt Frei reports, "Thirty years after the end of the war, Vietnam continues to divide and haunt America far more than the country that lost 50 times as many people." And so, the 30th anniversary of the end of the Vietnam War was marked in Vietnam with celebrations, but it was largely ignored in the U.S., where CNN led with the story of a runaway bride who went missing when she had second thoughts.

One reason for the lack of historical perspective is not simply media amnesia. Most TV news reporting follows templates, constructing action-oriented and picture-driven "breaking news" with little time and fewer resources allocated for background and context.

By July of 2004, much of what was left of the pretexts and rationalizations for the U.S. invasion of Iraq had unraveled. Public opinion had started to turn against the war. The press was filled with admissions of "failures." Some journalists and newspapers took a second look at some of their coverage and acknowledged it had been flawed. There were admissions of misreporting, especially on the issue of the existence of weapons of mass destruction in Iraq. The government of course had vociferously insisted that Iraq had WMDs, and the media believed it without hard evidence. As we know now, that turned out not to be the case.

Richard Clarke, President Bush's own terrorism coordinator, went public with a view of the war as evidence of a failure of policy. It was, he charged, not only NOT part of the War on Terror but undermining it. He accused the government of intentionally misleading the public by linking September 11th and Iraq and implying a close connection to Osama bin Laden. "It's not hard to understand," Clarke wrote in his book *Against All Enemies,* "why 70 percent of the American people believed that Saddam Hussein had attacked the Pentagon and the World Trade Center."

Critics and Cover-ups

Experienced military leaders like General Anthony Zinni and others condemned the war as a military failure. A Senate committee in the U.S. and a commission headed by Lord Butler in the U.K. catalogued extensive intelligence failures. U.S. senators condemned the pervasive group think, and later a presidential commission said the intelligence had been "dead wrong." Why had the media not been challenging the contrived case for war?

These critics—including the 9/11 Commission—remained relatively narrow in their approach by focusing on problems or process and organizational defects. Few looked at the larger picture or dared to hold politicians directly accountable. The Butler Commission specifically exonerated Prime Minister Tony Blair.

Critics consider most of these inquiries as part of a cover-up, not signs of serious investigation to expose wrong-doing and, more importantly, its consequences. In intelligence circles, this is called a "limited hang out," a technique in which some disclosures are dribbled out to avoid revealing more devastating ones. That phrase translates roughly as "you concede a little to hide a lot." The effect is an illusion, a lack of real accountability.

Take the *New York Times*. On July 16, 2004, it admitted in an editorial that "we were wrong about the weapons." But what about the rest of its coverage, which underplayed civilian casualties, missed many of the reasons for the Iraqi resistance, and initially what was behind the Abu Ghraib torture story?

The *Washington Post's* ombudsman Michael Getler selectively critiqued his newspaper's coverage, faulting for example the downplaying of demonstrations, as did media correspondent Howard Kurtz. Editorially the *Washington Post* said little and refused to mount an internal investigation of its own flawed coverage. The television networks that most Americans relied on for their news and information about the war also said little or nothing. They moved on to other stories without any acknowledgment that the modes of coverage that we saw during the war were manipulated and had not changed fundamentally over the last two years.

When these *mea culpas* appeared, I was delighted to see some limited confession about errors and omissions on the part of media outlets that, when it really counted, had become transmission belts for unsubstantiated government claims and pro-war propaganda. It gave me and other media critics faith in the capacity of our profession to acknowledge at least some wrongdoing, correct mistakes and admit that some of our top media outlets in effect drank the White House Kool-Aid.

Bear in mind that many of these same outlets often had been arrogant and self-righteous, impervious to war critics who they treated like lepers who were in denial about real threats and the need for a Washington-led preemptive strike. It took a long time for these admissions to come to the surface, alas, well after they could do any good in terms of influencing the decision to go to war.

In selling the Iraq War the Administration dipped into the playbook of Hollywood narrative techniques, relying on storytelling, not just sloganizing. They told stories of soldiers under fire as well as those tortured by Saddam Hussein. A master narrative was concocted to fit the good guy/bad guy formula that works so well on the silver screen. The narrative was simplified into themes justifying preemptive intervention as the only recourse, whatever its legality.

The Strategy Comes Home

Corporate PR pros helped plan and execute this strategy. Andrew Card, the President's top aid, compared the launch of the war to a "product roll-out." With some modifications, the Administration continued to use the same strategy for the Bush reelection campaign, on the theory that if "it ain't broke, don't fix it." This time their media plan relied on demonizing John Kerry, with repeated charges like "flip flopper" and distorted information that was rarely scrutinized in the same way as WMD claims had been accepted. Correcting misinformation has to be done immediately, before impressions become convictions. In the case of the Swift Boat Veterans, the Kerry people were slow in responding. By the time the charges were discredited, it was too late. The damage to his reputation had been achieved.

We saw and heard war rationalizations endlessly, simplified: "The war was forced on us"; "We will either fight them there or here"; "Saddam Hussein was a Weapon of Mass Destruction"; "Kerry was for the war until he was against it"; etc., etc. This approach mirrored techniques used earlier during the run-up to the war as Maureen Dowd of the *New York Times* explained:

> These guys figure, hey, these scare tactics worked in building support for the Iraq War, maybe they can work in tearing down support for John Kerry. They linked Saddam with terrorism and cowed the Democrats (including Mr. Kerry, who has never been able to make the case against the Bush Administration's *trompe l'oeil casus belli)* and fooled the country into going along with their trumped-up war. So why not link Mr. Kerry with terrorism and cow the voters into sticking with the White House they've got?

Only a few commentators in the media even commented on the "Iraqiazation" of our domestic election coverage. Paul Krugman of the *New York Times* was one of them, writing, "...the triumph of the trivial is not a trivial matter. The failure of TV news to inform the public about the policy proposals of this year's presidential candidates is, in its own way, as serious a journalistic betrayal as the failure to raise questions about the rush to invade Iraq."

The GOP convention climaxed the strategy, showcasing all of the techniques that were built around vicious personal attacks and distorted arguments; they blatantly ignored any and all information that had earlier debunked them. (The same Administrative operative, Jim Wilkinson, who managed media at the Coalition Media Center in Doha, and described by a *Houston Chronicle* reporter as a commissar straight out of Stalin, ran the GOP media operation in New York. The Iraq War media strategy became the GOP political strategy.)

A 9/11-Iraq connection was shamelessly exploited and reinforced as if the 9/11 Commission had never happened, or the Senate Intelligence Committee Report debunking the parallel had never been issued. The Republicans paid no respect for fact; instead they hammered home points and slogans that delegates could mindlessly repeat like a mantra of received truth. Once again "faith-based" information trumped "fact-based reporting."

Perhaps you could expect that from politicians but what of the media? Why weren't news organizations doing fact checks and debunking distortions? A few did, but most did not. When Zell Miller, the Republican keynoter finished his rant, he did find himself challenged aggressively by a few journalists–Chris Matthews on MSNBC and Wolf Blitzer on CNN. That was it. Jon Stewart featured the confrontations as a high point on his Comedy Channel show without mentioning that their challenges were the exceptions to uncritical coverage.

The *Washington Post's* sometime-liberal columnist Richard Cohen called Miller's diatribe a "Category Five Lie," and characterized the speech "as mad an eruption of hate as I have witnessed in politics. Some time back, Kerry must have dissed Miller. This was personal."

But was it? Miller actually published a book that most of the press corps had not bothered to dig out, called *A National Party No More.* In it he trashes all the Democratic White House hopefuls at the time in the nastiest terms. The Republicans knew where Miller stood even if the press corps hadn't bothered to find it out.

Most of the GOP convention was then treated as a Bush triumph because of his "likability." His speech was not scrutinized. The largest protest at any convention in American history, with more than 1700 arrests (as opposed to 600 in Chicago in 1968), contained by police-state tactics, treated as a nuisance by the GOP, and ignored in most of the press, except on the Sunday before the event began. The streets around Madison Square Garden in New York City came to resemble Baghdad's high security Green Zone. Later, court cases challenged police abuses and won compensation.

Protests against the media coverage in New York were also largely ignored. I know. I spoke at one rally outside Fox News headquarters in midtown Manhattan, just down the block from CNN studios. The wire story that I saw of the event was by Agence France Press on a Turkish news website. I was interviewed by Canadian Public Radio, not NPR. One American newspaper was there–the *Toledo* (Ohio) *Blade.*

Jim Drew reported:

Outside the arena, a swarm of protesters, ignored by most of the national press but united in their efforts to oust Mr. Bush from the White House and fearful of what will happen if the race is tight and Mr. Bush declares victory on election night. For those of us with the "limited access" credentials that couldn't get us on the convention floor, the streets were an option. And the guerrilla reporters found [that] by far the most important and interesting story. In the age of international terrorism, the patriotic right of political dissent in the United States is in crisis.

Drew also quoted Peter Hart, of Fairness and Accuracy in Media which had organized the march on the media:

Mr. Hart said activists "demand a more accountable media," and they marched to the headquarters of "corporate media" to celebrate the independent and alternative press. "These are the people who sold us a war. The biggest media companies get bigger and bigger based on favors from the government. They sell ideas: that assistance to the poor must be reformed, and free trade is the only way. These are the ideas that the mainstream media are selling—and we're not buying," he said.

I was quoted too: "I've never seen the level of defensiveness in the major media, the level of disenchantment, and the level of dread; journalists on the front lines representing the public in some way feeling they can't play that role."

And why? Because their bosses and the culture of corporate news make it impossible.

At least some media outlets have not lost the spirit of independence and crusading that the U.S. press used to be known for.

The *Toledo Blade's* coverage of the protests mirrored its relentless coverage of war crimes. Not the alleged "crimes" of John Kerry who was being blasted inside the Garden, but real crimes committed in Vietnam 35 years ago by an American military unit that had all but been ignored by major media then and now. The *Blade* uncovered massacres by U.S. troops and bravely made it news. Their hope was that the Pentagon would reopen the issue. They didn't.

And so, once again, the coverage of war, or lack of coverage, was linked in this case by a heroic example of a newspaper in a small Ohio city in the heart of an electoral battleground state. The media battle, the political battle and the fight for truth about war were being joined again.

Meanwhile, as the war ground on, the media hung on. Soon they had less access as the security situation deteriorated, with the news only reporting on incidents with little background analysis. The old truism "when it bleeds, it leads" was never more true. Even as more mainstream media outlets admitted to failures in covering the Iraq War, a question must be asked: What will it take to get media organizations and journalists to challenge the distorted language of war-speak?

In fact, even opposition politicians like John Kerry ducked the issue arguing, in effect, that none of these misrepresentations mattered. When questioned at the time, he said that knowing what he knows now, he would still have supported the war, even if all of its rationalizations were invented and/or deliberately deceptive. The Democrats' capitulation to the White House had many causes and fear of media retaliation was one of them. What politician would want his or her patriotism questioned?

To this day, the media and Administration won't let the facts undercut their deceptive approach to managing public opinion. That may be because the emerging debate about the media role remains narrowly focused, avoiding deeper questions about the media's overall performance.

In August, 2004, I was asked to appear on a national TV news program as part of a panel on the issues of media complicity. I was told that we would be talking about the pre-war coverage of WMDs. That call came, predictably, after the *Washington Post* had carried a story about its pre-war coverage, questioning only how it handled the run-up to the war. Once again TV producers were following a newspaper's lead. The producer loved me until the program didn't. I was dropped at the last moment for the usual Washington insiders. In this case, it was the PBS "News Hour" that limited the range of the debate.

Many news organizations had top editors and producers keeping their troops in line. *Post* media critic Howard Kurtz reported that a story in his paper that had challenged the evidence on Iraq's weapon stockpiles "ran into stiff resistance from the paper's editors." The *Post's* Managing Editor

Bob Woodward, author of two insider books that are largely positive about President Bush, admitted, "We did our job but we didn't do enough, and I blame myself mightily for not pushing harder."

In his story, Kurtz intimated that the *Post's* performance was understandable since its chief competitor, the *New York Times,* was just as bad. He took a subtle swipe at the *Times,* noting, "The *New York Times* ran an editor's note last month saying the paper's aggressive reporting on WMDS was 'not as rigorous as it should have been' and overplayed stories with 'dire claims about Iraq,' adding, 'editors at several levels who should have been challenging reporters and pressing for more skepticism were perhaps too intent on rushing scoops into the paper.'"

In an apparent response, the *Times* followed by casting a skeptical 'ours-was-better-than-yours' eye on the *Post* exposé, noting: "For all of its contrition, Mr. Kurtz's article does not represent an official statement on behalf of the *Post.* In an interview yesterday [8-15-05], Steve Coll, the paper's managing editor, said that the idea for the article had been Mr. Kurtz's, and that he and [Executive Editor Leonard] Downie had recused themselves from editing it. 'We did not make a determination from our offices that we needed to commission an investigation into these issues,' Mr. Coll said."

There you have it, no investigation needed. None!

To contrast his paper's efforts, Jacques Steinberg of the *New York Times* explained that the *Times* published a 1220-word article in which the newspaper's editors acknowledged that in the run-up to war they had not been skeptical enough about articles that depended "at least in part on information from a circle of Iraqi informants, defectors, and exiles bent on 'regime change' in Iraq whose credibility has come under increasing public debate."

So here we have the *Times* using its news columns to put down the *Post.* But both papers and most of the TV coverage are guilty of far more than what has so far been conceded. Complicity and collusion are two words that come to mind. A real investigation of the media role would probe deeper questions not only about the run-up to the war but the ongoing coverage up to the present day.

By the following week, the *Washington Post* started to hear from readers responding to Howard Kurtz's story about mistakes in the media coverage. His *mea culpa* had raised some concerns about the *Post*'s miserable performance. Kurtz seemed defensive, noting that liberals were outraged and sent him a "torrent of emails and online postings," arguing that "the *Post* and its ilk could have slowed the drive to war if only we had tried harder to uncover the truth about Saddam Hussein's weapons of mass destruction. This view deserves an unvarnished response." (The headline gave away the fatalistic approach: "Ultimately Newspapers Can't Move the Earth.")

So Kurtz responded with a *mea culpa* for a *mea culpa,* noting that he was not directed to do the story, which says a lot right there about the management of the *Post* and its slow off-the-mark lack of self-criticism. Kurtz explained that many of his readers (I was among them) felt he was "too soft." He went on to patronizingly "explain the culture of American newsrooms" so his readers would understand and hopefully restrain their rage. "Don't expect us to do any better," said the *Post* defensively.

Kurtz then restated his approach, relating about all the agonizing he encountered in interviews that resembled therapy sessions, and how other reporters and editors recalled frustration and acknowledged missteps. Look at the framing of language being used by a media critic! He was eliciting sympathy for his colleagues and was understanding of their missteps because they are good people who were trying hard. Here was Kurtz, talking about reporting on policies that led to thousands of deaths and a newspaper whose editorials and op-ed page sounded like an extension of Donald Rumsfeld's office, and he wanted understanding!

Kurtz then had the nerve to shamelessly rail at his critics for being stupid, naïve and uninformed: they believe his newspaper has more power than it does; they believe the paper had "nefarious" motives. "Ridiculous" was the word he used to dismiss those who suggested the newspaper wanted war. Why would a newspaper want that?

Kurtz did admit that journalists were reluctant to challenge a President who was mobilizing support against a mass murderer. Yet his assessment

betrayed a deeper bias than he may have realized. It's hard to even pene-
trate the density of this convoluted back and forth on the one hand or the
other apologia for the *Post's* "missteps" at all.

Howard Kurtz may nibble at the hand that feeds but won't take a bite.
No passion. No fire. And he is arguably our best known media critic.

"So were the media a band of pro-Bush, pro-war cheerleaders?" Kurtz
finally asked. It's a good question, but he never answered it, retreating even
further into sentences like: "The unexciting truth is that newspapers are
collections of human beings who don't always get it right." Translation:
Sometimes, we do this, sometimes that. We are flawed, we are good guys.
Don't judge us too harshly. Accept our limitations. And that's the view of
the leading media critic in America? It looks to me like more of the problem, not the solution. No wonder faith in the press has dropped to a new
low, just 37 percent in a recent Gallup poll.

Richard Nixon resigned, in part thanks to the *Post's* persistence; now
the *Post* has resigned in the face of Bush-era bullying. Kurtz had it wrong
from the beginning. What critics wanted was not just the truth about
Saddam, but the truth about Bush and his neo-con war machine.
Interesting isn't it how the newspaper that revels in its legacy of Watergate
reporting that helped bring down a President is now saying "they did all
they could do."

Big media's admissions of their errors and omissions in reporting never
rose to the level of institutional post-mortems or real *mea culpas.* And they
still haven't led to more diversity of perspective, investigative journalism or
dissection of government claims. The modalities of coverage continue. The
New York Times spent more time and space exposing the fraudulent but
minor inventions of a troubled reporter, Jayson Blair, than on its own role
in the selling of a war. Blair was forced to quit, but no one was discharged
over Iraq.

Ironically, it was the *New York Times'* Judith Miller, whose own coverage
of Iraq was heavily criticized, who went to jail allegedly to protect a source.
But not on the war story. Another journalist, Lesley Stahl, admitted on "60
Minutes" that she had been taken in by Ahmed Chalabi's (Chalabi was

head of the U.S.-backed Iraqi National Congress until May 2004) claims and did a follow-up story to rectify her error. Miller did not.

After a few prominent media institutions acknowledged their flawed coverage, few others followed. Despite the essential media support for U.S. foreign policy, and a propensity for news managers to follow the government's lead in setting the agenda, dissent is growing. Note that during the Vietnam War it was not until the anti-war protest had grown louder that the media frame changed. In Iraq today most of the media is trapped in hotel rooms and only one side is covered; in Vietnam, there was more reporting occasionally from the other side. In Iraq as in Vietnam, the media focus was on "progress" and "turned corners." If Iraq is to follow the pattern of the Vietnam War era, what was once a vocal minority's view will eventually work its way into the mainstream and find broad acceptance.

The German philosopher Arthur Schopenhauer was the first to identify this process of coming to terms with the evolution of accepted political realities. He wrote, "All truth passes through three stages. First, it is ridiculed. Second, it is violently opposed. Third, it is accepted as self-evident."

The process usually starts with a few individuals whose skepticism is rewarded with recriminations and even dismissal. In the news world, it began with the firing of small town newspaper editors and cartoonists who dared to dissent. Few nationally known news people came to their defense.

Popular TV talk-show host Phil Donahue came next, purged by MSNBC for his anti-war programming. MSNBC's most heavily promoted correspondent, Ashleigh Banfield, was taken to the woodshed for reprimanding by her bosses when she questioned the network's war coverage at a lecture at Kansas State University. She said in part: "It wasn't journalism, because it looked to them like a courageous and terrific endeavor. You did not see where those bullets landed. You didn't see what happened when the mortars landed. A puff of smoke is not what a mortar looks like when it explodes, believe me." The network later dropped a reporter who they had once promoted as a news star of NBC. (Something similar had occurred during the first Gulf War when NBC's "Scud Stud" Arthur Kent challenged the network and was fired; he later sued and collected a settlement.)

Soon after the reining in of Banfield, Pulitzer Prize-winning war correspondent Peter Arnett was fired for saying on Iraqi TV what he was also saying on American television: that the U.S. military was underestimating Iraqi resistance. That view, which later turned out to be correct, was branded then as treason and worse. Arnett was targeted first by Fox News and later made the subject of a campaign by the Free Republic website which flooded NBC executives with demands that he be fired. He was discharged even after a National Geographic executive investigated the smear campaign and told NBC that the campaign was orchestrated. Their response: the facts didn't matter. Arnett had lost the public's trust. Perception had triumphed over truth once again.

Critics of the war were not just ridiculed; they were ignored and marginalized. Former BBC chief Greg Dyke (later forced to resign because of an inflated scandal involving BBC reporting which was subsequently found to be baseless) said that of 800 experts interviewed on U.S. TV in the run-up to the war and during the U.S. invasion only six challenged the war. A Fairness & Accuracy In Reporting (FAIR) study of 1716 on-air sources cited by TV news in this period found that 71 percent supported the war while only 3 percent opposed it.

This lack of balance on TV—the medium that most Americans turn to for their news—has yet to be acknowledged, explained or apologized for even as some TV journalists reluctantly begin to admit they were wrong in their earlier assessments and coverage. When CNN's Christianne Amanpour charged that her own network and others were muzzled, no TV correspondents echoed her charge or offered their own experiences. CNN's Wolf Blitzer later admitted, "we just weren't skeptical enough." During the run-up to the war, Fox's Bill O'Reilly had said, "If the Americans go in and overthrow Saddam Hussein and it's clean, he has nothing, I will apologize to the nation, and I will not trust the Bush Administration again." To his credit O'Reilly admitted (not on Fox but on "Good Morning America") that he too was wrong on WMDs. His words fell short of an "apology to the nation," however, and he's still just as supportive of the Bush Administration. Most of our punditocracy and journalistic elite remain silent.

These media failures have opened the door to a mass market for counter-narratives and other media offering alternative and suppressed information. Speaking of Michael Moore's film *Fahrenheit 9/11,* George Monbiot, a columnist for the *Guardian,* said, "The success of his film testifies to the rest of the media's failure." *San Francisco Chronicle* writer Tim Goodman charged that *Fahrenheit 9/11* is rattling the cages of established journalism.

Yet Moore's film only tangentially touched on journalism. *WMD* confronts the failure directly.

And yet, even as I write in 2005, it is not a widely accepted proposition that the media coverage was as responsible for the war as the government policy. We are still in Schopenhauer's first stage—where truth is ridiculed. It is apparently easier to blame politicians than to recognize how many of us bought the media-fed rationalizations for the war.

"Why should we want to hear about body bags and deaths and [how many] get killed … I mean, it's not relevant. So why should I waste my beautiful mind on something like that?"

–Barbara Bush
Wife of President George H.W. Bush
"Good Morning America," ABC–TV, 2003

"For Dawes, professor of English at Minnesota's Macalester College, the military's traditional use of gaming metaphors–entering the red zone, rolling the dice–can be troubling. The retired generals serving as television analysts seem 'for all the world like NFL commentators,' he says."

–James Sullivan
Staff writer, *San Francisco Chronicle,* 2004

→4←

The Media Is the Issue

Challenging the War Is Not Enough

The media flaws and failures detailed in this book (and others) are part of a larger institutional problem anchored in our mainstream media system. The war coverage illustrates the way our corporate media covers the world. It will be hard to rectify the problem without a more fundamental reform of the media system. That's why discussions of specific inadequacies always bring us back to the need for a larger systemic transformation.

What gets covered and how it gets covered is often a bottom-line issue with priorities determined not by reporters but accountants, not by media managers but media executives.

Juan Cole, the Iraq scholar, examines the larger mainstream media problem in terms of the pressures exerted by the demands of big media companies:

> Would giving airtime to Iraq, where we Americans have 138,000 troops and are spending $300 billion that we don't have, be too depressing to bring in the audience and advertising and the 15 percent profit? Then we would dump it in favor of bread and circuses. We'd dump Afghanistan as a story even faster, since there are "only" 17,000 U.S. troops in that country, and it is only a place where Bin Laden may be hiding out and from which the U.S. was struck on 9/11, leaving 3000 dead and the Pentagon and World Trade Center smoldering.

He quotes CNN founder Ted Turner on the economics of international coverage, noting:

> How good journalism is when practiced in the service of a business depends on the owner's philosophy and economic goals.
>
> When CNN reported to me, if we needed more money for Kosovo or Baghdad, we'd find it. If we had to bust the budget, we busted the budget. We put journalism first, and that's how we built CNN into something the world wanted to watch. I had the power to make these budget decisions because they were my companies. I was an independent entrepreneur who controlled the majority of the votes and could run my company for the long term. Top managers in these huge media conglomerates run their companies for the short term. **After we sold Turner Broadcasting to Time Warner, we came under such earnings pressure that we had to cut our promotion budget every year at CNN to make our numbers.** Media mega-mergers inevitably lead to an overemphasis on short-term earnings.

As support for real journalism inevitably erodes in this environment, manipulation by self-interested political and economic interests becomes more prevalent and even unstoppable.

As I document in *WMD,* U.S. war strategy in Iraq has been presented like a political campaign with key message points and "message-of-the-day" perception management techniques. Behind the scenes, a small army of PR firms and perception managers were busy spinning the news, reinforcing certain stories and discrediting others while at the same time monitoring the coverage so that the Administration could respond rapidly and in a timely way, assuring what was information dominance. This "rapid response" approach is part of the underlying strategy to insure that every story considered unfriendly could be contested and every criticism discredited.

David Miller, editor of a book called *Tell Me Lies* (Pluto Press, 2003), explains:

> As Col. Kenneth Allard has written, the 2003 attack on Iraq "will be remembered as a conflict in which information fully took its place as a weapon of war." The interoperability of the various types of "weaponized information" has far reaching, if little noticed, implications for the integration of propaganda and media

institutions into the war machine. The experience of Iraq in 2003 shows how the planned integration of the media into instruments of war fighting is developing. It also shows the increased role for the private sector in information dominance, a role which reflects wider changes in the armed services in the U.S. and the U.K.

This approach continued beyond the invasion phase. It took a week for us to learn, for example, that the capture of Saddam was not the reported U.S. military intelligence coup, but rather the work of Kurdish groups bent on avenging the rape of a woman, not the country. (And even then it was not widely reported or believed.)

Unfortunately, at this point, we can expect more disinformation and misinformation to follow, with renewed efforts by the U.S. government to leapfrog over any semblance of critical media with news feeds bypassing the news networks and fed directly to local stations. Media control will intensify as perceived "bad news" threatens to disturb the domestic tranquility that the Administration is hell bent on preserving.

As the Bush Administration geared up for the election cycle in 2004, it applied the approach it used in the war. A carefully managed and manipulated narrative was constructed. It quickly became the template, a way of driving its issues in the media. The public by then had been well propagandized by repetitive defenses of the war. As many as 80 percent of Bush supporters told pollsters that they believed that there still were WMDs in Iraq even after the President dropped the issue.

The toxic media climate had long ago neutered the anti-war issue through underexposure and distorted coverage. Democratic challenger John Kerry, who had been an anti-war hero, became even more of a war supporter than the President seeking to "out-Bush Bush" with promises of being a more effective commander who would never cut and run.

Bush played the "patriotic card" with supporters questioning Kerry's patriotism and competence. A media campaign by the so-called Swift Boat veterans demonized Kerry with more than 1,000 media appearances. They shifted attention away from Iraq and back to Vietnam. Ultimately their arguments were discredited even as they achieved their goal of putting Kerry on the defensive, reinforcing the GOP charges that he was a "flip-flopper."

Paul Krugman of the *New York Times* condemned what he saw as bias and trivialization on the airwaves:

> Somewhere along the line, TV news stopped reporting on candidates' policies, and turned instead to trivia that supposedly reveal their personalities. We hear about Mr. Kerry's haircuts, not his health care proposals. We hear about George Bush's brush-cutting, not his environmental policies. ... And since campaign coverage as celebrity profiling has no rules, it offers ample scope for biased reporting.

In a TV system obsessed with such trivialization, it is no wonder the realities of war were rarely communicated clearly.

Charles Lewis of the Center for Public Integrity, an institute that promotes investigative reporting, explained in a speech why this is:

> To the "suits" who control the news, edgy enterprise journalism is not efficient or cost-effective. It simply takes too much time, requires too much money and incurs too many legal and other risks. This helps to explain why today we have so little independent, critical reporting and why instead we are mostly fed a steady diet of pap from morning to night.

> The line between truth and falsehood—between the facts and a veneer of verisimilitude—has become so blurred as to be indistinguishable. Increasingly, what the powers that be say has become the publicly perceived reality, simply because they say it is so.

Lewis documented how that worked in beating the drums for war with Iraq:

> Between 1999 and mid-2004, there were more than 700 specific utterances by George Bush or Dick Cheney mentioning Iraq, often banging the war drums in ominous tones; interestingly, there was not a single sentence explicitly linking Saddam Hussein to September 11. Instead, that was often slyly implied contextually.

> At the same time, with some notable exceptions such as Seymour Hersh of the *New Yorker* and Walter Pincus of the *Washington Post* and the Knight Ridder's duo of Jonathan S. Landay and Warren P. Strobel, investigative news coverage before March 2003 of the Bush Administration's ramp-up to the war in Iraq was

underwhelming, to say the least. Daily coverage of government policy pronouncements and rationales was largely uncritical, almost stenographic.

In an image-dominated media environment it was easy to intimate that the terrorists behind 9/11 (if that's who they were) had to somehow be connected with Iraq. After all, Osama bin Laden and Saddam Hussein both spoke Arabic and both hated America. Thus, they melded together almost as one person for viewers uneducated in making even simple distinctions.

Even after the infamous "trophy" photos documenting abuses of detainees at Abu Ghraib had been widely circulated and reported, the issue never got nearly as much visibility as the Michael Jackson trial. There was more outrage shown on television over the Terry Schiavo incident than continuing exposés of torture in U.S.-run prisons.

Facts on the ground and the feelings that powered the Iraqi resistance were downplayed as vaguer descriptions of a mindless "insurgency" that seemed to have no rhyme or reason. The Bush Administration reinforced this perception by placing emphasis on the terrorist threat. Only a few outlets reported that the terrorism that emerged in Iraq came after the invasion and not before it.

U.S. reports from Iraq generally have conveyed a distorted image of a home grown resistance movement fighting against illegal and tyrannical occupation. As Molly Bingham explained in *Vanity Fair* (June 2004): "There is an array of terms used to describe these fighters. They usually refer to themselves as *'mujahideen'* and to their side as the 'resistance.' The coalition authority often calls them 'insurgents' or, in some cases, 'terrorists.'"

After spending time in Iraq, Bingham found that reporting on the "other side" is hard but not impossible:

I discovered that members of the insurgency cannot be found. They must find you, and find me they did. ... Some of what I discovered about the insurgency is not so surprising. Its members are fighting for their freedom and for the sovereignty of their nation. They are fighting for their God against an occupying force of a different faith. They are also fighting for their dignity and *ghira*–an

Iraqi term meaning a sense of integrity, self-respect, and honor, rooted in the protection of one's country and family.

What I hadn't expected was that the insurgents would be so diverse. ...

Arab critics of the U.S. coverage of the Iraqi resistance denounced the distortions in harsh terms noting that the violence of those fighting the U.S. occupation is always in the news; the violence of the occupation itself rarely. Professor Ghali Hassan of Curtin University, Perth, Western Australia, argued that the "distortion of the image of the Iraqi Resistance has its purposes and [was] designed to discredit the name of the Resistance."

"It was a mistake to discount the Iraqi Resistance," a U.S. soldier, Lt. Col. Kim Keslung told the Wall Street *Journal* as far back as October 2003. "If someone invaded Texas, we'd do the same thing," he added.

It is striking that a country that celebrates its own revolution which started with a guerilla warfare campaign by Massachusetts farmers against British occupation finds this argument so inexplicable.

Hassan quoted Martin Luther King, Jr., to remind readers of the American roots of the principle he invoked. King said, "I could never again raise my voice against the violence of the oppressed without having first spoken clearly to the greatest purveyor of violence in the world today—my own government."

It was Arab media outlets that showed the most compassion and concern for civilians. Throughout the war, satellite channels like Al Jazeera and Abu Dhabi TV documented the war's costs and consequences while the U.S. media sanitized the war's impact. And they paid a price for it.

In our media there was ongoing prejudice against Arab journalists and official hostility toward their media outlets. One Arab journalist working for the Abu Dhabi channel was actually a former Reuters correspondent based in Washington, D.C. He lived in a suburb and his children went to American schools. He was, in fact, an American citizen. But once he was sent to Iraq, he told me that soldiers there suspected him of being one of "them." Some soldiers bullied him; one pointed a gun in his face. He was shocked to have his loyalty questioned, not to mention his credentials. He teared up as he told me about the way many Arab journalists were abused.

He at least survived. Many Arab journalists did not. Al Jazeera's Tariq Ayoub was killed when the Arab media center in Baghdad was bombed, even though the Pentagon had been given its coordinates. Al Jazeera correspondents took risks to get footage that was exclusive and that they could sell to western outlets that were happy to pay for pictures they did not have the courage to pursue. When the pictures aired, their narrative was stripped and replaced with voiceovers by TV generals and in-studio analysts. The full story of how the Arab media covered the war is told by Hugh Miles in his book, *Al Jazeera* (Grove Press, 2005). His account shows that Al Jazeera pursued a journalistic agenda, not a political one. Its audience was different than the western audience and demanded a different type of coverage.

The narratives of western media and Arab media were worlds apart. The U.S. networks increasingly came to be seen as voices for an extension of the invasion and occupation.

Perhaps this helps explain why the "insurgents" began to kidnap and target journalists, believing they were simply another tool of the Bush war. Not all are or were of course, but as the danger grew, many journalists resorted to the security of hiring stringers and relying on the news agencies hotel journalism. News organizations began pooling footage to try to insure the safety of their people. This led to even more uniformity of perspective and reporting in the coverage and daily attacks and incidents.

Americans who were relying on our media for their news and information couldn't understand what foreign critics were talking about when they accused the U.S. of war crimes or targeting journalists. These attacks were dismissed as "sliming our troops."

There were some voices in the media challenging the deluge of pro-war sentiment. Even media-watcher Howard Kurtz filed a mild dissent in a rare commentary critical of the coverage. He wrote, "Despite the investment of tens of millions of dollars and deployment of hundreds of journalists, the collective picture they produced was often blurry. Were readers and viewers well served or deluged with confusing information? And what does all of this portend for coverage of future wars?"

Paul Krugman of the *New York Times* had offered a more critical voice. In a broadcast on CNN, February 23, 2003, Kurtz challenged him: "Are you saying that CNN and Fox are essentially rooting for war?"

> Krugman responded: Fox is clearly. CNN is a little more ambiguous but both have—the point that I was trying to make is that both networks and MSNBC, as well, have essentially gone into war mode. They've treated this as a done deal. They've used essentially the kind of logos, martial music and so on that we saw after we saw Gulf War I had started. So from the point of view of the American public, Iraq is already the enemy, we're already at war. And the point I was trying to make in the *Times* column was that, you know, if you ask why do the Europeans see things so differently, well, one answer is not culture, not society, not politics but, just hey, they don't have, you know, "Countdown: Iraq," "SHOWDOWN IRAQ," "Target Iraq" on their screens nonstop.

BBC's Katty Kay and former Bush speechwriter David Frum joined the broadcast for some telling discussion about the portrayal of the anti-war movement.

> Kurtz asked: What's wrong with the idea of listening to a very important and burgeoning anti-war movement around the world?

> Katty Kay replied: In fact, I think that part of it is that, is that there isn't such a large anti-war movement here in America, and therefore there isn't so much reporting of it. I think that European networks felt that American networks missed a trick last weekend in reporting the anti-war protests, which were seen really talking to people back in Britain as epoch-making. That was the single, largest peace-time demonstration ever.

> David Frum challenged her: I didn't criticize you for covering it. I'm criticizing covering it without focusing on the content. You can't just cover the size of the crowd and ignore, for example, Tony Benn saying that—saying that Kurdish demonstrators are CIA stooges. That's …

> Kay: But the interesting thing about those demonstrations is that this was not just your classic anti-war demonstrators. These were middle-class people who

had never demonstrated before, many of them from the Conservative Party. This was—I think this was misportrayed, actually, by some of the American networks and certainly some of the cable networks as your—what were they described as?—your classic demonstrators. These were not your classic demonstrators. This was very different.

Later the *Washington Post's* ombudsman Michael Getler would accuse the newspaper he and Howard Kurtz work for of downplaying anti-war protests in the U.S. and abroad.

So yes, some journalists of conscience and a few media executives spoke up but often on campuses or conferences, rarely on the air or even in print. In April 2003 Greg Dyke, then head of the BBC said, "I was shocked while in the United States by how unquestioning the broadcast news media was during this war. If Iraq proved anything, it was that the BBC cannot afford to mix patriotism and journalism. This is happening in the United States and if it continues, will undermine the credibility of the U.S. electronic news media."

During the official phase of the war, CNN was as "on message" as the other networks. The World Socialist News Service (WSNS) reported:

> As for CNN, it sought unsuccessfully to close its ratings gap with Fox News by aping the chauvinist coverage of the Murdoch-owned cable network. CNN anchormen and embedded reporters regularly referred to U.S. troops as "heroes" and "liberators," and joined with the rest of the American media in downplaying reports of Iraqi casualties, civilian and military.

> CNN chief Eason Jordan, in an appearance on his own network's program on the media, "Reliable Sources," defended his use of military experts who had criticized U.S. tactics and strategy during the initial stages of the invasion. The Pentagon had vetted all these retired generals in advance, he revealed: "I went to the Pentagon myself several times before the war started and met with important people there and said, for instance, at CNN, 'Here are the generals we're thinking of retaining to advise us on the air and off about the war.' And we got a big thumbs-up on all of them. That was important."

But in January 2005, Jordan discussed military attacks on journalists in Iraq in an off-the-record meeting at the World Economic Forum in Davos,

Switzerland. Jordan created a firestorm by his reported remark that he thought journalists in Iraq had been targeted. Those comments led Jordan himself to be targeted and forced to resign. Even after 25 years at CNN, "his" network only vaguely came to his defense even though Reuters, the International Federation of Journalists and other press freedom groups had been pushing for independent investigations of what they considered suspicious killings of journalists. The Pentagon has refused to cooperate or permit journalists to interview any soldiers involved in the incidents. A transcript of the meeting has not been published to date.

When the World Tribunal on Iraq met in February 2005 in Rome, they issued a statement on Jordan's reported remarks. They found Jordan's sudden resignation "very troubling and suspicious in light of his recent comments suggesting that as many as 12 journalists were killed in Iraq by the U.S. military."

> It is clear that Mr. Jordan was intimidated and pressured into stepping down after intense criticism by some pro-war U.S. politicians and media outlets led by Rupert Murdoch's Fox News and *New York Post,* questioning his patriotism. His resignation calls into question freedom of speech within the media and the right to dissent.
>
> Are Mr. Jordan's claims accurate? Many journalists and press freedom groups believe that such targeting and killings have taken place in the Iraq War as we have heard in testimony before the Tribunal by journalists documenting massive abuses by the U.S. military against civilians in Fallujah and other Iraq cities. We have been told of the harassment of journalists and the barring of members of the media from covering aspects of the U.S. military campaign.
>
> We have also heard testimony from Danny Schechter, a former CNN producer and filmmaker who shows the killings of journalists under such circumstances in his film, *WMD: Weapons of Mass Deception,* that is being shown at the Tribunal.
>
> The World Tribunal on Iraq joins the calls by international media groups and the families of dead journalists for a full independent investigation by an international team of journalists who should be given the right to question members of the military. We demand that media outlets stop impugning the

integrity of journalists who raise these questions and that CNN examine the charges raised by its former head of news.

What actually happened to Eason Jordan? While no physical recording of Jordan's actual comments was ever released, a blogger disseminated his account of the event into the blogosphere, starting the firestorm. This was picked up by columnists in Murdoch media outlets who then claimed that Jordan was speaking for CNN itself–not just in a personal capacity–and thus CNN had "slimed our troops."

Leading the charge to trash Jordan was CNN competitor Fox News Channel and its sister publication, the *New York Post.* Members of Congress piled on with angry demands for evidence, although the tone of their remarks suggested a total denial of the possibility that Jordan may have information that they didn't have. Instead, Jordan's patriotism and CNN's integrity were attacked.

This incident raised three urgent issues:

1. Do media executives have a right to express opinions that deviate from the official line? Media companies should defend the rights of their employees to take part in democratic debate without fears of recriminations. The conservative editorial page of the Wall Street *Journal* and the World Editors Forum have rushed in to defend Jordan's right to express controversial opinions without intimidation.

2. Do media companies have an obligation to investigate and not just denigrate? CNN, Reuters, the Associated Press, Agence France Press and other media outlets should take a fresh look at these charges to determine their validity. At least 11 journalists have been killed by "friendly fire" since the Iraq War began, according to the Committee to Protect Journalists. (The statistics of war casualties are constantly changing, usually in an upward direction. For more accurate figures, consult online sources.) Thus far there has been little effort by the Pentagon to explain their deaths.

3. Are we who care about integrity in the media willing to stand up to protect free speech during a time of war? While this issue is often spun as a left-right story, it's about much more than that. We are all paying dearly

for this war. Shouldn't we Americans have a right to know what's being done in our name?

Jordan is not talking and may never tell his side of the story. A journalist interviewed in *WMD* who covered the war in Iraq and Afghanistan related that Jordan was furious with CNN for not standing up for him. He wrote to me: "I had breakfast with Eason after the event and he was glad to be out of CNN. I suppose when a corporation that owes its very existence to you refuses to stand up for you . . . then its time to move on.

> I never thought I would see the day when a news executive simply states that he knows of ten (and well-documented) incidents in which journalists have been targeted by U.S. forces. He also had tried to bring attention to the four journos (three locals from Reuters and one from NBC) who were arrested and tortured by U.S. forces in Fallujah. I was stunned when the faux journos a.k.a. bloggers began to tear apart Eason instead of looking into his charges (they were sparked by [Congressman] Barney Franks' comments that dead journos were just collateral damage).

> ... Anyone who knows [Jordan] or has benefited by his absolute unshakable dedication to journo safety is unshaken by the tiny tempest. CNN and the journalistic community [are] poorer for the experience.

Jordan was reportedly given a generous pay out, but with a gag clause forbidding him to speak on this issue. This is not unusual for media organizations; CNN has done it before in the case of the producers of its controversial "Operation Tailwind" story. Dan Rather's producer Mary Mapes said she was offered a similar deal, but turned it down. She is writing a book that will give her version of the "60 Minutes" program that became cast as 'Rathergate' and cost Mapes her job.

Purging the media of high-profile figures who were critical and willing to air their dissent was not new; it was already a pattern that besides Jordan included veteran war correspondent Peter Arnett, MSNBC talk-show host Phil Donahue, and MSNBC reporter Ashleigh Banfield. Some believe that Dan Rather's fall, aided and abetted by his own lapses in judgment, was part of the same orchestrated backlash.

As the Bush Administration switched their rationale for the war from a campaign to thwart WMDS and a threat to U.S. freedom to a campaign for delivering "Iraqi freedom," mainstream media coverage of the Iraq elections quickly pronounced not only a successful demonstration of democracy but repeated the Administration's claim that the election was the ultimate vindication of the war.

Two years into a continuing war, many people remained perplexed about why we went to war in the first place, what exactly happened there, and what was still going on. The reporters who were so high profile in the war's earliest days were long gone. Their replacements were cowering in hotels and relying on local staff. As the paradigm of coverage shifted from occupation to resistance, the coverage narrowed in scope.

Even local newspapers like the *Gainesville Times* (Florida) warned readers to expect little in-depth coverage in what was considered a murky situation. "Iraq War Provides Plenty of News But Few Clear Answers," was the headline of one editorial which noted:

> March 19 will mark the second anniversary of the United States-led invasion of Iraq. As the day approaches, the news media will bombard us with reports and analyses. We also will receive information directly and instantly from members of the troops. We have more information available to us daily about this war than any other in history.

> Secretary of Defense Donald H. Rumsfeld, testifying before the House Armed Services Committee last week, said, "Think of it: 24-hour worldwide satellite news coverage, including terrorist attacks, disasters, and combat operations; cell phones, digital cameras, global internet, emails, embedded reporters; an increasingly casual regard for the protection of classified documents and information; and a U.S. government that's basically still organized for the last century, not the information age."

Once again, the more we watched, the less we knew. All this media power has not quieted anti-war voices or fully dominated the discourse. Access to internet websites enables news consumers to seek out more diversity of opinion. Alternative news sites, Arab outlets like Al Jazeera, a vast array of blogs including some in Iraq and in the military, and even documentary films like *WMD* offer more critical perspectives. The more the mainstream media acts as a shill for the war makers, the more viewers and readers abandon it in pursuit of more honest news.

The implication here is ominous. Donald Rumsfeld wants the government to better organize for the information age. Recall that back in 2003 when some of the press exposed the creation of a new Office of Strategic Influence aimed at managing news and planting false stories in overseas news outlets, Rumsfeld insisted he would continue the practices even if the office itself would be closed to placate a storm of criticism. Washington has spent billions of dollars on all sorts of information dominance operations.

The government went from influencing coverage to actually creating and subsidizing their own TV stations in Iraq and other outlets to report the news their own way. In some cases, journalists resigned, charging blatant censorship and news management, protesting micro-management by media advisors at the Coalition Provisional Authority. In late April 2005, one of those advisors, Dorrance Smith, a former executive producer at ABC's "Nightline" published an op-ed piece in the Wall Street *Journal* blasting Al Jazeera's reporting. His article was conspicuous for a lack of evidence and did not identify his history as a political and media operative for the Bush campaign. Even though he is identified as a media consultant, he labels Al Jazeera as the enemy and writes in terms of "we." The BBC called me to explore the controversy. Smith refused to debate and then refused to appear at all. My interview was then promptly canceled. We can't have lack of balance, can we?

The Administration also tried to bypass the networks by feeding material directly to local stations and inviting those TV news reporters with the least background on Iraq to cover the conflict; these reporters had a tendency to be the most supportive of the troops and the war. This approach backfired when one such news team from a local station in Minneapolis embarrassed the Administration by airing footage of poorly guarded Iraqi arms dumps that were systematically looted. Their footage was shown while the Pentagon was denying charges of negligence by its military units.

Later, the Administration itself would be accused of planting news in the U.S. through video news releases produced to resemble news reports but without full disclosure of their sources. *Congressional Quarterly* reported in April 2005 that the Senate "voted unanimously to require federal agencies to add disclaimers to video news releases they produce, notifying viewers that the government is the source of the information." The 98-0 vote for the measure amounted to a sharp, bipartisan rebuke of a practice that had come under fire: the distribution of prepackaged news stories to television stations around the country that tout President Bush's policies but do not disclose that the government produced the material.

In some cases, Democrats charged that local news stations compromised themselves by carrying government-subsidized news reports that echoed Administration message points. The Bush Administration avoided comment on the revelations, but later some cabinet secretaries said they had exercised bad judgment (perhaps because this covert operation was exposed).

It was also found that a White House "reporter" called Jeffrey Gannon was working for a bogus Republican-funded press service and using his thinly veiled credential to raise highly politicized softball questions at presidential press conferences. It turned out that even his name was bogus; his real name is James A. Guckert. (He ran a gay dating site on the side.)

Guckert was not the only faux reporter at the White House. Many non-subsidized reporters were also deferential to a fault. As Paul Sperry wrote on World Net Daily after one Bush press conference: "It was comical, with Bush at one point actually saying out loud that he was following a 'script' in calling on establishment media types, passing once again over any new faces who might actually ply him with an outside-the-Beltway question the American people want to have asked as their government *starts* a war in the Middle East, and our oil-dependent economy teeters again on the brink of recession."

Jim Lobe who covers Washington for Inter Press Service told the Echo Chamber Project that mainstream reporters have to pull their punches to survive. "You just can't say certain kinds of things in certain kinds of atmosphere and expect that your editors are going to let it pass and it's going to be printed in a newspaper. I mean, I'm not saying there is active censorship. Most of it exists on a self-censorship level, I believe. And people become used to censoring themselves and feeling the political winds and figuring out what they can get away with and what they cannot get away with."

The CBS debacle, the Armstrong Williams payola scandal and fabricated newspaper circulation figures are signs of a deeper crisis. Trust in the news and journalism is on the wane. The discovery that the Administration planted phony news adds to the problem even though the "non-phony" news is often simplistic, superficial and unworthy of respect.

To be fair, not every news outlet misreported the run-up or the war itself. There were journalists in the alternative media and the mainstream who did their best to dig out facts and challenge government claims. Dahr Jamail, Amy Goodman and many others come to mind. There were also bloggers, gadflies, media watch groups and academic critics who tried to get the truth out. David Sirota of the Center for American Progress offered his analysis to the Echo Chamber Project:

> The media as a whole was intimidated since 9/11. They were in a posture that was more willing to accept what the government was telling them about the threat of terrorism than they had been previously about different issues.

> I think the print media—certain news outlets, certain reporters, did a very good job of trying to get to the bottom of some of the unsubstantiated things that were coming from the government—people like Walter Pincus, people like Johnathan Landay and others. But I think that—unfortunately, those were the exceptions, not the rules. The television media was far worse. The television media typically took the President's and the Vice President's myths about Iraq at face value.

It should be noted that these criticisms and concerns are not limited to the U.S. media. The war was covered (and slanted) differently in different countries. Pentagon media consultant John Rendon, shown on camera in *WMD,* explains the media wars in Iraq:

> There were five wars in Iraq. There really was the reality of combat operations from the air, on the ground and from the sea. The second war was the war the

United States saw, the third war was the war that Europe saw. The fourth war was the war that Arab audiences saw. And the fifth war was the war the rest of the world saw. And as we monitored that in real time, we found that none of them were in alignment.

All over the world, critics lashed out. Here's one of many examples found through a simple Google search:

Pacific Media Watch noted in March 2005: "Two media critics have strongly criticized New Zealand and some global media coverage of the Anglo-American war on Iraq—especially television—describing it as biased and 'failing spectacularly' to do its job.

The attacks came in two separate seminars in Wellington by Scoop Editor Alastair Thompson ('The Role of Media in the Second Gulf War') and in Auckland by Auckland University of Technology Senior Journalism Lecturer David Robie on World Press Freedom Day."

The Arab media was debating the coverage too as I learned when I covered the 2004 Arab Media Summit in Dubai for *WMD*. I also read assessments of the coverage by many Arab journalists like Muhammad Fhad Al-Harithy writing in *Arab News* in August 2004. He wrote:

I wonder why no bloodshed, no dead bod[ies] and no injured soldiers are seen in wars launched by superpowers. Only charred and destroyed military installations, empty of human victims, are seen. ... An American study carried out in collaboration with Columbia University analyzed the results of the experience of journalists being embedded with military units. Most reports produced by the journalists lacked photos of actual war. It was, according to the study, a war without blood. ... Withholding pictures with painful content is an issue being debated. Efforts to keep war reports free of blood and killing while thousands are in fact killed [are] tantamount to encouraging war because it makes people believe that war has no cost in terms of human lives.

Some more thoughtful U.S. journalists paid tribute to Al Jazeera: *Newsday*'s magazine ran a story that asked, "Who Covered the War Best?" Their answer: "Try Al Jazeera." Hugh Miles' book on "the Arab News Channel that is challenging the West" quotes the piece saying:

Al Jazeera's approach to covering the war—both critical and multi-dimensional with an ideological commitment to democracy, openness, and pluralism—has seriously threatened the political projects of the world's most powerful.

Critics in Great Britain accused the BBC of bias. Al Jazeera and Arabic satellite channels were criticized for being inflammatory. But the U.S. coverage was dramatically different from what viewers were watching all over the world. And many in the U.S. were influenced by propaganda and prejudice.

In 1927, sociologist Harold Lasswell raised issues that the current political climate forces us to return to. He explained that all sides rely on propaganda in every war. Why? Because it "engineers consent."

He wrote: "[A] new and subtler instrument must weld thousands and thousands and even millions of human beings into one amalgamated mass of hate, will, and hope. A new will must burn out the canker of dissent and temper the steel of bellicose enthusiasm. The name of this new hammer and anvil of social solidarity is propaganda. Talk must take the place of drill; print must supply the dance. War dances live in literature, and at the fringes of the modern earth; war propaganda breathes and fumes in the capitals and provinces of the world."

Perhaps it's time for our generation of embeds and loud-mouthed TV talking heads to become acquainted with Lasswell's findings and to examine what accounts for the pervasive complicity, compliance, and the conformity in the coverage of our timid corporate media. Was it a conspiracy or something else?

Deeper questions like the ones posed by the British-based Australian journalist John Pilger still need asking:

How does thought control work in societies that call themselves free? Why are famous journalists so eager, almost as a reflex, to minimize the culpability of political leaders such as Bush and Blair who share responsibility for the unprovoked attack on a defenseless people, for laying to waste their land and for killing at least 100,000 people, most of them civilians, having sought to justify this epic crime with demonstrable lies? Why does a BBC reporter describe the invasion of Iraq as "a vindication for Blair"?

Why have broadcasters never associated the British or American state with terrorism? Why have such privileged communicators, with unlimited access to the facts, lined up to describe an unobserved, unverified, illegitimate, cynically manipulated election, held under a brutal occupation, as "democratic" with the pristine aim of being "free and fair"?

Jean Rostand, a policy analyst quoted by *Le Monde Diplomatique* offers one answer: "Stupidity, outrage, vanity, cruelty, iniquity, bad faith, falsehood—we fail to see the whole array when it is facing in the same direction as we."

This is an old debate but one that remains timely and relevant. It takes us into a terrain that goes beyond the issue of Iraq War coverage: media reform.

Transforming the Media

By the end of 2003, media practices that once were casual complaints had become issues around which millions were organizing. The outcry against the pathetic cheerleading that called itself TV coverage of the war in Iraq, and the battle to stop new FCC rules allowing further media concentration demonstrated that there is a large constituency for media activism and organization. A citizens' Bill of Media Rights was introduced by organizations representing 20 million Americans, pinpointing the problem:

> In recent years, massive and unprecedented corporate consolidation has dangerously contracted the number of voices in our nation's media. While some argue we live in an age of unprecedented diversity in media, the reality is that the vast majority of America's news and entertainment is now commercially-produced, delivered, and controlled by a handful of giant media conglomerates seeking to minimize competition and maximize corporate profits rather than maximize competition and promote the public interest.

> According to the Supreme Court, the First Amendment protects the American public's right to "an uninhibited marketplace of ideas in which truth will prevail" and "suitable access to social, political, esthetic, moral, and other ideas and experiences." Moreover, it is "the right of the viewers and listeners, not the right of the broadcasters, which is paramount."

In November 2003, media activists converged in Madison, Wisconsin, demonstrating their commitment to make media reform a central concern. The war coverage was deplored. A second national conference in St. Louis in May 2005 drew 2500 activists. Many speakers cited the media coverage of the war as a prime example of why media reform is needed. They made an impressive, energetic and strong statement. In attendance were members of Congress, top journalists like Bill Moyers, legends like Studs Terkel, comedian Al Franken and other best-selling authors, pop stars, and a who's who among media reformers, including journalists Bob McChesney, Amy Goodman, John Nichols and myself. Their collective analysis was as powerful as their passion. New coalitions and campaigns are beginning to emerge.

But follow-up is key. The conferences were not important as events in themselves–they were important as a staging ground for a new offensive on media issues. By 2005 many organizations, like Common Cause, that had previously worked only election issues, became active on media reform, sparking news and insuring that the issue will receive more attention. Media reform on the legislative front and before regulatory bodies like the Federal Communications Commission has new energy and political supporters, but campaigns against corporate abuse of journalism are still to come.

The impressive mobilization of public sentiment signaled a wider dissent than had been acknowledged about the recent FCC policies that encouraged media concentration without addressing any conflicts of interest. There was an unreported context that is introduced in *WMD*: network lobbying for rule changes to permit big media companies to become bigger while downplaying criticism of Administration policies. As the networks uncritically waved the flag, the FCC waived the rules. Was there a connection? I think so.

Political maneuvers and compromises in Congress blocked the total rebuke to the FCC in 2003 that many had hoped for. The tricks politicians played seem to have taken the wind out of a well-orchestrated citizens' campaign. Many paid lip service to the cause but failed to roll back regulations. In the end it was a lawsuit that killed the FCC's ambitions.

Some activists tended to denigrate media activism as somehow secondary to the "real problems," especially during the elections when partisanship polarized politics along party lines. But media reform remains as one of the few issues with national bipartisan traction and offers an opportunity to galvanize support across the spectrum of political differences.

The Bush Administration has been intent on controlling the message, so it's no surprise that the FCC battle and the public rejection of proposed deregulation was the first issue that the President threatened to exercise a veto against. It was the first issue in the Bush Era that brought Democrats and some Republicans together. It signaled that media concerns are not marginal or to be marginalized.

The pubic concern about media issues has been ongoing. In early 2004 I received an email from a Mediachannel reader that asked: "What do we do when our TV and newspapers tell us lies but insist we should regard this information as truth? What do we do when the vast majority of people in our society accepts these lies as truths and ridicules us when we call these statements lies?"

These are good questions but there are also some good answers. They involve hard work and real action, day-to-day work in the trenches—not just sending checks to political parties or candidates. Bear in mind that part of the mess we are in goes back to the Telecommunications "Reform" Act of 1996, backed by the Clinton Administration and many liberal democrats. The bill was supposed to foster competition. It led instead to a massive wave of media concentration.

Very few politicos ever focus on media concentration or slanted coverage. They rightly fear that they would risk not getting coverage at all; they certainly will lose their "fifteen seconds" of fame if they piss off thin-skinned media moguls. (Many on the left believe that the Dean campaign lost its media support after Governor Dean made a high profile speech calling for media reform.)

Many people in the global justice movements realize that real power is exercised today not by governments but by private interests; therefore turning the focus on corporate interests makes sense. The corporate media deserve more attention than it has thus far received. Some examples:

At the end of 2003, the FCC gave Rupert Murdoch a thank-you present for services rendered in the form of a go-ahead to take over DirecTV, the largest satellite TV service in the United States. (It was owned by Hughes Electronics Corp. which had been bought by General Motors.)

As Space News explained, "the deal gives News Corp. a television distribution platform in the United States, where it already operates TV stations, the Fox television network, and several pay-TV channels." News Corp. immediately transferred its stake in Hughes to its majority-owned Fox Entertainment Group, which owns TV stations and other media properties in the United States, the statement said.

This is also part of a global strategy, as the trade newspaper explains: "In addition to DirecTV, which claimed 11.85 million subscribers as of the end of September [2003], Hughes operates a satellite hardware and networking company, Hughes Network Systems of Germantown, Md., and controls DirecTV Latin America, a satellite TV provider in Central and South America. Hughes also owns 81 percent of Wilton, Conn.-based satellite operator PanAmSat Corp."

Could this FCC decision have anything to do with comments by former FCC Chairman Michael Powell (son of the then-secretary of state, and originally a Clinton Administration appointee, by the way) that one reason we need big media is that "only big media can cover the war the way this one has been covered"?

Media institutions, which report on the corporate irresponsibility of others, like the endless stream of indicted Wall Street operators, need to turn the cameras on themselves. How socially responsible and accountable are they? How transparent? Had activists been paying attention, there would have been a protest against revelations in 2000 by the Alliance for Better Campaigns that showed how many local TV stations violated federal laws by overcharging candidates for air time on local stations while reducing their electoral coverage, especially of non-presidential races.

What this points to is the need for activists themselves to become better informed about the way big media works and the way the government works with it. That's where websites like Mediachannel.org and Mediareform.net and the research of groups like FAIR and Media Tenor come in. Media sources should be informing the public of the latest research and analysis of media manipulation, how media drive politics, and why we can now speak of America as a mediaocracy in which media rule, not a democracy in which the people decide.

One of the problems of our mediaocracy is that the government gets to control the public dialogue as well as the language. A dictionary website (www.yourdictionary.com) that tracks words found that "embedding" was the most-used new word in 2003.

Media coverage of politics is often shaped by media consultants who understand how manipulating media coverage and using the media is central to campaigning and governing. No wonder the Bush Administration practices "message discipline" with a religious intensity. Bush political guru Karl Rove is said to be a master at media management often relying on covert techniques. To write about how that works, I resorted to satire, imagining how these political operatives think based on what I know about their approach and methods. (My own experience years ago as an assistant to a big city mayor gave me some exposure to how techniques like these are "deployed" to advance political goals.)

(Disclosure: With tongue in cheek, Mediachanel.org obtained this document from usually unimpeachable sources. We cannot verify it. One document expert we consulted opined that its font style and syntax bears an uncanny resemblance to work written on the G4 Mac Powerbook used by News Dissector Danny Schechter. The Dissector was covering a hurricane in Texas and could not verify it either. Readers will have to judge it for themselves in terms of what they know or suspect.)

MEMO TO THE PRESIDENT

EYES ONLY

To: GWB
From: Karl Rove
Re: Remarks for the Confidential Media Mogul Appreciation Breakfast

Here is the advance draft of the remarks my office has prepared for your use at the "Media Mogul" breakfast we are having on the morning of the State of the Union address.

Let's call it the State of the Media.

Our friends will be seated in the room, strategically as usual, and will be provided with questions to ask you. I will give you the order to call on them and small photos so you know who's who. Please do not call on anyone else!

Tomorrow, I will be able to read the speech aloud to you and mark up the key message points for emphasis, the way we usually do.

As you know, we have been taking a bit of flak on that growing Armstrong Williams problem, so we need to keep these media moguls on the reservation. (Aside: These liberals are such hypocrites—Clinton didn't need to subsidize reporters because he had them in his back pocket, at least before Monicagate. Hah. Hah!)

Here's our expected guest list:

l. Rupert—we can always count on him. (Roger Ailes may not make it because he's on another diet and says he needs to preserve the appearance of that "Fair and Balanced" thing they have going. We talk all the time.)

2. Sumner—I wish he hadn't said Viacom would be better off with a Republican administration. It was too obvious. We do better when some of these Viacom guys appear, from time to time, to be attacking us because it makes their support seem more sincere and credible. I already passed on your thanks to Les Moonves at CBS for the way he handled that Rather mess. Didn't you just love that "document" drama and the way it shifted attention away from you? Wink. Wink. Also, Dickie Thornburgh has come through for us again on that "independent" investigation. Make sure you drop him a personal note. Your dad already has.

3. Bob Wright of NBC/GE will be there and, as always, can be trusted. Ask Bob how GE's reconstruction work is going in Iraq. We took care of them with a $600 million contract.

4. Reverend Moon of the *Washington Times* can't come personally for obvious reasons but will send a key member of his team. He's a very generous man in more ways than one. Don't refer to him as "Dear Father"—that's only for his people!

5. Dick Parsons, CEO of Time Warner is a definite. Be sure to thank him for the $250,000 corporate contribution he made toward the inauguration festivities. He's been a Republican for years and Colin Powell has been on his board. He did well in dumping Ted Turner, don't you think? (He will be the only black guy there. He doesn't like rap so don't tell him how much you like 50 Cents.)

6. The *Washington Post* company will be there—no journalists of course, but a top management player. They gave $100,000 to the inauguration. Make eye contact this time when you express your appreciation.

7. Pat Robertson will represent the religious broadcasting community. I asked Falwell and Dobson to miss this one because they tend to have loose lips. I told them they can serve the Lord more effectively by being more discrete.

8. Our friends at Sinclair Broadcasting and Clear Channel will be represented. They have been great although you might pull Clear Channel aside and ask them why they are letting that Air America network buy time on their stations?

9. I have bypassed Disney this time but I have already thanked Michael Eisner on your behalf for refusing to distribute that *Fahrenheit 9/11* hate-umentary.

10. Film director Jerry Bruckenheimer sends regrets. He's on location making a new action movie celebrating the War on Terror. He's a genius.

11. I asked Dick Cheney to stay away. You may not recall but he dropped in at a Washington correspondents' dinner after the Iraq invasion and thanked them all for a "job well done." But many felt he was too abrupt and could have said more. Media people find him too gruff even when he praises them.

Needless to say, there are hundreds of others in the industry who would want to join us but as we learned in the campaign, massaging the egos of fat cats is always best achieved in small exclusive groups.

These guys like to be in the "in-crowd" and on the top VIP guest lists. They like face time with the President. It makes them feel more important.

By the way, Rummy is leaking some details of an old intelligence operation to Sy Hersh to distract him and keep him far, far away. I hope to get some "documents" to him later. Helen Thomas will be far away also having a pre-scheduled visit with Laura at a library opening.

The rest of the White House press corps can be easily handled, as we know.

FYI: We are calling this event an off-the-record invitation-only "Tsunami Relief Thank You Gathering" for public consumption.

As you see, with the right staff preparation, this type of thing doesn't have to be that "hard." These media execs like candor. They are friends. You can level with them. They want to help and know it is in their interest to do so. They understand that.

Karl

P.S. Please shred after reading. Paper is dangerous.

DRAFT—CONFIDENTIAL
STATE OF THE MEDIA 2005 ADDRESS FOR GWB

Later tonight, I will be delivering the State of the Union Address. We have been rehearsing and I expect it will go well thanks to those fancy new teleprompters.

As you know sometime my English is not the best. (Laugh Line)

Remember how the State of the Union in 2001 turned public opinion around? A great phrase like "Axis of Evil" is sometimes all you need. As you know from your businesses, "branding" and repeating the right message points keep ratings high.

We all win when we stay on message.

As Karl keeps reminding me, perception is what matters. It has to be well-managed. PM is more important than PR. (Laugh Line)

By the way, Karl will drop by later with some of the key language we need to reinforce our policies this time around. Try avoiding words like "privatization" and instead stress "personal security accounts" when talking about Social Security. Sometimes people don't know what's good for them. To get through to them, we have to make it personal.

I don't have to tell you why more money in the stock market is good for all of us.

But before the public sees me talk about our nation tonight—and its state is good by the way—let me say a few things about our media. We need you. Our country relies on you.

I am sure you know that when some of our more enthusiastic supporters knock the "liberal media," they are not talking about you.

We know who our friends are—and that's why you are here.

Remember, that in his war plan, Tommy Franks renamed your fourth estate, the "fourth front." That's how we regard you.

Without your support, our Administration could never accomplish all it has.

So I'm here to thank you for keeping election coverage on a positive note and standing by our service members in Iraq and other fronts in the War on Terror.

(SINCERE) If you don't keep the flag flying, who will?

We need the country to stand behind our soldiers. I know you have to report our casualties but please keep the focus on the terrorists or insurgents or whatever we call them. That has been helpful. A little bit of fear is as good for politics as it is for the box office.

Thank you for your focus on the threats we face. More personal stories from the front line always foster audience identification.

People don't want to hear nay-sayers. They want to believe in America.

Thank you for your patriotism. And your understanding when things don't always go right. I am sure all of you have backed TV programs that fizzled. It's the same way with laws and wars. We all have our lemons. Practice makes perfect.

You don't go around apologizing for every mistake. Neither do I.

The only apology I would make to you has to do with the FCC. As you know Michael Powell and his dad are leaving. Sometimes, both went off message. Like father, like son.

As a result we lost those FCC rule changes that you all were counting on. We hope to do something about that once we have someone more trustworthy running the Commission.

Also I want you to know that I personally did not approve all the big so-called obscenity fines that the former chairman levied on your companies. I mean that Rupert. He overdid it … and as you notice, he's no longer here. Janet Jackson was a big thing but not in the way it was treated. (Smile.) We will make it up to you all.

Media matters to this Administration. It matters a lot. This is one thing Laura agrees with me on. She can get you a list of the best books on the subject. (Laugh Line)

We also want you to be successful in business and. …"

(At this point the document ends. Our efforts to find the rest of the speech were unsuccessful. Again, we do not vouch for its contents.)

"The ownership of mass media by giant conglomerates makes independent film one of the few places where criticism of corporate chicanery can reach a large audience.

–Kevin Lally
Editor, *Film Journal International,* June 2004

⇥5⇤

The Making of the Film *WMD*

The Inside Story

Some years ago, I was invited to meet with the PBS legend Bill Moyers, one of our country's most prolific program-makers. My partner at Globalvision, Rory O'Connor, and I were seeking his help in getting our documentaries on the air.

We met in his office in the late afternoon when the sun then setting across the river in New Jersey sent harsh rays glistening across shelves of his gold-plated Emmy awards. Talk about being "blinded by the light."

In response to our request, Bill blinked, paused for a quick New York minute, and then summed up in two words what he called his biggest problems: money and airtime.

Rory and I looked at each other: if Bill Moyers, who seemed to be on the air all the time, had these problems, where did that leave the rest of us? I thought about that meeting when I set out to make a film on the coverage of the war. I knew that only an independent film offered the promise of an uncensored platform that could document and challenge the blatant betrayal of journalism I was seeing. So I decided, in spite of the obstacles, that if I was really going to be true to my outrage, it was time to fight fire with fire: to use images to fight images, to deploy media against a media war.

I was immediately confronted with some key questions: Where would the money come from? What channel would ever show such a film even if I managed to make it? Furthermore, how do you get the story behind this story, especially months after the war had begun? Would news executives speak candidly? (I tried questioning Fox's John Moody at one event; he walked the other way when he saw me coming.) Would my fellow media mavens, especially high-profile journalists, go on camera to discuss their real experiences or make footage available? Few journalists privy to the behind-the-scenes chatter were likely to be forthcoming. Would there be a media market for a work that takes big media to task through the lens of a news veteran who's been there and done that?

These questions suggest the real-world obstacles confronting a film taking on the media itself. They also point to the first step in filmmaking: know your subject and commit yourself to understanding what you are up against and how to overcome the obstacles. Try to figure out the market. I knew all of this and still decided to go ahead. My partner Rory had figured it out, too—he thought I was nuts.

My first wake-up call: there is no such thing as independent production unless you are independently wealthy. If you are not, you are dependent. Period. I had to get used to it. I had to be willing to invest in my own ideas. If I didn't, who would? I thought maybe others would step up to the plate if I did so myself. How could I ask others to risk their money if I wouldn't risk my own?

When you want your say, sometimes you have to pay. If you don't have a rich uncle or a willing patron or funder/financier/drug dealer, you have to come up with hard cash. So I had to start off by financing my own movie in a world where OPM (Other People's Money) is an axiom, and for good reason. It didn't take long to go through $20,000 and we were just getting started. I considered dropping the project. My pockets weren't deep enough.

But then I'd see some war-related outrage on television, or a propaganda piece posing as news and it would force me onwards. I convinced myself this film was needed, that I had a solemn duty to journalism and the future to see it through. Maybe I inflated the film's importance, but if I didn't think it was important, no one else would.

I had to consider what I could do without a real budget. What opportunities were out there? Who could I beg to shoot for me? Fortunately, having been a producer for years at the networks and then as an independent, I had friends who were willing to help with their time, footage, and skills. This helped immensely in deferring costs and keeping them low.

I didn't have and couldn't afford the kind of professional team you need on a project like this. Necessity is the mother of invention so when Anna Pizzaro, a dedicated young woman with a marketing background, came to our company as an intern, she began working on *WMD*. She had never made films before, but she was bright, talented and dedicated. After lots of hard work, she became a producer. Later, volunteers with a wide range of experience joined our team to help place the film in festivals, build a website, handle press, coordinate my chaos, etc. Without them *WMD* would never have gotten going.

So we began going to and filming at conferences where journalists spoke about the war with each other. One was at the New School University in New York City; another was the Arab Media Summit in Dubai. There I was the only American asked to speak. Many of those in attendance had never heard an American rip into his own country's media before. I also sprinkled in some concerns about their media, especially the tendency to assume all Americans backed Bush in the same way that our media portrayed all of Iraq as Saddamland.

Production Hell

Reporting the film was easier than making it. There were a lot of elements, footage, scripting, editing and endless aggravation. Our budgetary and staff limits made it a slow go—but the details are relevant because they speak to the difficulties inherent in constructing counter-narratives to the nonstop output of a multi-billion-dollar news business. To take on major media, you have to be as professional and as credible as they are, and be careful to avoid being dismissed as inaccurate.

We soon began collecting footage from groups who were monitoring media and we reached out to independents like Robert Young Pelton and Gwendolen Cates who were brave enough to share footage and commentary from the frontlines.

We also reached out to international broadcasters who, after some coaxing, agreed to supply some footage. The BBC, CBC, ARD TV in Germany, France 3, Al Jazeera and South African Broadcasting shared some of their material to let me show the different ways they approached the challenge of covering the war. Independent filmmakers such as Stephen Marshall of the Guerilla News Network and Patrick Dillen, who had lived in Baghdad, supplied excerpts of their work. Some U.S. network people agreed to allow me to use their footage of a public forum shot by NBC. I shot anti-war demonstrations and conducted interviews in disparate locations. Before long we had over 350 tapes and hundreds of hours of material to log, transcribe and make sense of. It took a year of work to come up with a cut we were happy with.

Finally, a benefactor emerged but could only put money in as an investor, not a donor. Soon I was setting up a limited partnership. The legal work cost money I didn't have, but we needed the corporate structure to facilitate financing. Then there was the money needed for music clearances. When I attempted to get permission to use one popular song, I was told it would cost "SLOM." SLOM? Translation: "A shit load of money."

Eventually, over time a few new angels materialized who were willing to invest in the film. I still hope to be able to recoup their investments, but given the way the industry is organized, that may be harder than I anticipated. *WMD* lurched along from each infusion of cash to more shooting and editing.

First we had a 20-minute trailer, then a 57-minute cut and soon, an 89-minute version. Slowly, a structure came into focus. I was learning to ask for help and listen to others, in my case, a smart associate who challenged me when I wasn't challenging myself. I also had to give up being too attached to my first ideas which turned out to be unrealistic and unachievable. They were ultimately dumped. I also had to learn not to be too impressed with myself as a director. We made the mistake of sending out videos that weren't finished and attracted a predictable range of responses pointing out some obvious problems.

Michael Moore was still months away from releasing *Fahrenheit 9/11*. To his credit and based on his money-making track record with films such as *Roger and Me* and *Bowling for Columbine,* Moore was able to snag interest and investment money from Miramax, a Disney affiliate. It took a lot of money for Moore to make a lot of money. In *Disneywar,* a book on the "magic kingdom" of Michael Eisner, James Stewart reveals that *Fahrenheit 9/11* cost $6 million to make, $20 million to market and more than $60 million in distribution fees. Moore didn't rely on the largess of progressive philanthropy but went the corporate route.

No dummy he.

Moore believed correctly that there was a huge market for his outspoken views and bold approach. He believed in himself. The film's success reflected dissatisfaction with our social criticism-free media system where dissenters like him are rarely seen except when sanitized or "balanced." Not only was his bet on audience interest vindicated, but his film demonstrated that filmmaking affords an outlet for an extended critical argument unfiltered by the editorial vetting that goes on routinely at TV stations that end up homogenizing most of the programming. It showed a hunger for hard-hitting documentaries.

Moore was also able to break through the way he did because he had already been certified as a celebrity, a "name" in a celebrity-obsessed society. He had won an Oscar and had become a fixture in the limelight. He knew he could trade on that fame to promote his new film, aided and abetted by a brilliant marketing maneuver by his producers at Miramax, built around picking a public fight with Disney (which had earlier expressed its lack of interest in distributing the film) that made a big enough stink to push the story to page one.

"All the conditions for a public relations hurricane were now in place," writes Stewart in *Disneywar*. Even though Disney had already said it would not distribute the movie, it seemed to be caught off guard when what they thought was an old story suddenly had new legs, and it blew up in their corporate face, projecting Eisner as a censor at best.

There was more to the story.

Stewart quotes Eisner as saying, "I don't want to be political," and then adds Miramax's Harvey Weinstein's comment that "this was rank hypocrisy since Disney-owned stations broadcast conservative commentators Rush Limbaugh and Sean Hannity."

This free publicity, combined with the premium prize at the Cannes Film Festival and strategic guidance from movie maestro Harvey Weinstein and his brother Bob, were the savvy marketers behind the big breakthrough. So was some big money. They knew how to play the game in a way that most independents, like me, are clueless. They shaped a brilliant win-win strategy.

According to Edward Jay Epstein, an analyst of Hollywood movie practices, in a column for *Slate,* Disney, Miramax and Moore all profited from the documentary through clever maneuvers:

> In the case of *Fahrenheit 9/11,* Eisner wasn't about to let the windfall escape into the Weinstein brothers' pockets. Nor could Disney take the PR hit that would result from backtracking and distributing the movie itself.
>
> Eisner's solution: Generate the illusion of outside distribution while orchestrating a deal that allowed Disney to reap most of the profits. Here's how the dazzling deal worked. On paper, the Weinstein brothers bought the rights to *Fahrenheit 9/11* from Miramax. The Weinsteins then transferred the rights to a corporate front called Fellowship Adventure Group. In turn, that company outsourced the documentary's theatrical distribution rights (principally to Lions Gate Films, IFC Films, and Alliance Atlantis Vivafilms) and video distribution rights to Columbia Tristar Home Entertainment).
>
> Because of the buzz and prestige attached to *Fahrenheit 9/11,* Harvey Weinstein extracted extremely favorable terms from these distributors, about one-third of what distributors typically charge. Their cut amounted to slightly more than 12 percent of the total they collected from the theaters. As a result, *Fahrenheit 9/11*'s net receipts—what remains after the distributors deduct their percentage and their out-of-pocket expenses (mounting an ad campaign, making prints, dubbing the film)—would be much higher than those of a typical Hollywood film.

Epstein seemed to marvel at Moore's accomplishment even if the charge of censorship was overplayed or even invented. He was "very smart," he wrote to me. I asked him if there was truth to the charge that Disney suppressed the film. His response: "No, no truth whatsoever. 99.99% of documentaries are turned down for distribution because there is no back-end licensing. Disney saw it as a headache, said no. Weinstein said he would recover money by selling it at Cannes. Moore than brilliantly played the censorship card."

So there you have it, even in making a political statement, marketing is as important or more important than mission. I cite this not to criticize Moore, but to try to learn from his experience.

Moore's final *coup de grace* was getting MoveOn.org behind the film. They called on email list members to flood the theaters on opening weekend, which had been strategically positioned between the Democratic and Republican conventions in the summer of 2004. MoveOn.org had a large, active membership base, and Democratic hopes were high because Bush seemed very vulnerable at the time. The confluence of big money for marketing and PR, a big push from a popular grassroots organization and the right timing turned the film into an instant hit.

The lesson is obvious. You need to "align the stars" behind you. I marveled at his success (and wished him well) but a lower budget film like *WMD* didn't and couldn't mobilize the same combination of powerful forces behind it. We had the means of production, actually finishing *WMD* before *Fahrenheit 9/11* was released, but lacked the distribution and marketing clout that Moore was able to stitch together.

Distribution is never easy to find. I knew early on that many indy distributors are now tied into bigger companies and hence wouldn't be too receptive to a film critical of their own industry. Many of my worst fears came to fruition. Several networks "passed" at the idea. Ditto for some channels that I thought might agree to air it. (The reasons cited never responded to the content of the film; it was never, "what a stupid idea" or "it's badly done" but always, "just not for us," or even, "we are doing something similar.") PBS watched it and shared their "thoughts," which boiled down to "forget it." You soon learn that the term "pass" is a codeword for rejecting a project without comment, a cop-out.

I had decided that the film needed a fashionable, character-based storytelling approach. Without the staff and funds, however, I had to become the character that I didn't have who would tell the story. The rationale was this: I was making serious charges. The audience should know who I am and what I have done.

Some distributors didn't like me in the film; others wanted more. It was too personal, or not personal enough. Some said it was too talky; others, not talky enough. I was too serious or "shambling" or both. Some thought I was imitating Moore, others that I wasn't as funny. One viewer in Amsterdam called it a "*Fahrenheit 9/11* for adults."

As for comparisons with Michael Moore, who is also frequently bashed for personalizing his perspectives, I can only say as one who admires his work and envies his success, that he was not my main influence. I have been reporting as "The News Dissector" since 1970, well before Moore first emerged on the scene. *WMD* is a very different film and an expression of a slightly deeper struggle.

In the end, Bush bashing proved more popular than media critiquing even though, in my mind, the media coverage of the 2004 election campaign was hostile to the Democrats and helped thwart their efforts.

The Republicans were far more skillful in getting their message out into the main media and in keeping the Democrats on the defensive. When the Democrats held their fire on the war, so did the various groups outside the party structure that were aligned with them. *WMD's* fortunes were affected by the reluctance among liberals and Democrats to challenge the media and the war.

Finishing the Film

A film is never done until it is. The tinkering is endless. Some felt that *WMD* was too long at two hours; too short at 90 minutes. After a lot of back and forth, I settled on a 98-minute length for the theatrical version.

(A TV version is 58 minutes.) That led to restructuring, more editing and more expense. Happily we were able to find more investors to keep us going as well as talented editors willing to work at reasonable rates.

We started showing our final cut at screenings at festivals to generate "buzz." The initial response was good from Nantucket to Dallas to Sacramento and Chicago. The film won top prizes in film festivals in Austin and Denver, the only two places where we competed. We won a third documentary prize at the Durban Festival in South Africa in June 2005. Sundance never got back to me; the Freedom Cinema Festival, screening alongside Sundance, in January 2005 awarded me their George Orwell Award "for journalistic courage opposing tyranny."

After over a year of work, it felt good when audiences responded with enthusiasm. I soon found myself showing it worldwide. It was accepted and promoted at festivals and events in Holland, Denmark, Spain, Switzerland, Brazil and South Korea. Soon, it was generating interest in the press in Copenhagen, Paris and Tokyo.

Our last hurdle was a legal review. This was tricky because I was making a "fair use" claim to use copy-written network war footage off-air. Here's a definition of fair-use I found in a law library. I thought it was so important that I put it in the film:

> The non-competitive right to use of copyrighted material without giving the author the right to compensation or to sue for infringement of copyright. The common and accepted industry practice of permitting use of brief excerpts of news footage for legitimate purposes of media criticism and analysis in furtherance of freedom of press and opinion.

If there was ever a project that fit squarely into these definitions, *WMD* is it. By and large, my pro-bono lawyers agreed. Insurers were more reluctant, but we got a policy covering errors and omissions. (A few months later, two of the insurers I had approached were indicted and paid big fines for illegal business practices.)

A gutsy distributor, Cinema Libre Studio, agreed to handle the movie. We debated whether to release it before or after the election. I argued for before because of the heightened political environment, but it was hard to book theaters. Ultimately, we opened in early December 2004, and began showing *WMD* in commercial theaters. But we hadn't anticipated the incredible post-election depression that would sweep through the anti-Bush camp, where we thought we would draw most of our initial audience. As the air went out of the activist bubble, our own expectations and theatrical opportunities took a dive.

Now I had to step back and wait for the reviews to roll in. I knew that when I, as somewhat of a media insider and critic, took on the media system, the mainstream media, especially the *BIG* media, would not take too kindly to my efforts–especially when I sought to peer more deeply into the institutional pressures inside the media and shine a light on it. *OutFoxed* producer Robert Greenwald advised me not to read the reviews. "They will make you crazy," he told me. But as a critic myself, and an advocate, I couldn't ignore them.

I was not surprised then when the *Washington Post* and *New York Times*–two newspapers that had led the charge to war and, later, under immense pressure from critics and readers, acknowledged some of their own failings, would be nasty and dismissive. Apparently, they believe that only they have the right to sit in judgment on their peers. Neither paper mentioned my referencing their roles and *mea culpas.*

The tone of their reviewers illustrates the deep gap between the polished put-down artists in mainstream media, which largely backed the war with deceptive reporting, and the independent media that did not. More troubling has been the sniping in the attitude-driven formerly alternative press that is of course "hipper than thou" and believes everyone already knows everything I report because they think they do. That jaded assumption is not true of course. I was profiled in the *New York Times* and *Gay City News,* praised in *Le Monde,* smeared by Accuracy in Media, and delivered up as a hero with four pages and my name on the cover of *Hustler.* Buzzflash said I deserved an Academy Award. The *Nation* said nothing.

I can only say that being accepted into, and winning recognition from leading film festivals, was gratifying, as was watching the film with enthusiastic audiences around the world. Ultimately, those who see it will be the real judges. On the second anniversary of the war, we had house parties in 240 cities worldwide. The film has also been shown on TV in Japan, Australia, Spain and the Middle East–so far. A new ITN channel bought it in England. So has Czech Television. Closer to home, the Independent Film Channel in the U.S. acquired the film for a September 11th cablecast after an executive read my complaints in a *New York Times* interview about getting the film seen in America. He said he would run it if he liked it. Happily he did.

As the war in Iraq continues, as some news organizations finally acknowledge problems in their coverage, as the media continues to treat the war as a sports event with more focus on dead soldiers than a failed policy, *WMD* is, in my admittedly subjective opinion, never more timely or needed.

I knew that the odds were against realizing the kind of success *9/11* had achieved; although *WMD* had an important mission, there was so much going against it. "You are always tilting at windmills," my father said affectionately. The biggest consolation prize came from the encouragement I received from journalists I respected and letters from Iraqis like the blogger, Riverbend (who lives at the bend of a river):

> I saw you on Al-Arabia today!!! It was great. I was vaguely watching a documentary on American media prior to wars and the focus was Iraq. They were interviewing people (famous media people, I assume) about their views on the wars and the media. There were some media people justifying the war and the media, etc. Just as I was getting impatient with the whole thing and cursing Al-Arabia, they started talking about the anti-war media and they interviewed some big-shot who was saying that Americans couldn't oppose the war because they were instantly attacked as anti-American, especially after September 11, and he talked about some journalists and activists and authors who were attacked by the media for being anti-war, etc.
>
> So the commentator (in Arabic) went on to say something like this, ... and while the war drums were being beaten no one dared raise their voice to object because journalists would ruin their careers, except one man who spoke loud and long against the war–a journalist famous for his award-winning docu-

mentaries named Danny Schechter ..." and they showed clips from something you made on the war. The profile lasted a couple of minutes and they showed you in your office or something talking on the phone, etc. I was jumping up and down and saying, "That's Danny! That's Danny!" (The peas I was shelling went flying all over. ...) My aunt asked if you were an actor. An actor? No, more like an activist.

That's the kind of review a filmmaker lives for—from a great writer in Baghdad who has so far survived the bombs and the odds.

The final chapter of this saga is the hardest and is still unwritten—will the audiences keep coming? I want to pay back our investors. Will *WMD* have any impact or will I become a casualty of the Iraq War, too? I remember my old friend, writer Paul Goodman, saying, "In America, you can say anything you want—as long as it doesn't have any effect."

All I can say is that I have given the *WMD* project my best shot in a very uneven battleground. Over a year and a half after beginning the project, as *When News Lies* emerges, I realized that in the end it was never about money or fame. I had to stand up and speak out. Yes, Dad, someone has to tilt at windmills like these.

As I say to the audience at the end of *WMD,* "Now I have had my say. It's your turn."

Epilogue

I made it a point in my own "media war" with the war to try to bring into the media industry my assessment of the media coverage in hopes of reaching decision-makers. I was pleased when media trade and journalism magazines including *Nieman Reports, Broadcasting & Cable, Editor & Publisher* and *TV Week* carried my commentaries. (Others, like *Variety,* would not.) Unfortunately, the response was often silence from their readers, as if the issue was not debatable. It was the silence of the lambs all over again.

To be fair, there are few channels of dissent within the news business in an industry that claims the first amendment as its mission. Employees are rarely encouraged or allowed to exercise their freedom of speech, especially if they want to question the news practices of the company they work for. Some of the people who work for big media companies do so because they condone their policies and align themselves with their outlooks. But when they don't, they know that if they value their careers, it's often best to keep their concerns to themselves. Dissent is not encouraged in most newsrooms.

Perhaps that's because media professionals don't see their work as ideological or political and are therefore resistant to being challenged on those grounds. Craft and conservatism is common in the business; consciousness and conscience is not. Standing up for principles is not encouraged; getting along by going along is.

There is a parochialism in our news culture that screens out critical views that are perceived as coming from a separate but rarified parallel universe which includes the findings of media critics. Our own media don't bother to watch what is being presented in other countries. The assumption is Americans know best and know how to do it best.

World opinion does not influence news decisions. American TV news rarely covers the UN except when U.S. issues are dominant. Reporters from all over the world are stationed at UN headquarters but there are few American reporters unless a scandal is brewing. As the Bush Administration pressed the UN to sanction war, TV trucks turned the front of the building into a parking lot. I watched all the reporters line up in front of their trucks to do live shots for their newscast, all seeming to echo the same script. No one bothered to point to the irony of using the UN, a world body whose *raison d'être* is to make peace not war, as a backdrop for a push to war.

Many observers were incredulous at the lack of logic and inconsistency of the argument that in some media outlets turned into attacks on "surrender monkeys." Author Paul Freudlich noted, "We are going to ignore the United Nations in order to make clear to Saddam Hussein that the United Nations cannot be ignored. We are going to wage war to preserve the UN's ability to avert war."

Colin Powell's performance at the Security Council was praised for its shocking evidence until months later when Powell admitted that most of it was bogus. Where were the journalists to question and challenge all of this at the time?

As the Administration carefully managed their message, controlling what government spokespeople could say, they were also busily hiring PR companies to control the spin and stay ahead of any alternative stories. These external influences meshed easily with the fast moving news cycles. They were synchronistic and synergistic. The PR types generated stories and planted experts on the air; they provided special "sources" and access for journalists considered "friendlies." They understood how TV news had moved into a post-journalism era where entertainment values trumped information values.

The fast paced nature of 24/7 news meant that a story could surface quickly and just as quickly disappear with few remembering what had come before.

If the run-up to the war was treated almost as comedy, the war itself became a tragedy.

The political writer and philosopher Phillip Green writes in his book, *Primetime Politics,* "It is simply the case that nowhere in what might loosely be called the democratic world, even very few places in the rest of it, could one find out less about events in Iraq than one could find from American television."

But that indictment would not resonate with those responsible for the coverage. They were proud of it. They were giving each other awards for the "best live war coverage by an embed," etc.

It is significant that most of the interpretation of what we were seeing came from Pentagon-approved "TV generals" and experts from inside the military and intelligence world. (Some Canadian viewers called them "war heads.") They became our guides. They told us what to think about the news, rarely quibbling with what the Administration presented in terms of the "progress" of the military campaign.

So when ex-General Barry McCaffrey appeared on NBC-TV and questioned whether enough soldiers had been deployed, or suggested that a "quagmire" was possible, he was surprised by the enmity he encountered. The Pentagon did not just disagree but denounced the very idea. "It was either their way or the highway," is how he described their attitude. (McCaffrey was hardly a hero in my eyes; he had played a reactionary role in the War on Drugs and was exposed for war crimes during Gulf War I by Seymour Hersh in *The New Yorker.)*

Yet McCaffrey too was bullied by the Administration. He told me that even as he was perceived by some viewers as fronting for the Pentagon, he was fighting Pentagon decision-makers to get credible information. He presented himself to me as a beleaguered man in the middle pressured on all sides. He (along with other TV generals) found that because he often mistrusted the official DOD line, he not only had to act as a commentator, but he had to become a journalist to dig out facts—a role he was not qualified to play. The TV news organizations that used these "experts" rarely questioned their conclusions; after all, they were supposed to be the experts. In fact, many weren't.

War critics were largely excluded from most TV broadcasts so a counter-narrative could never be suggested much less constructed. Just as the TV experts identified with the "mission" set out for our soldiers, so did many viewers. It was a process of electronic osmosis. Many of the well-dressed and articulate pundits and "experts," who held strong, even extreme points of view, were presented as neutral analysts not advocates. They were shown to be above the fray, offering facts not opinions. This is how ideology gets masked as objective fact, how it gets transmitted and absorbed into the public psyche.

This is how TV news works, not only in wars. It creates a framework. Viewers tend to respond less to specifics than to the overall media environment. Justin Lewis, Michael Morgan and Sut Jhalley from the University of Massachusetts studied the media's impact on public attitudes and found through an analysis of survey data that there are "consistent systemic misperceptions among the public. ... People are less likely to be informed by particular details of news coverage than by an overall oft-repeated framework," they wrote.

Media professionals tend to work in an environment where they are convinced that their understanding of events and the world has been reached through the lens of an objective media system. Their support for that system is cultivated over time. When you join big media, big media tends to join you as well. Whatever your grumbles and complaints, you become a part of a corporate team flying well-branded corporate logos. As media employees get caught up in the desire to please their bosses, the public winds up with milquetoast passed off as objective reporting.

Investigative reporting often gets lost in this environment as well. Faced with this type of approach, it is no wonder that TV viewers tend to believe what they watch. Writes Canadian scholar Paul Rutherford in his book on the marketing of the war, *Weapons of Mass Persuasion,* "most Americans were not aware of how one-sided and biased the coverage had been. They believed the news media had served the country well." They also had few opportunities to compare and contrast what they were seeing with what others outside the U.S. watched.

And even if the public did watch other broadcasters, interpreting the differences takes some skill. Television shares the same templates and formats worldwide, often relying on a small number of consultants for advice while using similar sets, anchors, graphics and pacing. Also television does not call attention to its techniques of sanitizing war or in Frank Rich's words "airbrushing" the conflict. Even as television news brought us closer to the war, it distanced us from it. In fact it became part of the war. Phillip Green asks, "Are the television cameras the witnesses to war or are they part of the weaponry? Or both?"

I would say both.

"Television cannot ever adequately convey the sheer brute force of war, the noise and the utter violence," NBC's Tom Brokaw told the *New York Times.* "It somehow gets filtered through the TV screen and that's probably just as well." In short, the network news machine says "trust us." I say, if you think you can trust the mainstream media, think again.

Media can be deployed as an effective military weapons system because it is already a tool of cultural indoctrination. And it's not just the news that constructs and reinforces points of views. Entertainment programming can be even more effective in this regard as propaganda. It doesn't have to be informative or factual but it can and does transmit messages.

Of course the Pentagon has regularly used entertainers like Bob Hope and others to entertain the troops. In the aftermath of 9/11, Hollywood was enlisted in the war on terror. Karl Rove was sent to Los Angeles to meet with studio heads and producers. Some were supportive. It's clear that Hollywood's approach to storytelling influenced government propagandists who emulated many of their techniques.

The Iraqi blogger, Riverbend, who calls herself a "girl blogger" writes anonymously from Baghdad. I became a fan of her "Baghdad Burning" blog and she very kindly wrote about my own book, *Embedded: Weapons of Mass Deception,* when I sent it to her. She has offered a consistent counterpoint to the U.S. coverage, but it has rarely, if ever, been picked up by U.S. mainstream outlets that rely on their own correspondents rather than more informed locals. She shares my concerns about the U.S. media but had never really seen it in action until it became a part of her own world when the American forces "liberated" Iraqis from Saddam-controlled TV, substituting corporate America's version of the news.

The circle then became complete: a media system used to incite Americans to go to war against Iraq was now being used to pacify Iraqis and seduce them with an American cultural offensive.

In the Spring of 2005, Riverbend described how in the beginning of the war, Iraq was bombarded with high-tech military weapons and now it is being bombed by American media, including American music, TV and movies. She wrote:

> Two years ago, the major part of the war in Iraq was all about bombarding us with smart bombs and high-tech missiles. Now there's a different sort of war— or perhaps it's just another phase of the same war. Now we're being assailed with American media. It's everywhere all at once . . . it's not just Iraq that is being targeted—it's the whole region and it's all being done very cleverly.

I was most intrigued by how she saw U.S. style "news" as part of this larger media environment aimed at cultivating Iraqi support of the larger strategy of winning minds and hearts, a strategy that has been successful in America for years. She observed:

> The thing that strikes me most is the fact that the news is so clean. It's like hos- pital food. It's all organized and disinfected. Everything is partitioned and you can feel how it has been doled out carefully with extreme attention to the por- tions—two minutes on women's rights in Afghanistan, one minute on training troops in Iraq and 20 minutes on Terri Schiavo! All the reportages are upbeat and somewhat cheerful, and the anchor person manages to look properly con- cerned and completely uncaring all at once.

Don't journalists recognize these problems? Many do. But are they will- ing to stand up to change their news practices? Bill Moyers quotes his col- league Jim Lehrer of PBS on how government spin and framing continues to influence news coverage:

> Why were journalists not discussing the occupation of Iraq? Because the word "occupation" was never mentioned in the run-up to the war. Washington talked

about the war as a war of liberation, not a war of occupation. So as a consequence, those of us in journalism never even looked at the issue of occupation.

In other words, says scholar Jonathan Mermin in an essay in *World Journal,* "if the government isn't talking about it, we don't report it."

Whose fault is this? We can't blame the government for all the stenography posing as journalism, can we? Journalists have to be more conscious and take responsibility for their reporting or be condemned, as many are, as accomplices to war and deception.

So as you can see, or have yet to see, the media war is not over. The challenge of confronting it remains. And that will take challenging the media makers as well as the policy makers. A media system that claims to strengthen democracy is eroding it both here in the U.S. and in Iraq. That is what makes the media problem so central to all the others. The war of words and images will go on even when the Iraq War ends, as it will.

The Iraq War has bombed us all with a torrent of lies, half truths, infotainment and marketing. It has decapitated the ability of many to even see what has happened to Iraq and to us. We are inundated and seduced by a media message that is often effective because we don't recognize its techniques and how it affects us.

In an age of seamless TV packaging, enhanced through slick editing and graphic formats and presented by authoritative anchors—familiar celebrities in their own right—its hard to for most viewers to recognize the impact of the editorial and production techniques, or the process that selects some information, transmits some sources and excludes others. This is not a new problem—and it is not just found in the electronic media.

No less a supporter of a free press in America than Thomas Jefferson, an author of the Bill of Rights, recognized the way newspapers can manipulate opinion without the readers realizing they are being deceived. He wrote about this in a letter in 1785:

The most effectual engines for [pacifying a nation] are the public papers. ... [A despotic] government always [keeps] a kind of standing army of newswriters who, without any regard to truth or to what should be like truth, [invent] and put into the papers whatever might serve the ministers. This suffices with the mass of the people who have no means of distinguishing the false from the true paragraphs of a newspaper."

–Thomas Jefferson to G. K. van Hogendorp
Oct. 13, 1785. ME 5:181, Papers 8:632

No wonder Jefferson demanded that eternal vigilance is the only way to safeguard our democracy. Who can doubt that these weapons of mass deception will be deployed again and again in this era of permanent warfare?

That is, unless and until, we recognize the danger and enlist in the fight for a media that serves the cause of democracy and social justice. My film *WMD* closes with a challenge to its viewers to fight back and asks, "Can we afford not to fight back?"

I would like to think that there is a conscience in the news business and that journalists will ultimately realize how they have been had, and how our democracy has been damaged. I hope they will ultimately speak up and join the fight for better media. I can only hope that once media professionals recognize the scale of our war-related failures, changes and reforms will be introduced to assure that it can't happen again.

But, truth be told, it sounds a bit naïve given how firmly media companies are managed and how easy it is for them to silence dissenters or just move on to the next story without looking back at their own responsibility for the misinformation that continues to be taken seriously.

Media companies make a big deal about freedom of the press when their issues are challenged or their employees are being forced to disclose sources–but they don't do much to ensure that critical voices are heard within their organizations. At times it seems as if the guardians of a free press are seeking to limit free speech.

In a statement recorded for the launch of Mediachannel.org, Walter Cronkite, once considered the "most trusted man in America," expressed a concern about the group think stultifying discussion in our news rooms. He said:

We have all been supportive for years of dissidents around the world who take great risks to stand up for what they believe in. But here at home, in our own industry, we need to make it possible for people to speak out when they feel they've been wronged, even if it means shaming news rooms to do the right thing. Journalists shouldn't have to check their consciences at the door when they go to work for a media company. It ought to be just the reverse.

As I've said on other occasions, the strength of the American system is possible and can be nurtured only if there is lively and provocative dissent. In a healthy environment dissent is encouraged and considered essential to feed a cross-fertilization of ideas and thwart the incestuous growth of stultifying uniformity. We need to encourage and support those around us who face either overt or covert threats—or even more subtle absence of encouragement to search out the truth.

This comment anticipated the issues raised in this book about the coverage of the war. That is why we need an investigation of media failures more earnestly than an investigation of intelligence failures. We need to challenge our journalistic community and put it in the dock of public opinion, along with the spooks and politicians who went along or looked away.

We also need to mobilize the American public to demand truth and integrity in the media.

This, I believe, is why *When News Lies* will have value in the years ahead and why I hope *WMD* gets the audience it deserves.

Biography

Danny Schechter: News Dissector/
Investigative Journalist/Producer/Director

Danny Schechter is a television producer and independent filmmaker who often writes and speaks about media issues. He is the executive editor and blogger-in-chief of Mediachannel.org, the world's largest online media issues network.

Schechter is co-founder and executive producer of Globalvision, a New York-based television and film production company now in its 18th year, where he co-produced 156 editions of the award-winning series "South Africa Now" and "Rights & Wrongs: Human Rights Television." In 1998, a human rights special, "Globalization and Human Rights" was co-produced with Rory O'Connor and shown nationally on PBS.

A Cornell University graduate, he received his Master's degree from the London School of Economics, and an honorary doctorate from Fitchburg College. He was a Nieman Fellow in Journalism at Harvard, where he also taught in 1969. After college, he was a full-time civil rights worker and then communications director of the Northern Student Movement; he worked as a community organizer in a Saul Alinsky-style War on Poverty program, and, moving from the streets to the suites, served as an assistant to the mayor of Detroit in 1966 on a Ford Foundation grant.

He has won two national News Emmy awards for his TV work with ABC News "20/20" (and two nominations); two regional Emmy's, a National Headliner award, and the Society for Professional Journalists award for an investigative documentary. Amnesty International honored him for his human rights television work.

Schechter's professional journalism career began in 1970, when he was named news director, principal newscaster and "News Dissector" at WBCN-FM in Boston, where he was hailed as a radio innovator and won many industry honors, including two Major Armstrong Awards. His television producing career was launched with the syndicated "Joe Oteri Show," which won the New England Emmy and a NAPTE IRIS award in 1979. In 1980, he created and produced the nation's first live late-night entertainment-oriented TV show, "Five All Night, Live All Night" at WCVB in Boston.

Schechter left Boston to join the staff at CNN as a producer based in Atlanta. He then moved to ABC as a producer for "20/20," where during his eight years he won two National News Emmys. Schechter has reported from 47 countries and lectured at many schools and universities. He was an adjunct professor at the Graduate School of Journalism at Columbia University. Schechter's writing has appeared in leading newspapers and magazines including the *The Nation, Newsday, Boston Globe, Columbia Journalism Review, Media Studies Journal, Detroit Free Press, Village Voice, Tikkun, Z,* and many other newspapers, magazines and websites.

Other Works by the Author

Books

Embedded: Weapons of Mass Deception–How the Media Failed to Cover the War on Iraq (Prometheus Books, 2003; ebook version–coldType.net, August 2003)

Media Wars: News at a Time of Terror (Roman & Littlefield, 2003)

News Dissector: Passions, Pieces and Polemics (Akashic Books, 2001; ebook version–electronpress.com, 2001)

Hail to the Thief: How the Media "Stole" the 2000 Election, Ed. with Roland Schatz. (Inovatio Books, Bonn, Germany, 2000; ebook version–electronpress.com, 2000)

Falun Gong's Challenge to China (Akashic Books, 1999, 2000)

The More You Watch, the Less You Know (Seven Stories Press, 1997, revised 1999)

Films and TV Documentaries

Weapons of Mass Deception (2004)

We are Family (2002)

Counting On Democracy (2002)

Falun Gong's Challenge to China (2000)

Nkosi: Saving Africa's AIDS Orphans (2000)

A Hero for All: Nelson Mandela's Farewell (1999)

Globalization and Human Rights (with Rory O'Connor) (1998)

Sowing Seeds, Reaping Peace: The World of Seeds of Peace (1996)

Prisoners of Hope: Robben Island Reunion (1995), co-directed by Barbara Kopple

Countdown to Freedom: Ten Days that Changed South Africa (1994), narrated by James Earl Jones and Alfre Woodard

Sarajevo Ground Zero (1993)

The Living Canvas (1992), narrated by Billy Dee Williams

Beyond JFK: The Question of Conspiracy (1992, co-directed with Barbara Kopple)

Give Peace a Chance (1991)

Mandela in America (1990)

The Making of Sun City (1987)

Student Power (1968)

TV Series

South Africa Now (Executive Producer) 1988–91

Rights & Wrongs (co-produced with Rory O'Connor; anchored by Charlayne Hunter-Gault) 1993–1997

TV Programs

Editorial Producer, "Topic One with Tina Brown" (CNBC), 2004

Broadcast Producer, "The Last Word" (ABC), 1986

Producer, "20/20" (ABC News), 1981–1988

Producer, "Sandi Freeman Show" (CNN), 1980

Producer, "Five All Night, Live All Night" (WVCB, Boston), 1980

Producer, "The Joe Oteri Show" (WLVI, Boston), 1979

Reporter, "The Ten O'Clock News" (WGBH, Boston), 1978

For continuing coverage and updating on the issues
discussed in this book, visit Mediachannel.org

Feedback welcome: dissector@mediachannel.org

"It's not surprising that documentary-makers have usually worked in a spirit of advocacy. They are people sufficiently committed to a point of view to go to the trouble of obtaining expensive equipment, carting it into the field, shooting miles of film under often unpleasant or dangerous conditions, and spending months or years splicing the results into a coherent movie. It's easier to write an editorial. It's easier, even, to write a book. People who make documentaries don't make them because they believe that 'reasonable people can disagree,' or that there are two sides to every question. They believe that there are, at most, one and a half sides—a right side and a side that, despite possibly having some redeeming aspects, is, on balance, wrong. They make movies because they are passionate about their subjects and they want to arouse passion in others, many others."

–Louis Menand
Staff writer, *The New Yorker*, August 2004

Script of the Film:
WMD: Weapons of Mass Deception

1. SECTION: TEASE

BLACK SCREEN ONLY MUSIC. REPORTER ROBERT YOUNG PELTON GOING THROUGH CHECKPOINT IN IRAQ	**SOT: REPORTER ROBERT YOUNG PELTON GOING THROUGH CHECK POINT IN IRAQ:** This is a checkpoint. Here is what is interesting. We all have guns, right? I don't have a gun, but my driver has a gun, my security guy has a gun, and they're looking for guns. And so, they're going to search us. So now they start to, and then when I say, "Hey, look I am American," they kind of go "Oh," and let you go.
CHECKPOINT INTERAC-TION	**SOT: CHECKPOINT INTERACTION:** **Soldier:** You all keep going. It is a free country. Where are you all from? **Journalist in car:** I'm from LA, I'm with CBS News. **Soldier:** CBS? **Journalist in car:** Yah.
CYRON: FAIR USE: (FÂR-YÜS), FUNC-TION NOUN	MUSIC

1. The non-competitive right to use of copyrighted material without giving the author the right to compensation or to sue for infringement of copyright.

CHECKPOINT BACK-GROUND

WAR PROMO, BILL O'REILLY ON SCREEN	**SOT: BILL O'REILLY, FOX NEWS HOST–OFF-AIR AUDIO:** There is a school of thought that says we should have given the citizens of Baghdad 48 hours to get out of Dodge and flatten the place. The war would already be over and we could have done that in two days.
CYRON: FAIR USE: 2. The common and accepted industry practice of permitting use of brief excerpts of news footage for legitimate purposes of media criticism and analysis in furtherance of freedom of press and opinion. SHOWDOWN WITH SADDAM PROMO	MUSIC POLARITY1
IRAQ WAR NEWS PROMOTION NBC PROMO	**SOT: TOM BROKAW, NBC NEWS ANCHOR:** One of the things we don't want to do is to destroy the infrastructure of Iraq because in a few days we're going to own that country.

IRAQ WAR NEWS PROMO-TION	**SOT: NBC NEWS ANCHOR:** Target Iraq. Operation Iraqi freedom

2. SECTION: TITLE SEQUENCE

CYRON: GLOBALVISION PRESENTS WMD WEAPONS OF MASS DECEPTION WMD A PERSONAL FILM, A MEDIA CHALLENGE WMD A DANNY SCHECHTER DISSECTION MEDIA MEDLEY FOLLOWED BY SCRATCH	**MUSIC: MEDIA WAR:** "We're gonna fix that, that technical problem" "Tick tock its time for shock / Are you bored/ It's time to get awed/ ABC/NBC/CBS/CNN/FOX News/ Breaking news/ Faking news/ Da media war/It's time to get sore."

3. SECTION: "READ MY APOCA-LIPS"

DS: IN A SCENE SATIRIZ-ING *APOCALYPSE NOW* **CYRON:** "READ MY APOCA-LIPS" MARCH 2003 **CYRON:** "READ MY APOCA-LIPS" MARCH 2003 DANNY SCHECHTER'S OFFICE, NEWS COVERS HEADLINES OF WAR ON THE TABLE	**MUSIC: THE DOORS,"THE END"** **SOT: TED KOPPEL** Wreak havoc and unleash the dogs of war. And there they start moving into Iraq.

US SOLDIERS EMBARKING,
US SOLDIERS IN TANK CON-
VOY IN IRAQ, DANNY
SCHECHTER'S BOOKS

US SOLDIERS MOVING BY DAWN, NIGHT VISION FOOTAGE, DANNY SCHECHTER DREAMING, SOLDIER WALKING	**SOT: MEDLEY OF NEWS RECORD-INGS:** **TV CORRESPONDENTS:** We got rockets coming in on us. Tom, we're under attack right now. PFC Jessica Lynch who's being held … The battle of Basra is still raging along this way …
DANNY CLOSE-UP SOLDIERS WITH GAS MASKS RUNNING IN SLOW MOTION, DANNY SCHECHTER DREAMS ON, DESERT STORM BOMBS EXPLODING, TANKS ROLLING, NIGHT VISION GUN FIGHT, DANNY UPSIDE DOWN, CEILING FAN HELICOPTERS FLYING	**V/O: DANNY SCHECHTER:** <u>THE INVASION OF IRAQ HAS INVAD-ED MY BRAIN. IT'S LIKE I AM UNDER ATTACK–WAR IS ALL I SEE. I DREAM OF AN ENDLESS DESERT …</u> <u>… DISSOLVING INTO BOMBS FALLING, INTO TANKS ROLLING, INTO SOLDIERS SHOOTING, INTO PEOPLE DYING, INTO REPORTERS REPORTING–IF THAT IS WHAT THEY ARE REALLY DOING.</u> MUSIC: THE DOORS "THE END" TAKES OVER
EMBEDDED REPORTER REPORTING FROM HELI-COPTER	**SOT: REPORTER:** Just this second, we've crossed over the border into Iraq.
DANNY UPSIDE DOWN, FLASH OF RUNNING SOL-DIER, BUSH, SADDAM STAT-UE FALLING, RUMSFELD AT THE STAKE-OUT, TV SHOTS OF ROADSIDE	**V/O: DANNY SCHECHTER:** <u>TALK ABOUT EMBEDDING…. EVEN MY BED OFFERS NO ESCAPE FROM THE 24-HOUR NEWS CYCLE, SPIN CYCLE, IRAQI FREEDOM CYCLE–THE PENTAGON HAS INVADED MY LIV-</u>

DANNY SCHECHTER WATCHING TV, TV SHOTS OF TANKS ROLLING, CLOSE-UP DANNY SCHECHTER, BATHROOM, BLACK AND WHITE WAR FOOTAGE

AMERICAN SOLDIER WAVING THE FLAG, BLACK/WHITE WAR FOOTAGE, RUMSFELD

DANNY WASHING HIS FACE

ING ROOM. THEIR GENERALS HAVE TAKEN OVER MY TV SET.

IS IT NEWS OR PROPAGANDA? OR IN THIS AGE OF MEDIA MERGERS, HAS THE MEDIA MERGED WITH THE MILITARY? YOU DON'T HAVE TO GO INTO THE JUNGLE ANYMORE TO FIND"THE HORROR." IT HAS COME HOME!

I FEEL LIKE I'M LIVING THROUGH MY OWN MEDIA APOCALYPSE—UNDER FIRE ON THE POLLUTED RIVER OF TV NEWS.

THIS IS MEDIA WAR WITHOUT END. I'M A MEDIA CRITIC... MY JOB: TO DISSECT THE NEWS.

SCRATCH

DANNY SCHECHTER AT HIS COMPUTER, SOLDIER BY DAWN, BOMBS GOING OFF, FF OF STAND-UPS BEING SET UP, TV STAFF/ JOURNALISTS' MAKE-UP, TV STAFF EDITING, FILMING, PEOPLE WATCHING TV, JOURNALISTS TYPING, DANNY SCHECHTER TYPING

DANNY SCHECHTER AT HIS COMPUTER, IMAGES OF INTERNET NEWS SITES, NEWSPAPERS AND MAGAZINES

V/O: DANNY SCHECHTER
THERE WERE TWO WARS GOING ON IN IRAQ—ONE FOUGHT WITH SOLDIERS, BOMBS,"SHOCK AND AWE." THE OTHER WAS FOUGHT ALONGSIDE IT, WITH CAMERAS, SATELLITES, AND ARMIES OF JOURNALISTS; THEY WERE FIGHTING A MEDIA WAR—THAT WAS THE ONE I COVERED.

THROUGHOUT THE WAR I WAS"SELF-EMBEDDED" AT THIS COMPUTER, WRITING ABOUT MEDIA COVERAGE WORLD-WIDE FOR THE MEDIACHANNEL.ORG WEBSITE.

CUT-AWAYS OF DANNY SCHECHTER IN OFFICE WATCHING WAR NEWS SHOWS OF THE BOMBING OF BAGHDAD	EVERY DAY I READ NEWSPAPERS AND MAGAZINES, SIFTED THROUGH WEBSITES, LISTENED TO THE RADIO AND STUDIED THE TV COVERAGE.
PETER ARNETT COVERING THE WAR	**SOT: PETER ARNETT IN BAGHDAD, WAR REPORTER:** "Right in front of us, an amazing sight ..." "It's just like out of an action movie, but this is real."
NEWS SHOTS OF THE BOMBING OF BAGHDAD, ANCHOR REPORTING ON WAR, SADDAM FOOTAGE	**V/O: DANNY SCHECHTER:** THE WAR WENT ON FOR 720 HOURS. I WATCHED AS MUCH AS I COULD STAND, AND WAS NOT THE ONLY CRITICAL JOURNALIST.
ASHLEIGH BANFIELD GIVING A LECTURE AT KANSAS STATE UNIVERSITY **CYRON:** DROPPED BY NBC A YEAR LATER	**SOT: ASHLEIGH BANFIELD, MSNBC: KANSAS STATE UNIVERSITY** So, was this journalism or was this coverage? There is a grand difference between journalism and coverage. And getting access does not mean you're getting the story, it just means you're getting one more arm or leg of the story. And that's what we got.
NBC NEWS REPORTER INTERVIEWED BY MAYVIN KALB (HARVARD UNIVERSITY) **CYRON:** ATTACKED FOR NAMING US WAR DEAD	**SOT: TED KOPPEL, NBC NEWS REPORTER:** Live coverage of a war, to describe that, as"live journalism" is, I think, an oxymoron. **SOT: TED KOPPEL, NBC NEWS REPORTER:** I think it's bad journalism.

YOUSEF IBRAHIM	**O/C: YOUSEF IBRAHIM, FORMER NEW YORK *TIMES* REPORTER:** I thought the entire American media, print as well as audio and video, was seduced by this run-up to the war. There was an envelopment in the American flag, a patriotic sweep.
MEDIA WATCH AUSTRALIA	**SOT: DAVID MARR, MEDIA WATCH AUSTRALIA:** "Say what you like about Rupert Murdoch's Fox network—its strange intimacy with God and the US administration—but it takes real flair to put this on national television ..."
REPORTER IN FIELD DIS-CUSSES HOW JOURNALISTS RELIEVE THEMSELVES	**SOT: FOX NEWS CHANNEL REPORTER:** "Using the facilities when there aren't any facilities. How are you going to the bathroom, buddy?"
REPORTER MAKES SOLDIER DEMONSTRATE THE PROCE-DURE	**SOT: MEDIA WATCH AUSTRALIA ANCHOR:** "So the reporter called the soldier over ..." **SOT: FOX NEWS CHANNEL REPORTER:** "You want to demonstrate for us how you sit on that shovel? You want me to do it? Go ahead. There you go, there you go. Isn't that something?" **SCRATCH**
DANNY SCHECHTER ON FOX NEWS WITH BILL O'RIELLY	**O/C: BILL O'REILLY, FOX NEWS:** In the second "Back of the Book" segment today, a book called *The More You Watch, the Less You Know*. With us

is the author of *The More You Know,* Danny Schechter, who has had many TV news jobs, including being a producer for"20/20."

STILLS FROM DANNY SCHECHTER'S YOUTH AS A JOURNALIST	**V/O: DANNY SCHECHTER:** <u>YEARS AGO I BECAME A NETWORK REFUGEE, CHALLENGING THE SUPERFICIALITY OF MAINSTREAM NEWS, ESPECIALLY IN ITS TREATMENT OF WAR.</u> <u>EVEN WHEN COVERING WARS IN VIETNAM AND CAMBODIA, I ALSO CRITIQUED THE COVERAGE.</u>
FOOTAGE FROM GLOBALVISION PRODUCTIONS IN SOUTH AFRICA AND BOSNIA	<u>I DID THE SAME WHEN I WORKED AT CNN AND ABC NEWS, AND THEN WITH COLLEAGUES ON GLOBALVISION'S TV SERIES ABOUT SOUTH AFRICA THAT TOLD UNREPORTED STORIES.</u>
ARCHIVE SADDAM FOOTAGE	<u>DITTO FOR HUMAN RIGHTS COVERAGE OF BOSNIA</u> <u>IRAQ TV AND SADDAM'S TERRIBLE CRIMES AND ABUSES.</u>
SHOT OF REPORTER COVERING GULF WAR VICTORY PARADE 1991	<u>WARRING WITH THE REPORTING OF WAR HAS BEEN AN OBSESSION FOR YEARS.</u> <u>I LAMBASTED MEDIA FAILURES DURING ALL THE HOOPLA AROUND THE FIRST GULF WAR</u>
GULF WAR SOLDIER AT PARADE	**GULF WAR SOLDIER:** The majority is saying thumbs up, y'know ... and I like that!

VICTORY PARADE	**V/O: DANNY SCHECHTER:** SO HERE I GO AGAIN …

4. SECTION: THE PAST IS NEVER PAST

UNIVERSAL NEWSREEL REPORT ON VIETNAM, WOUNDED SOLDIER CARRIED INTO BARN, WOUNDED ON THE FLOOR RECEIVING HELP	**SOT: UNIVERSAL NEWS REEL:** UPI Cameraman Abe Keller came down with the GI's—took these dramatic scenes while the dead and dying covering the floors…
WOUNDED ON THE FLOOR, SOLDIERS SHOOTING FROM TRENCHES, THROWING GRENADES	**V/O: DANNY SCHECHTER:** IT WAS THIS HISTORY OF COVERING WARS THAT LED ME TO LOOK AT THE RELATIONSHIP BETWEEN THE MEDIA AND THE MILITARY.
SOLDIER FIRING A ROCKET LAUNCHER, WINDOW BREAKS IN HOUSE, SOLDIERS RUNNING IN EMPTY STREETS, STREET SHOTS FROM TANK, HELICOPTER DIVING, SOLDIERS EMBARKING FROM HELICOPTERS, TANK ON THE STREET	TO UNDERSTAND WHY PEOPLE RALLY AROUND THE FLAG THE WAY THEY DO, YOU HAVE TO CONSIDER THE INFORMATION THAT SHAPES THEIR OPINIONS AND IMPRESSIONS. HOW WARS ARE COVERED, OR COVERED UP, IS KEY.
VIETNAM FOOTAGE GENERAL WESTMORELAND, BULLET GOING OFF, SOLDIER RUNNING IN JUNGLE	**SOT: GENERAL WILLIAM WESTMORELAND, FORMER VIETNAM GENERAL:** I can say without reservation that these magnificent young Americans are as fine as any fighting men our nation has ever sent into battle.
SOLDIERS RUNNING IN JUNGLE, SOLDIER WITH HELMET, OTHER SOLDIERS WITH HELMETS, A WOUND-	**V/O: DANNY SCHECHTER:** THE PENTAGON'S EFFORTS TO CONTROL PRESS COVERAGE WERE A RESPONSE TO THE LOSS OF THE

ED CARRIED BY RUNNING SOLDIER, WOUNDED PUT ON A STRETCHER, HELI-COPTER NIGHT SHOT, SOLDIER SNEAKING IN RICE FIELD, STILL OF MASS GRAVE, STILL OF ARNETT	WAR IN VIETNAM. MANY OF THE MILITARY TO THIS DAY BELIEVE THAT THE MEDIA COVERAGE WAS RESPONSIBLE FOR AMERICA'S DEFEAT—NOT THE ARMED FORCES OR THE POLICY. IN THAT ERA, REPORTERS WERE FAR MORE AGGRESSIVE IN EXPOSING WAR CRIMES AND DUPLICITY. PETER ARNETT WAS ONE OF THEM.
CONTINUED STILL ARNETT, ARNETT O/C, BLACK/WHITE SHOT OF US SOLDIER IN COFFIN, B/H HELICOPTER, O/C ARNETT	**O/C: PETER ARNETT, WAR REPORTER:** In Vietnam, the reporters did not get on the team. We challenged generals, governments. We challenged, we demanded their accountability, we challenged their findings. Vietnam is seen by the right wing as a war in which the American media sold out to the communist side.
MEDIA PANEL 1994	**SOT: DAVID HALBERSTAM, NY *TIMES* VIETNAM REPORTER:** Well you should be a pain in the ass, I mean any reporter, in a time like Vietnam … you ought to be a pain in the ass, because that's when it counts.
MEDIA PANEL 1994	**SOT: SEYMOUR HERSH, INVES-TIGATIVE REPORTER:** Generally, it is my belief that Richard Nixon was much more of a national security threat to the United States than any reporter I know.
PANORAMA SHOT OF THE PENTAGON, MEDIA ON THE BATTLEFIELD EXERCISE VIDEO	**V/O: DANNY SCHECHTER:** AFTER VIETNAM, THE PENTAGON LIMITED MEDIA ACCESS TO ITS WARS, WHILE IMPROVING OUT-

REACH TO JOURNALISTS WITH
TRAINING EXERCISES LIKE THIS:

CYRON: MEDIA ON THE BATTLE- FIELD EXERCISE MEDIA ON THE BATTLE- FIELD EXERCISE VIDEO SOLDIER PRACTICING TO GET RID OF JOURNALISTS SOLDIERS GIVEN INSTRUC- TIONS IN HOW TO SPEAK TO THE PRESS	**SOT: BATTLEFIELD EXERCISE:** I'm sorry ma'am, I'm really busy, I need to attend to these people. Excuse me please. **SOT: MILITARY OFFICER:** Remember everything you say is on the record. Even if the camera is off. It doesn't matter; it's on the record. You say it, it can be used. **SOT: MOCK INTERVIEW:** Ma'am, basically all the soldiers here are heroes in one way or another.
GULF WAR PROMO 1991, STUDIO ANCHORS, MAP OF KUWAIT CITY, TRUCK CONVOY, TANKS ROLLING	**V/O: DANNY SCHECHTER:** WARS MAY DESTROY PEOPLE AND COUNTRIES, BUT THEY CAN BE PROFITABLE TO COVER. CNN WON THE 1991 GULF WAR IN THE SENSE THAT ITS COVERAGE PROPELLED A STRUGGLING CABLE NEWS OPERATION KNOWN IN THE INDUSTRY AS THE "CHICKEN NOODLE NETWORK" INTO A TOP GLOBAL NEWS BRAND; REVENUES FOLLOWED AS RATINGS SOARED.
TANKS ROLLING	**SOT: CNN NEWS REEL:** Iraqi forces in Kuwait. Iraq claims the attack is failing.
CHENEY AT PRESS BRIEF-ING 1991, FOG AT SEA, ANCHOR ROCKET LAUNCHER,	**V/O: DANNY SCHECHTER:** AND SO DID PATRIOTIC FERVOR... EVEN AS MEDIA OBJECTIVITY ERODED, THAT OLD TRUISM—"TRUTH IS THE FIRST CASUALTY IN WAR"—WAS

CHAIN OF TANKS FIRING, SHOTS FROM MILITARY CONVOY, CHRISTIANE AMANPOUR REPORTING	<u>NEVER MORE TRUE.</u> <u>JOURNALISTS WERE DENIED ACCESS TO MOST OF THE 1991 GULF WAR, WRITES CNN'S CHRISTIANE AMAN-POUR:</u>
CYRON: <u>"BEHIND OUR BACKS, BEHIND THE BACKS OF THE FIELD REPORTERS, FIELD PRODUCERS AND CREWS ON THE GROUND, OUR BOSSES MADE A DEAL WITH THE ESTABLISHMENT TO CREATE 'POOLS'—WHAT I CALL 'BALL AND CHAIN,' HANDCUFFED, MANAGED NEWS REPORTING"</u> **—CHRISTIANE AMANPOUR, CNN** TRUCK CONVOY BACK-GROUND	**V/O: DANNY SCHECHTER:** <u>BEHIND OUR BACKS, BEHIND THE BACKS OF THE FIELD REPORTERS, FIELD PRODUCERS AND CREWS ON THE GROUND OUR BOSSES MADE A DEAL WITH THE ESTABLISHMENT TO CREATE 'POOLS'—WHAT I CALL 'BALL AND CHAIN,' HANDCUFFED, MANAGED NEWS REPORTING.</u>
JET FIGHTER, SMART BOMB, BOMBS, US SOLDER IN COF-FIN COVERED BY THE FLAG	**V/O: DANNY SCHECHTER:** THE RESULT? WE LATER LEARNED THE"SMART" BOMBS USED THEN WERE NOT SO SMART—ONLY ONE OUT OF FIVE HIT TARGETS. MOST US CASUALTIES WERE CAUSED BY "FRIENDLY" FIRE.
O/C JOHN DONVAN	**O/C: JOHN DONOVAN, ABC NEWS"NIGHTLINE":** I've covered enough wars to be in a position to say this, that we have never, I, including me, have never shown the viewer what it's really like—how horrible war is. And partly you can't show it, because the camera can't

capture it, but even at a certain level the camera may capture it and they won't let you show it. There are certain kinds of close-ups that we won't show, there's certain blood spatters, dead children that we don't show people partly because it violates certain long-standing practices: 'Don't put gore on television.'

SADDAM HUSSEIN FOOTAGE, SADDAM GREETING HIS PEOPLE, SADDAM GREETING FROM TRIBUNE, TANKS PARADING, IRAQI KID PLAYING IN THE RUBBLE	**V/O: DANNY SCHECHTER:** THE COVERAGE OF THE GULF WARS LACKED MORE THAN GORE: CONTEXT AND BACKGROUND WERE MISSING. LIKE THE ROLE THE US PLAYED IN PUTTING SADDAM HUSSEIN IN POWER AND ARMING HIM FOR YEARS.
GIRL PLAYING IN RUBBLE, MOTHERS WITH BABIES IN THEIR ARMS, NEWS ARTICLE ON THE GULF WAR SYMPTOMS	AMERICA'S WAR ON IRAQ DID NOT END WITH THE END OF THAT WAR. WASHINGTON INITIATED, AND THE UN IMPOSED SANCTIONS WHICH, COUPLED WITH THE CRUELTY OF SADDAM'S REGIME REPORTEDLY LED TO A MILLION CHILDREN DYING...AND THE SPREAD OF NEW DISEASES....
SICK VETERAN FOOTAGE, FIGHTER JETS READY FOR TAKE-OFF, JET AT BASE, FLYING JETS, HELICOPTERS	...A MYSTERIOUS GULF WAR SYNDROME STRUCK VETERANS.... THE US AND BRITAIN IMPOSED NO FLY ZONES, USING THEM AS A COVER FOR WAR-LIKE BOMBING RAIDS YEARS BEFORE THE 2003 INVASION... NONE OF THESE STORIES RECEIVED THE FULL COVERAGE THEY DESERVED.

CYRON: SEPTEMBER 11, 2001 NEW YORK CITY WTC COLLAPSING	**SOT: 9/11 FOOTAGE:** "Huge explosion now raining debris on all of us; we better get out of the way"
911 FOOTAGE, WTC COL- LAPSING, DEBRIS SPREAD- ING, GROUND ZERO, FIRE FIGHTERS AT GROUND ZERO, THE US FLAG AT GROUND ZERO	**V/O: DANNY SCHECHTER:** AND THEN CAME 9/11— THE BUSH ADMINISTRATION USED THE ATTACK AS A PRETEXT TO PUT IN PLACE SECRET PLANS TO INVADE IRAQ, DRAWN UP BEFORE 9/11. THE MEDIA WAS MOBILIZED BEHIND THE WAR ON TERROR…
ANCHORS WITH FLAGS IN THEIR LAPELS, SHOT OF DANNY SCHECHTER'S BOOK *MEDIA WARS,* MAGAZINE AND PAPER COVERS "CRUSADE" AND"WANTED DEAD OR ALIVE" FRONT PAGES	IN POST 9/11 AMERICA, A"PATRIOTIC CORRECTNESS" SWEPT THROUGH THE NEWS BUSINESS. TV ANCHORS PUT FLAGS IN THEIR LAPELS. I WROTE A BOOK SHOWING HOW THE COVERAGE ADVANCED THE GOVERNMENT'S PLAN TO RESPOND MILITARILY. SOME STORIES EXPLAINING"WHY THEY HATE US" GAVE WAY TO THIS:
SCOTT RUTTER FORMER MILITARY COMMANDER	**O/C: SCOTT RUTTER—FORMER US MILITARY COMMANDER:** It all became very personal with 9/11. I was in command of my battalion at that time; I was in the training meeting when that happened. The unspeakable acts against pillars of strength being hit by aircraft. You can imagine what it was like. It all became, you know, very, very personal.

NY STREET FOOTAGE REACTION TO PEACE ACTIVISTS	**V/O: DANNY SCHECHTER:** <u>MUCH OF THE COVERAGE FUELED DEMANDS FOR RETALIATION. THERE WAS OFTEN MORE DEBATE IN THE STREETS THAN ON TV.</u>
VIDEO AT GROUND ZERO	**SOT: CONFRONTATION AT GROUND ZERO: WAR CRY: ACTIVIST:** The same hatred that killed so many people.
"YOU WRITE WHAT YOU ARE TOLD" POSTER	**V/O: DANNY SCHECHTER:** <u>MANY NETWORKS SAID THEY DID-N'T WANT TO GET AHEAD OF PUB-LIC OPINION, OR BE BAITED AS SOFT ON TERRORISM.</u>
NY STREET FOOTAGE REACTION TO PEACE ACTIVISTS	**SOT: CONFRONTATION AT GROUND ZERO, WAR CRY: Woman:** They don't love me and I don't love them, okay. **Activist:** Love they neighbor? **Woman:** They don't love me and I don't love them. **Activist:** Well I love them.
NY STREET FOOTAGE REACTION TO PEACE ACTIVISTS	**V/O: DANNY SCHECHTER:** <u>THIS CONFRONTATION AT GROUND ZERO IN NEW YORK SHOWS WHAT HAPPENED WHEN A PEACE ACTIVIST CALLED FOR GLOBAL UNDERSTANDING:</u>
NY STREET FOOTAGE REACTION TO PEACE ACTIVISTS	**SOT: CONFRONTATION AT GROUND ZERO: WAR CRY: Older woman:** What about us? Do you care about every human being here? **Young man:** It's September 11, you're at Ground Zero. **Young woman:** If they do something

to us, we're not going to do nothing back? We're not going to do nothin' back?

ACTIVIST: They didn't do anything. Iraq did not do shit to America.

Activist: So you're saying it's okay to kill innocent people.

Another man: Listen. If it's for a better good. Let's do it.

Third man: Yeah I volunteered. You know why?

Third man's friend: To keep your ass free. To keep your hippie ass free, he puts his life on the line.

O/C PETER ARNETT, WTC COLLAPSING, GROUND ZERO, US FLAG, AFGHAN WAR FOOTAGE— MUJAHIDEEN	**SOT: PETER ARNETT, WAR REPORTER:** Don't forget the American media is based in NYC. Every reporter in NYC saw the World Trade Towers collapse— they took it personally. There was a sense of revenge and fear, and that was reflected in the coverage of Afghanistan War and the War on Terrorism.
NEWS CAST	**SOT: CBS NEWSCAST DAN RATHER:** We may be wrong in some of the things we pass along …
CYRON: "I AM WILLING TO GIVE THE PRESIDENT AND THE MILITARY THE BENEFIT OF ANY DOUBT" –DAN RATHER, SEPTEMBER 22, 2002 SOURCE: CNN	**V/O: DANNY SCHECHTER:** CBS's DAN RATHER SEPTEMBER 22 2001: "I AM WILLING TO GIVE THE PRESIDENT AND THE MILITARY THE BENEFIT OF ANY DOUBT."

O/C ARNETT FIGHTER JET TAKING OFF	**SOT: PETER ARNETT, WAR REPORTER:** As we moved into Iraq, a more pre-emptive strike, the media maintained this sort of romance, you might say, with government.

5. SECTION: THE "RUN-UP" TO WAR

ERIC ALTERMAN, MEDIA CRITIC	**O/C: ERIC ALTERMAN, MEDIA CRITIC:** But the fact that they allowed the Bush administration to manipulate the truth so grossly and so nakedly in the run-up to the war made the war possible.
BUSH STATE OF THE UNION SHOT OF WHITE HOUSE	**SOT: PRESIDENT GEORGE W. BUSH, STATE OF UNION ADDRESS:** The United States of America will not permit the world's most dangerous regimes to threaten us with the world's most destructive weapons.
WHITE HOUSE, SADDAM IN CROWD, SADDAM POSING IN CHAIR, SADDAM GREET-ING, SADDAM IN CIVILIAN CLOTHES SADDAM AND THE IRAQI FLAG	**V/O: DANNY SCHECHTER:** <u>ALL THE WHILE WASHINGTON INSISTED IRAQ HAD TO BE DIS-ARMED, THAT IT HAD PROOF THAT SADDAM HAD WEAPONS OF MASS DESTRUCTION THAT THREATENED THE WORLD. THE DEMONIZATION OF SADDAM WENT ON FOR FIVE MONTHS.</u>
BUSH AT THE STAKE-OUT, TIMES SQUARE, NEW YORK TIMES, RUMSFELD ON TV, IRAQ CITY IMAGE	**V/O: DANNY SCHECHTER:** <u>DURING THE RUN-UP TO THE IRAQ WAR, AMERICAN MEDIA OUTLETS INCLUDING MOST TV NETWORKS AND THE *NEW YORK TIMES* RELAYED THE ADMINSTRATION'S SPIN ON THE THREAT POSED BY</u>

	IRAQ WITHOUT MUCH QUESTION. WITHOUT THEIR CHEERLEADING, THERE COULD HAVE BEEN NO CONSENSUS FOR WAR.
BOMBS GO OFF IN THE BACKGROUND, CLOSE UP OF THE NEW YORK TIMES ARTICLE	IN MAY 2004, THE *NEW YORK TIMES* ACKNOWLEDGED ITS PRE-WAR REPORTING HAD BEEN DEEPLY FLAWED. A *TIMES* EDITOR CALLED IT AN "INSTITUTIONAL PROBLEM" INDICTING EDITORS AND REPORTERS WHO QUOTE, "CODDLED SOURCES" AND PRACTICED "HIT AND RUN JOURNALISM." HE SAID AMERICA'S SELF-STYLED "NEWSPAPER OF RECORD" HAD NOT JUST REPORTED THE STORY BUT WAS PART OF IT; QUOTE, "COVERING THE WAR WAS NOT THE *TIMES* AT ITS BEST."
O/C ERIC ALTERMAN	**O/C: ERIC ALTERMAN, MEDIA CRITIC, THE NATION** Only now of course we're learning so much of the stuff that we simply assumed must be accurate wasn't accurate at all.
WASHINGTON POST BUILDING **CYRON:** "IT'S CLEAR NOW THAT THE PRESS, AS A WHOLE, DID NOT DO A VERY GOOD JOB IN CHALLENGING ADMINISTRATION CLAIMS."	**V/O: DANNY SCHECHTER:** THE OMBUDSMAN OF THE WASHINGTON POST LATER ADMITTED: "IT'S CLEAR NOW THAT THE PRESS, AS A WHOLE, DID NOT DO A VERY GOOD JOB IN CHALLENGING ADMINISTRATION CLAIMS."

–MICHAEL GETLER, *WASH-INGTON POST* OMBUDS-MAN

O/C JAKE LYNCH	**O/C: JAKE LYNCH, BBC REPORTER:** Critical perspectives, perspectives about alternatives to war, all the kind of efforts and discussion of the peace movements virtually disappeared from the media at that very point where, notionally, a society was making up its mind as to whether to go to war or not.
STILLS OF FAIR STUDY **CYRON:** FAIR STUDY US MEDIA SOURCES PRO-WAR: 71 % ANTI-WAR: 3 %	**V/O: DANNY SCHECHTER:** THE MEDIA MONITORING GROUP FAIRNESS AND ACCURACY IN REPORTING OR FAIR STUDIED 1,617 ON-CAMERA SOURCES BETWEEN MARCH 20TH AND APRIL 9TH, 2003. THEY FOUND 71 PERCENT OF ALL SOURCES WERE PRO-WAR–ONLY 3 PERCENT ANTI-WAR.
UN PANEL	**SOT: GREG DYKE, FORMER BBC DIRECTOR:** I saw a figure the other day. I forget the exact figures but something like there were 800 experts used during the war on all the American broadcasts outlets. And only 6 were opposed to the war. Now, that seems a pretty odd state of affairs.
SHOTS OUTSIDE UNITED NATIONS, UN FLAG, INSIDE SECURITY COUNCIL, JOUR-NALISTS WAITING AT THE STAKE-OUT	**V/O: DANNY SCHECHTER:** IN THIS PERIOD, I WAS HOPING WAR COULD BE AVERTED. UN DELIBERA-TIONS WERE COVERED BUT DISMIS-SIVELY. INTERNATIONAL OPINION WAS NOT TAKEN SERIOUSLY. THE

	MEDIA FRAME BECAME"US" VERSUS"THEM."
O/C DANNY AT THE UN	**O/C: DANNY SCHECHTER:** THERE WAS A BUZZ HERE FOR MANY WEEKS, ONE JOURNALIST TOLD ME. THAT BUZZ IS GONE. INSTEAD, THERE IS A PALL, A FEELING OF TOTAL FRUSTRATION.
JOURNALIST READING PAPER, STAKE-OUT AT THE UN, SECURITY COUNCIL, BUSH AND BLAIR SHAKING HANDS AFTER JOINT STATEMENT	**V/O: DANNY SCHECHTER:** THE UNITED NATIONS WANTED TO GIVE THE ARMS INSPECTORS TIME TO FINISH THE JOB. BUT THE BUSH ADMINISTRATION BYPASSED THE UN, CLAIMING TO ACT IN ITS NAME BY LAUNCHING A PREVENTIVE WAR–UNILATERALLY, AS AN ACT OF SELF-DEFENSE. BRITAIN AND A FEW OTHER NATIONS JOINED WHAT WAS OFFICIALLY BRANDED A"COALITION OF THE WILLING"; CRITICS CALLED IT A"COALITION FOR THE DRILLING."
DANNY SCHECHTER AT UN PRESS CONFERENCE	**SOT: DANNY SCHECHTER:** How can the United Nations survive this failure?
FRENCH FOREIGN MINISTER AT THE STAKE-OUT	**SOT: DOMINIQUE DE VILLEPIN, FRENCH FOREIGN MINISTER:** The United Nations is more important than ever. We need collective responsibility.
FRONT PAGES DENOUNCING FRENCH NEWSPAPER HEADLINES	**V/O: DANNY SCHECHTER:** WHEN COUNTRIES LIKE FRANCE CALLED FOR MORE UN INSPECTIONS, THEY WERE DENOUNCED AS"CHEESE-EATING SURRENDER MONKEYS" IN SOME MEDIA OUTLETS.

UN SECURITY COUNCIL, AL DOUHRI SPEAKING	**O/C: IRAQ AMBASSADOR AL DOUHRI:** And despite the fact that we have no weapons of mass destruction, the US armies have crossed the Atlantic and they have prepared hundreds of thousands of soldiers.
UN SECURITY COUNCIL, CLOSE-UP AL DOUHRI	**SOT: DANNY SCHECHTER QUESTIONS IRAQ AMBASSADOR AL DOUHRI:** The United States insisted they were there. What happened to those weapons?
AL DOUHRI O/C, IRAQI GOVERNMENT CLAPPING, SADDAM STROLLING, WEAPONS INSPECTION, MAN WITH GAS MASK INSPECTING WEAPONS, WEAPONS PILES, AL DOUHRI O/C	**SOT: IRAQ AMBASSADOR AL DOUHRI:** Well, I think it has been destroyed. It has been destroyed by the Iraqi government. Because they felt at that time that there is no need for it. Anyway they cannot use it because if they would like to use this chemical weapons, the other side will destroy the whole Iraqi people and the whole Iraqi country. So I think they did realize that, and for this reason they destroyed it. And they destroyed earlier: '91–'92.
WIDE ANGLE IMAGE OF DANNY SCHECHTER INTERVIEWING AL DOUHRI FRONT PAGE OF MEDIA STUDY **CYRON:** "EXAGGERATED""INACCURATELY" "IRRESPONSIBLY	**V/O: DANNY SCHECHTER:** THIS CLAIM, RIDICULED BY MEDIA THEN, IS LARGELY ACCEPTED NOW. AN EXHAUSTIVE MARCH 2004 UNIVERSITY OF MARYLAND STUDY ON THE COVERAGE OF WMDs FOUND THAT THREAT WAS EXAGGERATED, REPORTED INACCURATELY AND IRRESPONSIBLY.

MEDIA AT WAR CONFERENCE, NEW SCHOOL, NEW YORK	AFTER THE INVASION PHASE OF THE WAR ENDED, JOURNALISTS DEBATED THEIR ROLE IN FUELING A WAR CLIMATE.
CYRON: JULY 24, 2003 NEW SCHOOL UNIVERSITY, NEW YORK	**SOT: JOURNALISTS DEBATING** **V/O DANNY SCHECHTER** ON ONE PANEL *HARPER'S* RICK MACARTHUR CHALLENGED TIME'S MICHAEL ELLIOT.
FOOTAGE FROM CONFERENCE	AFTERWARDS I SPOKE WITH BOTH:
O/C JOHN MACARTHUR PUBLISHER, *HARPER'S*	**O/C: DANNY SCHECHTER:** IS IT THE NEWS CULTURE? IS IT LACK OF CRITICAL THINKING? IS IT ECONOMIC INTERESTS? IS IT ALL OF THE ABOVE?
O/C MACARTHUR	**O/C: JOHN R. MACARTHUR, PUBLISHER, *HARPER'S*:** Well, it's all those things, but it's mostly owners who don't care about journalism
SOT: ELLIOT ONSTAGE	**SOT: MICHAEL ELLIOT, EDITOR *TIME MAGAZINE*:** I think the American media has done a fabulous job since September 11th.
O/C MICHAEL ELLIOT	**O/C: DANNY SCHECHTER:** WASN'T THIS A MEDIA SYSTEM THAT WAS CHEERLEADING FOR THE WAR?
O/C MICHAEL ELLIOT	**O/C: MICHAEL ELLIOT, EDITOR *TIME MAGAZINE*:** I think, undoubtedly, what you saw in the war was a sharper distinction

between the print media and the TV media than I've ever seen before, or maybe I should have said that in the session just now.

| O/C MACARTHUR | **O/C: MACARTHUR, PUBLISHER, *HARPER'S:*** THEY HAVE GOT TO WATCH WHAT THEY SAY. IF MICHAEL ELLIOT GETS UP THERE AND SAYS,"YEAH, *TIME* DIDN'T DO A VERY GOOD JOB COVERING THE WAR, OR COVERING THE RUN-UP TO THE WAR," HE'S OUT OF A JOB. HE'S GETTING IN TROUBLE WITH HIS BOSSES. I CAN SAY IT BECAUSE I'M A PUBLISHER. |

6. MUZZLING DEBATE

DEMONSTRATIONS NEW YORK	**V/O: DANNY SCHECHTER:** IN THE RUN UP TO WAR, DISSENT WAS MARGINALIZED, DEBATE WAS LIMITED, PROTEST AND PROTESTERS SEEN, BUT RARELY HEARD.
RECORDED NEWS BROADCAST IN LONDON	**SOT: NEWS BROADCAST** More than a million demonstrators turned out in London. The march is thought to be the largest ever in Great Britain.
JAKE LYNCH O/C DEMONSTRATIONS IN THE UK, BANNERS ON BUS, DEMONSTRATION	**O/C: JAKE LYNCH, BBC REPORTER:** Sadly, the coverage was at its worst in the period when it mattered most. The period bracketed by the world-wide demonstrations on February the 15th and actually going to war was one in which British public opinion turned 'round from being approximately

60–40 against the war to approximately 60–40 in favor of the war.

DEMONSTRATIONS IN NEW YORK STILL MICHAEL GETLER **CYRON:** "UNDERREPORTING OR POORLY DISPLAYING...COVERAGE OF BIG DEMONSTRATIONS HERE AND ABROAD" —MICHAEL GETLER, *WASHINGTON POST,* OMBUDSMAN	**V/O: DANNY SCHECHTER:** *WASHINGTON POST* OMBUDSMAN MICHAEL GETLER BLASTED HIS OWN PAPER FOR: "UNDERREPORTING OR POORLY DISPLAYING.... COVERAGE OF BIG DEMONSTRATIONS HERE AND ABROAD."
O/C LESLIE CAGAN ON STREET FOOTAGE OF PROTESTS	**O/C: LESLIE CAGAN ANTI-WAR ORGANIZER:** There was fairly decent coverage of the fact that there was an anti-war movement. What there was not decent coverage of was the analysis of what we were trying to say about what was wrong with the war, why we never should've gone to war, why the war needed to end, what was driving sort of the motor force behind the war. That analysis never got into the mainstream media. SCRATCH
NYC DEMONSTRATION FOOTAGE **CYRON:** NEW YORK CITY FEBRUARY 15, 2003	**V/O: DANNY SCHECHTER:** IT WAS FREEZING IN NEW YORK DURING THE HUGE FEBRUARY DEMONSTRATION.

ANTI WAR DEMONSTRA- TION IN NEW YORK CITY O/C IAN WILLIAMS	**O/C: IAN WILLIAMS:** It's ironic it's taken George W. Bush to revive the progressive movements in the United States and Western Europe.
ANTI WAR DEMONSTRA- TION IN NEW YORK CITY, DESMOND TUTU GREETS DANNY SCHECHTER	**V/O: DANNY SCHECHTER:** SOUTH AFRICA'S BISHOP TUTU WAS A FEATURED SPEAKER.
TUTU AT THE PODIUM	**SOT: DESMOND TUTU:** What do we say to peace? Yeah!
O/C DANNY SCHECHTER MEDIA AT THE DEMON- STRATION IN NEW YORK	**O/C: DANNY SCHECHTER:** ... THE MAINSTREAM MEDIA SORT OF GHETTOIZES THIS KIND OF COVERAGE, AND DOESN'T ALLOW IT TO REALLY ENTER INTO THE MAINSTREAM DISCOURSE... I THINK THAT THEY'LL REPORT IT. THEY'LL SHOW THE CROWDS AS A MASS. THEY MIGHT SHOW SOME SOUND BITES, BUT THEY WON'T REALLY GET INTO WHAT THE SIGNIFICANCE OF THIS MOVEMENT IS.
CYRON: NEW YORK CITY MARCH 22, 2003 ANTI-WAR DEMONSTRA- TION STREET SHOTS, MARCH 21, 2003	**V/O: DANNY SCHECHTER:** AT LATER PROTESTS, I SPOKE WITH JOURNALISTS AND ACTIVISTS ABOUT THE COVERAGE WE WERE THEN BEING BOMBARDED WITH.
SOT CURTIS ELLIS ON STREET	**O/C: CURTIS ELLIS RADIO JOURNALIST:** The purpose of journalism is to question the prevailing wisdom ... The journalism we see in this country for the most part in the mainstream media does not question anything.

SOT MARC LEVIN ON STREET	**O/C: MARC LEVIN FILM DIRECTOR:** But that scares me to think that here it is, it's a war, people's lives, the whole world is changing, and most of us are just watching it like another entertainment channel.
ANTI-WAR COMMERCIAL *WHY RUSH THE WAR?*	ANTI-WAR COMMERCIALS **SOT: NOT IN OUR NAME TV AD:** If we invade Iraq, there's a UN estimate that says there will be up to half a million people killed or wounded. Do we have the right to do that to a country that has done nothing to us? **V/O: DANNY SCHECHTER:** <u>FROZEN OUT OF THE NEWS, ACTIVISTS TRIED TO BUY AIRTIME FOR ANTI-WAR COMMERCIALS LIKE THIS:</u> **SOT: BISHOP MELVIN TALBERT, NATIONAL COUNCIL OF CHURCHES:** No nation under G-d has that right. It violates international law. It violates G-d's law. **V/O: DANNY SCHECHTER:** <u>MOST NETWORKS WOULDN'T RUN THE SPOTS, EVEN FOR THE MONEY.</u>
INTERNET NEWS SITES, ANTI-WAR SITES FOREIGN NEWS OUTLETS NEWS CAST	**V/O: DANNY SCHECHTER:** <u>MANY ACTIVISTS SOURED ON MAINSTREAM NEWS, TURNING TO HUNDREDS OF INTERNET SITES.</u> <u>THEY ALSO TURNED TO FOREIGN TV OUTLETS, ESPECIALLY THE BBC.</u>

FIORE ANIMATION IRAQ–SADDAM	**FIORE ANIMATION** **SOT:** IRAQ–SADDAM ANIMATION
INTERNET NEWS SITES, THE ONION, COMEDY CHANNEL	**V/O: DANNY SCHECHTER:** <u>MANY YOUNG PEOPLE ABANDONED THE NEWS ALTOGETHER, PREFERRING SATIRICAL NEWSPAPERS LIKE THE ONION AND COMEDY NEWS SHOWS.</u>
CLIP FROM COMEDY CHANNEL	**SOT: JON STEWART,"THE DAILY SHOW," COMEDY CENTRAL CHANNEL:** Hey everybody
JOURNALIST AMY GOODMAN INTERVIEWING IN THE STREET	**V/O DANNY SCHECHTER** Many turned to alternative, independent media.
AMY GOODMAN O/C, DEMONSTRATION IN NEW YORK AND SHOTS OF JOURNALISTS	**SOT: AMY GOODMAN, DEMOCRACY NOW:** It's up to the media to challenge those in power, not to cozy up to power. So you have this media that's embedded now in the government, in the military. And, yet at the same time there's hope, because there is a response to that, and that is the independent media movement.

6. SECTION: THE MEDIA INVASION

IMAGES FROM BAGHDAD, CITY SHOTS, STREET TRAFFIC	**V/O: DANNY SCHECHTER:** <u>A GLOBAL NEWS ARMY WAS PUT IN PLACE BEFORE WAR ERUPTED … ON ALL SIDES OF THE CONFLICT, MEDIA OUTLETS WERE SPUN OR CONTROLLED BY GOVERNMENTS.</u> <u>IN BAGHDAD, MAINSTREAM JOUR-</u>

	NALISTS SAY IT WAS TOUGH TO GET THE TRUTH; SOMETIMES, INDEPENDENT REPORTERS WERE ABLE TO DO BETTER.
IMAGES FROM THE STREETS OF BAGHDAD, JEREMY SCAHILL O/C, FOOTAGE OF IRAQI MINISTER FOR INFORMATION GRAPHIC: SADDAM'S PRESS MINDERS	**O/C: JEREMY SCAHILL, REPORTER,"DEMOCRACY NOW":** Every foreigner is followed by the secret police, but journalists are watched even closer; there was an army under Saddam Hussein of government officials whose only job it was, was to spy on journalists. So, you have no way to avoid being under the control of the Iraqi Ministry of Information.
O/C JANINE DI GIOVANNI	**O/C: JANINE DI GIOVANNI, THE *LONDON TIMES*:** They tapped my phone in my office, my hotel room. There was a small camera in my hotel, which watched my every movement. I used to have to go to the loo to get changed.
O/C JEREMY SCAHILL	**O/C: JEREMY SCAHILL, REPORTER,"DEMOCRACY NOW":** I determined that the best thing was to not get accreditation as a journalist in my visa and to go in as a humanitarian worker.
IRAQI INFORMATION MINISTER AL-SAHAF PRESS CONFERENCE	**SOT: MOHAMMAD SAEED AL-SAHAF, IRAQI INFORMATION MINISTER:** They are not near Baghdad don't believe them. They are nowhere. This is silly.

AL-SAHAF AT VARIOUS PRESS BRIEFINGS, NEWSPAPER ARTICLES ABOUT AL-SAHAF, DRAWINGS OF AL-SAHAF	**V/O: DANNY SCHECHTER:** <u>IRAQ'S MEDIA MINDERS WORKED FOR IRAQ'S MINISTER OF INFORMATION MOHAMMAD AL SAHAF, KNOWN IN THE WEST AS COMICAL ALI FOR HIS FALSE CLAIMS.</u> <u>MOST OF HIS THREATS OF IRAQI RESOLVE WERE TREATED AS A JOKE. LATER, AS RESISTANCE EMERGED, SOME NOW SEEM ALMOST PROPHETIC.</u>
O/C JANINE DI GIOVANNI, *LONDON TIMES*	**O/C: JANINE DI GIOVANNI, *LONDON TIMES*:** The bribery system was appalling. Some television crews were paying up to $5000 per visa.
O/C JEREMY SCAHILL	**O/C: JEREMY SCAHILL, REPORTER,"DEMOCRACY NOW":** So, in the case of Rupert Murdoch, he has a tremendous number of media outlets, probably the most of any single other company or person in the world operating in Iraq under Saddam Hussein, more than any other media outlets. One colleague who works in a Murdoch news operation estimated that Rupert Murdoch was giving as much as half a million dollars to Saddam Hussein's government during the lead up to the war, just for permission for his news outlets to operate there. And there was a running joke that Rupert Murdoch was the second greatest source of cash for Saddam Hussein—second only to oil smuggling

REPORTER LIVE FROM IRAQ	**SOT: *NEW YORK TIMES* REPORTER JOHN BURNS ON CNN:** …There are pockets like Tikrit…
IRAQ CORRESPONDENT REPORTING, INTERNET NEWS SITES, FOOTAGE OF IRAQIS GRIEVING BY MASS GRAVE STILL EASON JORDAN, CNN	**V/O: DANNY SCHECHTER:** IF IRAQIS WERE CORRUPT, SO WERE SOME WESTERN MEDIA OUTLETS. NEW YORK TIMES CORRESPONDENT JOHN BURNS AND OTHERS ACCUSED WESTERN MEDIA COMPANIES OF COMPETING THROUGH CORRUP-TION–LITERALLY BUYING ACCESS FOR THEIR CORRESPONDENTS AND CAMERAS, WHILE NOT COVERING HUMAN RIGHTS ABUSES AND THE SUFFERING OF THE PEOPLE. CNN LATER ADMITTED THAT IT DID NOT REPORT ABUSES OF ITS OWN STAFF MEMBERS IN ORDER TO KEEP ITS OFFICE OPEN IN IRAQ.
EMBED REPORTING, EMBED JOURNALIST CLOSE-UP, REPORTER ROBERT YOUNG PELTON ON THE ROAD STILL PELTON'S TRAVEL BOOK *THE WORLD'S MOST DANGEROUS PLACES*	**V/O: DANNY SCHECHTER:** FEW OF THE JOURNALISTS WHO COVERED THE WAR COVERED THE WAY IT WAS REALLY COVERED. INDEPENDENT REPORTER ROBERT YOUNG PELTON, AUTHOR OF THIS BEST SELLING TRAVEL BOOK *THE WORLD'S MOST DANGEROUS PLACES,* HAD HIS EYE ON THE MEDIA EYE.
O/C PELTON, SHOWDOWN WITH SADDAM PROMO, MAP OF IRAQ, ARCHIVE FOOTBALL, WAR IN IRAQ, THE ROAD TO BAGHDAD PROMO	**O/C: ROBERT YOUNG PELTON, REPORTER:** There was never any sense that we might go to war. It was always like,"We're gonna attack Saddam Hussein and here's why."

There was very much a script on how this war was handled. There was a kick-off.

BUSH 48 HOURS COUNT-DOWN TO WAR	**SOT: PRESIDENT GEORGE W. BUSH:** Saddam Hussein and his sons must leave Iraq within 48 hours.
TROOPS WATCHING TELEVISION, GRAPHIC, O/C PELTON, GENERAL DRAWING DIAGRAM ON MAP OF IRAQ, ANIMATED MAP OF IRAQ, ARCHIVE FOOTBALL, TROOPS RUNNING, ARCHIVE FOOTBALL, ARTILLERY SHOOTING, ARCHIVE FOOTBALL, US SOLDIER WAVING THE FLAG, FOOTBALL	**O/C: ROBERT YOUNG PELTON, REPORTER:** And then there was a countdown; you got 48 hours to get out of town. Then it was like everyone tuned in for the opening kickoff. As the war progressed, it was done on linear scale. We're going from here to there. It's almost like we're running a pass. There were people actually drawing diagrams, generals drawing diagrams on a map that looked just like a football play. You know,"We're gonna go sneak around here and do this, and we're coming up there and doing that."
ARCHIVE FOOTBALL, PELTON IN BUS, VIEW FROM THE BUS, PELTON IN PRESS, STREET BY NIGHT	**V/O: DANNY SCHECHTER:** <u>THIS SPORTS METAPHOR OFFERED A SIMPLIFIED NARRATIVE MIMICKING A FAMILIAR TV FORMAT.</u> <u>WHEN PELTON WAS DELAYED GETTING INTO IRAQ, HIS FOCUS BECAME THE PRESS.</u>
HOTEL EXTERIOR, PELTON TALKING IN HOTEL LOBBY, SHOTS OF OTHER JOURNALISTS GETTING ACCREDITATION, JOURNALIST	**O/C: ROBERT YOUNG PELTON, REPORTER:** So, I ended up being the only person embedded with journalists during the war in a fancy hotel in Jordan.

HANGING OUT AT HOTEL, SLEEPING IN LOBBY CHAIR HOTEL LOBBY, PELTON O/C, BAR SHOTS, JOURNALISTS SMOKING WATER PIPE	Right now there's apparently 4000 journalists—everywhere from Kuwait to Baghdad, to Jordan, to Syria, to Turkey—all waiting for the war to start. And some of these people had been sitting around for nine weeks.
HOTEL NEWS ROOM	They lived in very nice hotels. They were all on expense accounts. They met at the bar every night. They worked 24 hours a day.
ARI FLEISHER WHITE HOUSE STAKE-OUT	**SOT: ARI FLEISHER, WHITE HOUSE SPOKESMAN:** The President will address the nation at 10:15.
BUSH DECLARES WAR FROM OVAL OFFICE, NEWS FRONT PAGES DECLARING WAR STILL OF HEADLINES	**SOT: PRESIDENT GEORGE W. BUSH** My fellow citizens at this hour American and coalition forces are in the early stages of military operations to disarm Iraq, to free its people, and to defend the world from grave danger.
FIELD NEWSROOM	**SOT: ABC JOURNALIST ON PHONE:** The level of protection would be minimal, and if I were a news president or a news executive, right now, I would be pulling my people out.
FIELD NEWSROOM	**V/O: DANNY SCHECHTER:** WHEN THE WAR HAD FINALLY BEGUN, THE NETWORKS BEGAN PULLING THEIR REPORTERS OUT OF BAGHDAD.
ARNETT IN IRAQ WITH NATIONAL GEOGRAPHIC	**V/O: DANNY SCHECHTER:** Peter Arnett WAS in the Iraqi capital

with a National Geographic documentary team. He decided to stay.

O/C PETER ARNETT	**O/C: PETER ARNETT, WAR REPORTER:** Covering wars are a dangerous business. You can die. And those companies feel responsible for their people in harm's way. They sometimes order them out.
NEWSROOM	**SOT: ABC JOURNALIST JUSTIFIES LEAVING:** I think there is something to be said for staying; however, from a news executive standpoint, the risks are enormous.
O/C: PETER ARNETT	**O/C: PETER ARNETT, WAR REPORTER:** I sort of have a genetic tick that allows me to go into dangerous areas without too much concern.
BOMBS GOING OFF IN BAGHDAD BOMB EXPLOSIONS, US TROOPS MARCH ON BAGHDAD,"PHOTO OPS" OF SOLDIERS MARCHING, BURNING US AND ISRAELI FLAG, PELTON O/C	**O/C: ROBERT YOUHNG PELTON, REPORTER:** The interesting thing was, is that the American military were trying to intimidate these journalists. They were saying,"You know you're going to be a target." And the journalists were working overtime to say,"Look we're here, this is our coordinates, don't fire," and everybody knew the journalists were at these hotels. That's why they were at these hotels. It was also known that if you're going to have"shock and awe," you're going to need someone to record it. I mean

the one thing that they left out was that they needed the media to fight this war. The war was set up to be filmed and recorded by the media. So there was this bizarre symbiotic relationship.

FOOTAGE OF BOMB EXPLOSION, TOMAHAWK MISSILE GRAPHIC	**V/O: DANNY SCHECHTER:** <u>WHEN THE AWESOME BOMBING OF BAGHDAD BEGAN WHAT WAS SHOCKING WAS THE WAY NEWS ANCHORS LOVINGLY DESCRIBED LETHAL WEAPONS–THEY BECAME BOYS WITH TOYS.</u>
LIVE NEWS COVERAGE MARCH 25, 2003–JOKING ABOUT THE USE OF DEADLY WEAPONS	**SOT: FOX NEWS ANCHOR:** Should they have used more? Should they use, a MOAB, the mother of all bombs, a few daisy cutters? You know lets not just stop at a couple of cruise missiles. I want to see them use that MOAB.

8. SECTION: PENTAGON MEDIA MANAGEMENT

"EVENING NEWS" WITH DAN RATHER	**SOT: DAN RATHER,** CBS's David Martin at the Pentagon is following the planning and has the latest on a possible plan ...
REPORTER REPORTS FROM THE PENTAGON, COLIN POWELL AT THE STAKE-OUT, SHOWDOWN WITH SADDAM PROMO, NETWORK ANCHOR REPORTING ON THE WAR, PANORAMA SHOT OF THE PENTAGON	**V/O: DANNY SCHECHTER:** <u>TO PROMOTE ITS WAR, THE PENTAGON MADE MEDIA MANAGEMENT A PRIORITY. THEIR STRATEGY WAS SOPHISTICATED, CLEVER AND ALMOST ALWAYS COVERT. FEW MEDIA OUTLETS EXPOSED IT. MOST PARTICIPATED WILLINGLY FOR THEIR OWN POLITICAL AND ECONOMIC REASONS.</u>

RUMSFELD AND GENERAL WALKING DOWN STAIRS, RUMSFELD IN OFFICE, RUMSFELD WALKING THE CORRIDORS, RUMSFELD ON TV, SOLDIERS WALKING THE CORRIDOR, OUTSIDE SHOT OF PENTAGON.	PENTAGON STRATEGY WENT BEYOND TRADITIONAL PR, USING MARKETING STRATEGIES AND"PERCEPTION MANAGEMENT." ADMINISTRATION OFFICIALS LIKENED THEIR WAR PLANNING TO A PRODUCT"ROLL-OUT. IT WAS ALL TO GUARANTEE THERE WOULD BE ONLY ONE STORYLINE IN THE MEDIA, AND IN THE MINDS OF AMERICANS: THEIRS. A PENTAGON ADVISOR TOLD ME IT WAS INTENTIONAL.
STILLS FROM THE OVAL OFFICE; BUSH, SADDAM AND HIS GENERALS FROM"FACE THE NATION"; SOLDIERS MARCHING BY DAWN; SHIP FIRING MISSILE; WEB PAGE ARAB/ENGLISH	THEY KNEW THAT TV NETWORKS PREFER STORY-TELLING TO SLOGANIZING. THEIR STORY LINE BECAME A MASTER NARRATIVE, DEFINING IRAQ AS THE PROBLEM AND US MILITARY INTERVENTION AS THE ONLY SOLUTION.
RUMSFELD AND MEYERS AT THE PENTAGON STAKE-OUT	TRADITIONALLY, PROPAGANDA IS TARGETED AT THE ENEMY. IN THIS WAR, IT WAS SMOOTHLY INFILTRATED INTO THE NEWS AIMED AT AMERICAN AND GLOBAL PUBLIC OPINION.
SHOT OF RUMSFELD AND PRESS CONFERENCES	**SOT: DONALD RUMSFELD, SECRETARY OF DEFENSE:** … that there are known knowns; there are things we know that we know. There are known unknowns; that is to

	say, there are things we now know we don't know. But there are also unknown unknowns; there are things we do not know we don't know.
FRANKS AT THE STAKE-OUT DOHA,	**SOT: GENERAL TOMMY FRANKS:** This platform is not a platform for propaganda; this is a platform for truth
STILLS FRANKS	**V/O: DANNY SCHECHTER:** IN HIS WAR PLAN, TOMMY FRANKS, THE US MILITARY COMMANDER, DESCRIBED THE PRESS, ONCE KNOWN AS THE FOURTH ESTATE, AS"THE FOURTH FRONT." HE KNEW THAT A SUPPORTIVE MEDIA WAS ESSENTIAL FOR VICTORY, AND HE CULTIVATED ONE.
STILL FRANKS	**SOT: GENERAL TOMMY FRANKS:** This will be a campaign unlike any other in history.
STILLS OF FRANKS	**V/O: DANNY SCHECHTER:** THE PENTAGON FOCUSED ON WINNING THE MEDIA WAR, LEAKING THEIR PLAN TO REPORTERS THEY COULD TRUST.
GREG KELLY O/C	**O/C: GREG KELLY, FOX NEWS EMBED:** We knew the plan. And, I think the military benefited as far as positive coverage during the war, because we knew what the plan was. So we reported that things, basically things, were on plan or we weren't worried when we were delayed two or three days, because we knew overall it was very successful.

STILL FRANKS, TORI CLARKE	**V/O: DANNY SCHECHTER:** <u>EARLIER, WHEN THE MEDIA PRESSED FOR ACCESS, FRANK'S TEAM CAME UP WITH THE IDEA OF EMBEDDING REPORTERS. A FORMER CORPORATE PR PROFESSIONAL TURNED PENTAGON OFFICIAL RAN THE PROGRAM.</u>
STILL TORI CLARKE VICTORIA CLARKE AT PANEL AT RADIO AND TELEVISION MUSEUM	**SOT: VICTORIA CLARKE, FORMER PENTAGON MEDIA CHIEF:** One of the things we did, it wasn't rocket science, but it was hard work. We took the same kind of planning and training and discipline that you put into military operations and put it into this aspect of the military operations. And Rumsfeld and Myers, being enlightened guys, had included people like me in the war plan from the very earliest stages.
O/C JOHN STAUBER, STILLS OF THE CONTRACT BETWEEN NEWS ORGANIZATIONS AND THE PENTAGON, O/C STAUBER, SHOTS FROM EMBEDDED JOURNALISTS IN BUS	**O/C: JOHN STAUBER, AUTHOR** *WEAPONS OF MASS DECEPTION:* Victoria Clarke got major networks and news organizations to sign the twelve-page contract agreeing to certain ground rules that actually kept the Department of Defense, public affairs people in the driver seat. And you got reporters in with these young, idealistic troops who really believed all the spin of what was going on, we're going to liberate Iraq…. that the reporters would overall identify with the troops and their reporting was very positive.
EMBEDDED REPORTERS ON BUS INSTRUCTED BY SOLDIER	**O/C: BRITISH SOLDIER:** When we get there, any sort of incident happens, please keep calm and

	remain on the bus. We will deal with the situation, no matter what it is, as swiftly as possible
BUS OF EMBEDDED REPORTERS	**SOT: VARIOUS INTERNATIONAL JOURNALISTS IDENTIFYING THEIR STATIONS/NEWSPAPERS:** **Q:** What news organization do you work with Tim? **A1:** Sat Eins, German Television Network **A2:** BBC **A3:** CNN **A4:** *LA Times* **A5:** Japan Broadcasting Corporation **O/C: GWENDOLEN CATES, *PEOPLE* MAGAZINE:** I'm Gwendolen Cates and I'm here on assignment for *People* magazine, and I'm embedded with the 205th battalion 165th.
BUS FOOTAGE, SOLDIER WAVING AT GWENDOLEN, O/C GWENDOLEN	**O/C: GWENDOLEN CATES, *PEOPLE* MAGAZINE:** I was the only journalist embedded with a military intelligence unit. They were part of the fifth corps based in Germany. And I was invited in fact to be embedded by this unit because one of the commanders had gotten to know me and felt that I could be trusted and would really tell the story.
ATROPINE INJECTOR KIT CLOSE UP, SOLDIER GIVING INSTRUCTIONS TO EMBEDS	**SOT: MILITARY OFFICER DEMONSTRATING ATROPINE SHOT:** These are your atropine injector kits. Should you become contaminated and start to feel the symptoms of nerve poisoning.

SOLDIER GIVING INSTRUCTIONS TO EMBEDS, GWENDOLEN PUTTING ON A GAS MASK	**V/O: DANNY SCHECHTER:** THE PENTAGON PUT THE EMBEDS THROUGH A TRAINING COURSE OSTENSIBLY TO TEACH THEM HOW TO SURVIVE—BUT IT WENT FURTHER…
INSTRUCTOR HELPING GWENDOLEN WITH GAS MASK	**SOT: INSTRUCTOR:** It's on, there so when you pull it tight.
GWENDOLEN STRUGGLING WITH THE GAS MASK; SOLDIER INSTRUCTING HER HOW TO BREATH	**V/O: DANNY SCHECHTER:** JOURNALISTS WERE GIVEN EXAGGERATED FEARS OF CHEMICAL ATTACK DESIGNED TO REINFORCE THE THREAT OF IRAQI WEAPONS OF MASS DESTRUCTION. THE PROPAGANDA WAS ALSO AIMED AT THE MILITARY. IT WAS A THREAT THAT WASN'T THERE.
GWENDOLEN WITH A GAS MASK ON	**SOT: CATES AND INSTRUCTOR:** **Cates:** Ready to go? **Instructor:** You look lovely.
CAMP FOOTAGE, GWENDOLEN O/C	**SOT: GWENDOLEN CATES, *PEOPLE MAGAZINE*:** I lived, ate, slept with the soldiers. And the bond that was established between us was very, very strong and very personal. And we shared the sandstorms together and the lack of food and people talked to me about their fears and their children they left behind and their fear of death and all those things. So I became very personally involved with them as individuals; at the same time I was observing this with journalistic detachment, but I did place their safety above any sort of journalistic

	responsibility I had, professional responsibility I had, and I would not have done anything to endanger any of them.
MILITARY BRIEFING OF EMBEDS	**O/C: MILITARY BRIEFING OF EMBEDS:** What we're saying is, help us tell the truth of what happens …
CLIPS OF REPORTERS BEING BRIEFED BY THE MILITARY	**V/O: DANNY SCHECHTER:** <u>UNMENTIONED BY MOST MEDIA: THE PLAN ACTUALLY BETRAYED AN EARLIER AGREEMENT MADE AFTER THE FIRST GULF WAR THAT SAID QUOTE"OPEN AND INDEPENDENT REPORTING WILL BE THE PRINCIPAL MEANS OF COVERAGE." THE PENTA-GON SIGNED OFF ON THAT POLICY ON MARCH 1, 1992.</u>
FOOTAGE OF JOURNALISTS AT PRESS CONFERENCES IN THE FIELD O/C SHELDON RAMPTON ARMED MILITARY	**O/C: SHELDON RAMPTON, CO-AUTHOR, *WEAPONS OF MASS DECEPTION*:** There is an interesting issue, of conflict of interest there, because one of the standard rules of journalistic ethics is that journalists should not accept any-thing of value from the sources they're covering. Well, all of their transporta-tion and indeed their very lives were being protected by those soldiers they were covering.
GWENDOLEN INTERVIEW-ING A 21-YEAR-OLD SOL-DIER	**SOT: GWENDOLEN CATES, *PEOPLE MAGAZINE*:** **Q:** And how old are you? **A:** I'm 21. **Q:** What is your birthday? **A:** 3rd of 10th 81

	Q: 'Cause we want to send you a birth-day card …
YOUNG SOLDIER, OLDER LAUGHING SOLDIER, O/C GWENDOLEN	**O/C: GWENDOLEN CATES, *PEOPLE* MAGAZINE:** When I was there it's funny because I was not so much scared for myself, … I thought what, how would I be able to handle it if one of my soldiers dies or is injured? I kept thinking about that. How will I be able to handle it?
ROBERT YOUNG PELTON O/C, CLIPS OF EMBEDS IN ARMY GEAR REPORTING; JOURNALIST REPORTING FROM HELICOPTER, REPORTER AT ROADSIDE, GWENDOLEN ROADSIDE	**O/C: ROBERT YOUNG PELTON, REPORTER:** The idea of embedding is essentially the Stockholm syndrome. If you take an unarmed individual and place him amongst armed people, he becomes sympathetic to their cause. So the idea was, look, slap a helmet on these guys, stick them in a jeep or a Humvee, head them in that direction and let them do whatever the heck he wants, and he will become sympathetic to our cause.
GWENDOLEN ROADSIDE, CONVOY, NBC EMBED HELI-COPTER SHOT	**V/O: DANNY SCHECHTER:** <u>MANY EMBEDS DID A CONSCIEN-TIOUS JOB BUT THEY COULD ONLY PROVIDE A LIMITED AND ULTIMATE-LY MISLEADING PICTURE.</u>
PANEL AT MUSEUM OF RADIO AND TELEVISION	**SOT: BILL ARKIN, NBC NEWS:** The debate from the left and right about embedding–from the left that these were going to be lapdogs of the Pentagon, from the right that this was going to be loose lips sinking ships–I think neither proved to be true. But we haven't had the debate about what the embedding process did to our under-standing of the war.

EMBEDDED JOURNALIST CRAWLING WITH HELMET AND LIPSTICK	**SOT: SOLDIER TO NBC REPORTER:** Stay down! Stay down!
EMBED CRAWLING WITH HELMET AND LIPSTICK, REPORTER IN MILITARY OUTFIT REPORTING IN FOG **CYRON:** "DEADLINE IRAQ"	**V/O: DANNY SCHECHTER:** FAR TOO MANY JOURNALISTS WERE GUNG-HO ABOUT COVERING THE WAR... SOME ROMANTICIZED IT, SEDUCED BY THE SPIRIT OF ADVENTURE; OTHERS SOUGHT GLORY AS CANADA'S CBC EXPLAINED IN A STUNNING SPECIAL "DEADLINE IRAQ." DURING THE WAR NO US NETWORK RAN ANYTHING LIKE IT.
"DEADLINE IRAQ": FOOTAGE (INTERVIEW) **CYRON:** CBC "DEADLINE IRAQ"	**SOT: MATTHEW FISHER, *NATIONAL POST*, CANADA:** I think so many journalists have this fascination—"I must do this and then I can call myself a war correspondent the rest of my life." It's as if they had a checklist of things to do in their life, and this is one of them. But they are absolutely not prepared for the reality.
"DEADLINE IRAQ": FOOTAGE (INTERVIEW) **CYRON:** CBC "DEADLINE IRAQ"	**SOT: PATRICK GRAHAM, *NATIONAL POST*, CANADA:** People didn't want to miss this war, and it had a lot to do with people's careers, there is no question.
"DEADLINE IRAQ": FOOTAGE (INTERVIEW) **CYRON:** CBC "DEADLINE IRAQ"	**SOT: PATRICK BROWN, CBC:** This is a thrill ride if you want to turn it into a thrill ride. I mean, you can go to places in order to get shot at, in order to have the excitement of feeling what its like to get shot at. I mean, you can go play in the traffic, too, if you want.

SHOTS OF CENTCOM, ALL SOLDIERS RISE, MILITARY PLANNING, CONTROL ROOMS, AIR WAR FOOTAGE—B/W EXPLOSIONS	**V/O: DANNY SCHECHTER:** <u>THERE WERE FEW EMBEDS WITH THE MILITARY PLANNERS, WITH THE COVERT ACTION TEAMS, THE CIA, SPECIAL OPS, OR WITH THE AIR WAR. THE US MILITARY UNITS THAT DID THE MOST DAMAGE WERE COVERED THE LEAST.</u>
CHRISTIANE AMANPOUR AT CNBC"TOPIC A" WITH TINA BROWN	**SOT: CHRISTIANE AMANPOUR, CNN REPORTER:** I mean it looks like this was disinformation at the highest level.
CHRISTIANE AMANPOUR ANCHORING	**V/O: DANNY SCHECHTER:** <u>LATER, CNN'S CRISTIANNE AMANPOUR ADMITTED HER OWN NETWORK MUZZLED THE NEWS.</u>
CHRISTIANE AMANPOUR AT CNBC"TOPIC A" WITH TINA BROWN **CYRON:** <u>CNBC"TOPIC A WITH TINA BROWN"</u>	**SOT: CHRISTIANE AMANPOUR, CNN REPORTER:** Yes, I think the press was muzzled, and I think the press self-muzzled. I'm sorry to say, but certainly television and, perhaps, to an extent, my station was intimidated by the administration and its foot soldiers at Fox News. And it did, in fact, put a climate of fear and self-censorship, in my view, in terms of the kind of broadcast work we did.
SOT TORI CLARKE AT RADIO AND TELEVISION MUSEUM PANEL	**SOT: VICTORIA CLARKE, FORMER PENTAGON MEDIA CHIEF:** Talk about letting people know that ratings have gotten under your skin. Umm, nothing could be further from the truth, obviously, and I will let the news media defend themselves, but I promise you, five, ten, 15 years from now people who study these things

will say,"you never saw such real, you never saw such accurate, you never saw such hard-hitting coverage of military conflicts ..."

TORI CLARKE AT RADIO AND TELEVISION MUSEUM PANEL	**V/O: DANNY SCHECHTER:** <u>A WEEK LATER CNN HIRED THE PENTAGON'S MEDIA FLACK VICTORIA CLARKE AS AN ON-AIR CONTRIBUTOR</u>
SOT CLIVE MYRIE REPORTING IN BATTLE	**SOT: BBC EMBED CLIVE MYRIE TALKING DURING BATTLE:** It seems that gunfire has been coming from the police station down there.
O/C CLIVE MYRIE	**O/C: CLIVE MYRIE, BBC:** I think a lot of journalists did lose courage. A lot of embedded journalists did lose their ability to be critical, to emphasize the fact that there might be problems going on here because they didn't want to be kicked off the team. They wanted to stay embedded, and I think that was part of the problem.
STILL OF GREG KELLY AS EMBEDDED. O/C GREG KELLY	**O/C: GREG KELLY, FOX NEWS:** Look, you do what you can do with what you are given. I did the best that I could with my assignment covering the 2nd brigade. I think overall if you have, what were there, 600 journalists embedded throughout, that is definitely a plus.
O/C: MAX ROBBINS, EMBEDDED REPORTER REPORTING, EMBEDDED JOURNALIST IN BASE, ROBBINS O/C	**O/C: MAX ROBBINS, EDITOR,** *BROADCASTING & CABLE* **MAGAZINE:** By and large, people who are covering this story, who were at the frontlines

STILL WASHINGTON D.C., TIMES SQUARE, SATELLITE ANIMATION	actually doing the actual reporting, did an admirable job. They were doing what they were sent out to do. However, they don't have ultimate control—the control is someplace else, the control might be back in Washington or in New York, or in edit bays in New York or Qatar.
GREG KELLY AT PANEL	**SOT: GREG KELLY, FOX NEWS:** Once this war started—we wanted the US to win … we got to know the soldiers and wanted them to be successful

9. SECTION: NEWS BUSINESS AS SHOW BUSINESS

AIR SHOT PENTAGON, NEWS PROMOS, VARIOUS NEWS ANCHORS PROMOTING IRAQ COVERAGE.	**V/O: DANNY SCHECHTER:** IF THE PENTAGON HAD AN AGENDA, THE NETWORKS HAD ONE TOO. AND, IT WENT BEYOND ATTRACTING AUDIENCES.
DANNY SCHECHTER STAND-UP OUTSIDE NEWS BUILDING, FOOTAGE OF SOLDIERS AT WAR	**O/C: DANNY SCHECHTER:** WHEN I WAS IN NETWORK NEWS HERE AT ABC, I WATCHED THE CLOSING OF FOREIGN BUREAUS, THE DOWNGRADING OF DOCUMENTARIES, THE DUMBING DOWN OF NEWS. THERE IS NOTHING LIKE THE SCARY THREAT OF WMDs AND A GOOD WAR TO PROVIDE THE BASIS FOR ACTION-ORIENTED TV COVERAGE.
TIME'S SADDAM AND HITLER COVERS, STILL CLOSE-UP BUSH, BOMBS GOING OFF IN IRAQ, GIVES IMPRESSION OF THE"BEST OF THE BOMBS" CHANNEL,	**V/O DANNY SCHECHTER** *TIME* MAGAZINE'S SADDAM COVER WAS MODELED ON AN EARLIER HITLER COVER; PRESIDENT BUSH WAS PRESENTED AS AN AVENGING ANGEL.

SOLDIERS FIRING ARTILLERY	WAR IS ONE OF THOSE ACTION-ORI-ENTED SPECTACLES THAT TV NEWS LIVES FOR, AND THRIVES ON IN A POST-JOURNALISM ERA.
JON ALPERT O/C SHOWDOWN WITH SAD-DAM PROMO	**O/C: JON ALPERT, FORMER NBC NEWS CONTRIBUTOR:** All the networks wanted to have was a countdown to war; if you looked at every network it was virtually indistin-guishable. Forty-eight hours to war, dun, dun, dun, showdown to Saddam.
URBAN WARFARE ANIMA-TION	**V/O: DANNY SCHECHTER:** WITH ENCOURAGEMENT FROM THE PENTAGON, THE NEWS NETWORKS FASHIONED THEIR COVERAGE TO MAXIMIZE PRODUCTION VALUES, TO MAKE IT EXCITING. TIME MAGA-ZINE CALLED THE APPROACH:"MILI-TAINMENT." JOURNALIST ROBERT PELTON DESCRIBES HOW IT WAS DONE:
PELTON O/C BEST OF THE BOMBS FOOTAGE, PELTON O/C FOOTAGE DEMONSTRATING WHAT VERITÉ COVERAGE AND FOOTAGE LOOKS LIKE	**SOT: ROBERT YOUNG PELTON, REPORTER:** I was in some of the initial phone meet-ings between New York and the people in the field, and this was being set up like a movie shoot. There was a channel called,"Best of the Bombs." That's exactly what it was called"Best of the Bombs," and every piece of good footage from any network would be tossed onto this feed, this is satellite feed, so if you're doing about,"Hi, I'm standing in the middle of nowhere and let's roll to the footage," you would have this feed that had only good explosions.

Secondly, they told people to take the camera off the sticks. We want to have that cinema-verité look, you know—move it around, move it, we want to see where you are. We want you to walk and talk and make people feel you're in the middle of something.

"ACTION" FIELD FOOTAGE, SOLDIERS LYING, SHOOTING AND RUNNING, EMBED CRAWLING WITH LIPSTICK	**V/O: DANNY SCHECHTER:** <u>THIS IS TRUE. A DEFENSE DEPARTMENT MEMO URGED MILITARY COMMANDERS TO ENCOURAGE ACTION COVERAGE QUOTE:</u>
CYRON: <u>"USE OF LIPSTICK AND HELMET MOUNTED CAMERAS ON COMBAT SORTIES IS APPROVED AND ENCOURAGED TO THE GREATEST EXTENT POSSIBLE."</u>	<u>"USE OF LIPSTICK AND HELMET MOUNTED CAMERAS ON COMBAT SORTIES IS APPROVED AND ENCOURAGED TO THE GREATEST EXTENT POSSIBLE."</u>
REPORTER CRAWLING WITH LIPSTICK	**O/C: ROBERT YOUNG PELTON, REPORTER:** If you were to pick a generality, they were there for the big story. And keep in mind that Iraq is unusual, because in the early days of CNN, one of the most memorable images were people like Peter Arnett sitting on the rooftop, calling the war like a football game.
PETER ARNETT REPORTING	**SOT: PETER ARNETT, WAR REPORTER:** This is the sixth cruise missile to have come over our head in the last half-hour.

IRAQIS EXTINGUISHING FIRE, PELTON O/C, JOURNALIST STAND-UP, CREW SETTING UP STAND-UP, JOURNALIST STAND-UP, PELTON O/C, JOURNALIST STAND-UP, JOURNALIST IN HELICOPTER STAND-UP, BOMBS GOING OFF, BEST OF BOMBS, JOURNALIST AT THE STAND-UP

O/C: ROBERT YOUNG PELTON, REPORTER:
The entire population of the planet focused on one journalist.
So this was a wet dream for any journalist that went to Iraq. To be in that spot for a well-known, predicted war to happen.

If you're the guy holding that microphone, and that thing happened behind you, that's what you're known for.

You're not known for careful research for, for—it's the face. It's all about the face. And where that face is a measure of who you are.

So they were looking to get bullets flying, bombs going off, and that microphone, and that face on TV.

SCRATCH

REPORTER LICKING LIPS, CORRESPONDENT IN FIELD WITH LIPSTICK, GUY GIVING THUMBS UP, GUY BY PARKED CAR, GIRL WATCHING MONITOR, BACKSTAGE AT STAND-UP PODIUM, BAD SIGNAL, RAINBOW, COUNTDOWN, NEWS PROMOS, VARIOUS NEWS ANCHORS PROMOTING IRAQ COVERAGE, ARABS SMOKING IN BAR WATCHING TV, SADDAM WALKING, BUSH SPEAKING RECORDED OFF

MUSIC:
DANNY SCHECHTER/ POLAR LEVINE:"NEWS GOO"

GOT REMOTE CONTROL TO CHOSE THE SHOW
BUT THE MORE WE WATCH THE LESS WE KNOW
IGNORANCE GROWS ON THE SPIRIT LIKE A TUMOR

SCRATCH

... TILL FREEDOM IS A RUMOR

THE TV. BUSH, SADDAM, BOXING IMAGES, SADDAM BUSH, BOX, SADDAM, BUSH, THE REMOTE CONTROL, SCRATCH, BUSH BLAIR SHAKING HANDS, NEWS PROMOS, VARIOUS NEWS ANCHORS PROMOTING IRAQ COVERAGE, GIRLS DANCING IN STREET SCRATCH	NEWS GOO–WHAT WE WANT TO KNOW NEWS GOO–WHAT WE THINK WE KNOW GOT REMOTE CONTROL TO CHOSE THE SHOW BUT THE MORE WE WATCH THE LESS WE KNOW IGNORANCE GROWS ON THE SPIRIT LIKE A TUMOR SCRATCH
PELTON O/C	**O/C: ROBERT YOUNG PELTON, REPORTER:** … and that's what generates money. I mean, you look at who moved up the food chain in the journalism world over the last four or five years, you have basically two fast tracks: you have entertainment or war. And entertainment—who cares? If you're a journalist really, you focus on war.
GRAPHIC ANIMATION OF MOAB BOMBS, GRAPHICS AND EYEWITNESS PROMO	**V/O: DANNY SCHECHTER:** THE NETWORKS WORKED OVER-TIME TO PRODUCE SO-ALLED"VIDEO ENHANCEMENT" ELEMENTS LIKE GRAPHICS, PROMOS AND SPECIAL MUSIC.
EYEWITNESS PROMO	**SOT: ABC NEWS PROMO:** We want you to know that"Eyewitness News" is there.
EYEWITNESS PROMO WITH JIM DOLAN, HELICOPTER ANIMATION, WAR IN IRAQ PROMO, GRAPHIC OF	**V/O: DANNY SCHECHTER:** THEY WERE PREPARING FOR WHAT THEY CALLED"NEWS IMMERSION."

MISSILE IMPACT, NEWS PROMOS, VARIOUS NEWS ANCHORS PROMOTING IRAQ COVERAGE, EMBED-DED REPORTER STAND-UP, MAP OF IRAQ, AIR FIGHTER GRAPHIC, BLACK/WHITE IMPACT SHOTS

THEIR WAR WAS FOR, RATINGS AND REVENUES.

A CNN GRAPHICS DESIGNER IN ATLANTA CONFIDED TO A FRIEND THAT HE WAS TOLD TO"SEX IT UP."

WAR COVERAGE SOON DEVELOPED ITS OWN ROUTINES—WITH ANCHORS TOSSING TO CONSTANT UPDATES FROM EMBED REPORTERS AND IN-STUDIO ANALYSIS BY NET-WORK "GENERALS."

ONE RESULT: GLITZY ROUND-THE-CLOCK FAST-PACED COVERAGE THAT WAS OFTEN MISLEADING, INACCURATE AND RARELY COR-RECTED—JUST MORE MILITAIN-MENT.

CYRON:
INTERNET PROMO
KUMA.COM

KUMA PROMOTIONAL
VIDEO GAMES SHOTS

THESE ENTERTAINMENT VALUES STIMULATED A DEMAND FOR EVEN MORE EXCITEMENT—FROM VIDEO GAME MAKERS—LIKE KUMAWAR.COM, WHO TURNED THE WAR INTO AN INTERACTIVE COM-MERCIAL EXPERIENCE.

THROUGH BRITISH EYES, THE US CHANNELS LACKED JOURNALISTIC DISTANCE

GARY YOUNGE ON NEW SCHOOL UNIVERSITY PANEL

SOT: GARY YOUNGE, *THE GUARDIAN*:
By and large in the American net-works, you would hear people talking about"We.""We" as though the American, as if the network was actual-ly in the war.

O/C JOHN KAMPFNER	**O/C: JOHN KAMPFNER, PRODUCER, WAR SPIN, BBC:** In the States, as far as I can ascertain, there is a presumption that politicians are right and honest and truthful. That is the default from which everything else operates.
NEWSPAPER FRONT PAGES	**V/O: DANNY SCHECHTER:** <u>SOME UK JOURNALISTS LIKE JOHN PILGER AND ROBERT FISK OPPOSED THE WAR; OTHERS FELT CON-STRAINED</u>
O/C JAKE LYNCH	**O/C: JAKE LYNCH, FREELANCE REPORTER, BBC:** If say, for example, you cease to base your news agenda on the words and deeds of official sources, of the Prime Minister, of the government and start to base it instead on gathering alternative perspectives, on gathering news from unconventional sources. Then you will be somehow exposing yourself to the risk that you will be accused of being biased.
NEWS PROMOS PROMOT-ING IRAQ WAR COVERAGE	**V/O: DANNY SCHECHTER:** <u>EVEN AS THE MILITARY ENCOUR-AGED ACTION COVERAGE, PENTA-GON ADVISOR JOHN RENDON RECOGNIZED THE DANGERS</u>
WAR IN IRAQ PROGRAM RENDON AT PANEL DISCUS-SION	**SOT: JOHN RENDON, PENTAGON ADVISOR:** There is a convergence of content. News, information, and entertainment need to be separated. Right now there is a blurring of the lines on all three and if you could just think about it

	just in terms of how music comes up underneath news pieces, as a form of dramatization it changes the dynamic, and if the vehicle that delivers this information is all the same, then the viewer, the listener, or the reader will find a hard time distinguishing between the three.
OPERATION IRAQI FREE-DOM PROMO, SOLDIERS UNLOADING FROM AIR-CRAFT	**V/O: DANNY SCHECHTER:** UNDAUNTED THE CHANNELS PRO-DUCED BRANDING LINERS, SOME TAKING THE GOVERNMENT CAM-PAIGN THEME—THE WAR FOR IRAQI FREEDOM—AS THEIR OWN. ONE PROPOSAL TO CALL THE WAR OPERATION IRAQI LIBERATION WAS DISCARDED BECAUSE THAT SPELLS OIL.
SOLDIERS RUNNING, SOL-DIER SMOKING CIGAR, HELICOPTER FLYING BY DAWN, SOLDIERS POINTING AT MONITORS, COLIN POW-ELL AT PODIUM, RUMSFELD AND MYERS AT PENTAGON PODIUM, JETS TAKING OFF, ANIMATION OF APACHE ATTACK, OIL PIPES, MAP ANIMATION OF IRAQ	**MUSIC: DAVID ROVIC SONG"O-I-L COLLAGE":** It's Operation Iraqi Liberation Tell me what does that spell? Operation Iraqi Liberation: O.I.L

9. SECTION: INFORMATION DOMINANCE

DANNY'S AT GARDINER'S HOUSE	**O/C: DANNY SCHECHTER:** WE'RE ABOUT TEN MILES FROM THE PENTAGON, IN VIRGINIA, AT THE HOME OF A RETIRED AIR FORCE COLONEL WHO'S BEEN INVESTIGAT-

	ING THE STORIES OF THE IRAQ WAR, HOW THEY WERE MANUFACTURED, DISTORTED AND MISREPRESENTED BY THE MEDIA.
DANNY WALKING UP TO THE HOUSE	**O/C: SAM GARDINER, FORMER AIR FORCE COLONEL:** When I heard things, I heard military guys say things about the Iraqis…there's something wrong here.
STILLS OF GARDINER	I'm Sam Gardiner. I'm a retired air force colonel, and I had taught strategy and military operations at the National War College, the Air War College, and the Naval War College.
IN SAM GARDINER'S HOUSE GARDINER AND DANNY SCHECHTER LOOKING AT DOCUMENTS BUSH AT THE STATE OF THE UNION, COMBAT EXPLOSIONS, US MILITARY PATROLLING FROM TANK, SADDAM IN ARMCHAIR, TV SCREEN BLUR, EYES WATCHING TV	**V/O: DANNY SCHECHTER:** GARDINER DID A STUDY THAT READS LIKE THE PENTAGON PAPERS OF THE IRAQ WAR. HE AND OTHERS—REVEALED HOW INFORMATION DOMINANCE PROMOTES STRATEGIC INFLUENCE, HOW IT DROVE THE BUSH ADMINISTRATION'S PRE-EMPTIVE WAR USING DECEPTIVE INFORMATION AS AN INTEGRAL COMPONENT OF MILITARY AND POLITICAL COMBAT. THIS GOES BEYOND JUST INFLUENCING WHAT WE THINK, IT AIMS AT CONTROLLING WHAT WE THINK ABOUT. CORPORATIONS SEEK MARKET SHARE; THIS ADMINISTRATION SOUGHT MIND SHARE.
O/C SAM GARDINER	**O/C: SAM GARDINER, FORMER AIR FORCE COLONEL:** Every morning at 9:30 they would have the message phone call, and it

would involve the White House Office of Global Communications, the Pentagon Press Office, a media advisor, the people at Central Command, and sometimes the people in the State Department.

And their notion for that day was to coordinate the message, and after that they would talk to the Brits, so that the message in London matched the message in Washington.

O/C GARDINER	**O/C: DANNY SCHECHTER:** ONE MESSAGE, ONE IDEA, PUSH IT OUT INTO THE MEDIA.
O/C GARDINER	**O/C: SAM GARDINER, FORMER AIR FORCE COLONEL:** Right. Dominate today's message with . . . and you can almost identify by day what the message was.
JOURNALISTS ARRIVING AT THE DOHA MEDIA CENTER, PRESS BRIEFING IN DOHA, GENERALS AT THE STAKE-OUT JOURNALISTS ASKING QUESTION WE LOVE OUR TROOPS SIGN, BROOKS AT THE STAKE-OUT, WILKINSON AT PRESS BRIEFING, CLOSE-UP OF WILKINSON IN ARMY CLOTHES, WHITE HOUSE HOME PAGE, GOP HOME	**V/O: DANNY SCHECHTER:** <u>EVERY DAY, THERE WAS LIVE COVERAGE FROM THE PENTAGON'S HI-TECH MEDIA CENTER IN DOHA BUILT BY A HOLLYWOOD SET DESIGNER.</u> <u>UNKNOWN TO MOST TV VIEWERS, THE WHITE HOUSE DIRECTLY STAGE-MANAGED THE DOHA MEDIA CENTER THROUGH, JIM WILKINSON, A REPUBLICAN OPERATIVE WHO HAD WORKED FOR A RIGHT-WING CONGRESSMAN AND THEN HELPED RUN THE BUSH MEDIA OPERATION IN FLORIDA IN 2000.</u>

PAGE, FLORIDA ORCHES-TRATED ANTI-VOTE RE-COUNT DEMONSTRATION, WILKINSON AT THE STAGED DEMO	THAT STRATEGY INCLUDED STAG-ING EVENTS SUCH AS THIS ANTI-VOTE RECOUNT PROTEST IN MIAMI._ IT LOOKED LIKE A PUBLIC PROTEST BUT IT WAS ACTUALLY LED BY RIGHT-WING POLITICAL STAFFERS
WILKINSON AT THE STAGED DEMO, WILKINSON IN ARMY CLOTHES AT BRIEFING	**SOT: HARVEY RICE, REPORTER,** *HOUSTON CHRONICLE:* This is the guy they put in charge of the media operation; he's the guy that engineered it … he is the guy who thought about these things.
HARVEY RICE ON STAGE	**V/O: DANNY SCHECHTER:** *HOUSTON CHRONICLE* REPORTER HARVEY RICE WATCHED HIM IN ACTION.
STILLS OF WILKINSON	**SOT: HARVEY RICE, REPORTER,** *HOUSTON CHRONICLE:* He was nothing more than a political commissar. I mean this is straight out of Stalin. And that's what he was there for. He was there to make sure the military and as he put it … He said:"I'm here to keep them on message" …. So, he was running the information on the war like a political campaign.
CLOSE UP WILKINSON, *NEW YORK OBSERVER* ARTICLE	**V/O: DANNY SCHECHTER:** After the war Wilkinson was brought back into the White House and then picked to run media at the 2004 Republican convention.
PRESS BRIEFING DOHA JOURNALIST ASKING QUES-TION, FOOTAGE FROM PRESS BRIEFING	**SOT: NEWS BRIEFING, DOHA:** **Q:** A missile attack on a residential sec-tion of Baghdad that killed 14 civil-ians, can you confirm that?

	A: Military spokesperson: We think it is absolutely possible that this may have been in fact an Iraqi missile that either came up and went down or ....
DOHA JOURNALISTS, MICHAEL WOLFF IN THE CROWD, JOURNALIST WRITING ON NOTE PAD, JOURNALISTS RAISING THEIR HANDS TO ASK QUESTIONS	**V/O: DANNY SCHECHTER:** WAR WATCHERS MAY REMEMBER MEDIA WRITER MICHAEL WOLFF CHALLENGING MEDIA BRIEFERS AT THE CENTRAL COMMAND.
SOT MICHAEL WOLFF AT DOHA	**SOT: MICHAEL WOLFF, MEDIA COLUMNIST:** Why should we stay, what's the value to us for what we learn at this million-dollar press center?
MILITARY GUY MAKING SIGNS TO SILENCE SPEAKER	**V/O: DANNY SCHECHTER:** WOLFF WAS LATER TOLD TO SHUT THE FUCK UP BY A MILITARY BRIEFER.
MICHAEL WOLFF O/C	**O/C: MICHAEL WOLFF, MEDIA COLUMNIST:** Sometimes your jaw drops and it's hard to figure out why are American journalists so, uh, maybe not even uncritical, self-satisfied, I think is the word.
HARVEY RICE ON STAGE, BANK OF CAMERAS, PEOPLE WATCHING. LIGHTS TURNED ON. PEOPLE EATING AND WATCHING TELEVISION. TANK DRIVING. SOLDIERS MARCHING. HARVEY ON STAGE	**SOT: HARVEY RICE, REPORTER, *HOUSTON CHRONICLE*:** So the first day of the war, it's on CNN where they've got this bank of cameras there, and everybody goes in and they're watching these explosions and tanks rolling across and guys with M-16s, M-14s. And we go, is the war started? And these PR guys there say:"I'm

sorry, I can't talk to you about that, I don't want to endanger the lives of our boys." I said,"But it's on television."

O/C PELTON, GROUP OF JOURNALISTS EAGER TO INTERVIEW OFFICIAL IN DOHA. JOURNALISTS ATTENDING DOHA PRESS BRIEFING. DOHA PRESS BRIEFING. BROOKS SPEAKING AT STAKE-OUT. PELTON O/C	**O/C: ROBERT YOUNG PELTON, REPORTER:** If you can give the media more content than they can handle and, as far away from the battlefield as possible, they will focus their energies where the source of that fire hose is. So, Doha is the center of the fire-hose. And the idea is, you simply have press conferences every day, and every once in awhile you throw a little tidbit—you hand out videotapes, free coffee, whatever. So that if you leave, you're gonna miss the story that everybody else is covering …. Fire-hose coverage and fire hose delivery blocks out all the secondary sources.
O/C SAM GARDINER	**O/C: SAM GARDINER, FORMER AIR FORCE COLONEL:** My research of the threads of stories from the war, which takes it from the beginning through the end, the way they were created, the way they were used, the way they were repeated, that research leads me to say that there were 50 or 60 stories that were either created or manipulated for the purposes of distorting the truth.
TV SHOT OF SADDAM, STILLS OF BIN LADEN, JESSICA LYNCH	**V/O: DANNY SCHECHTER:** GARDINER CITED FALSE STORIES, LIKE THE LINK BETWEEN SADDAM AND AL QAEDA, AS WELL AS THE JESSICA LYNCH STORY, WHICH THE BBC ALSO DEBUNKED.

JESSICA LYNCH PICTURE	**O/C: DANNY SHECHTER:** WHAT WERE THE TWO NARRATIVES?
O/C JOHN KAMPFNER NEWSPAPER ARTICLES ABOUT JESSICA LYNCH, US DEPARTMENT OF DEFENSE PROMO RESCUE VIDEO, FOOTAGE FROM HOSPITAL, KAMPFNER O/C	**O/C: JOHN KAMPFNER, PRODUCER, WAR SPIN, BBC:** In the American narrative she's well-known as the great hero, the great heroine who was captured under fire, who was then taken to hospital, potentially mistreated. American special forces went in, all guns blazing, rescued her against hostile fire. ....There was no resistance; the Iraqi doctors had been caring for her, given the circumstances as well as could have been. And, a lot of the more dramatic elements of the story may have been embellished.
O/C SAM GARDINER, RUMSFELD AT PRESS BRIEFING	**O/C: SAM GARDINER, FORMER AIR FORCE COLONEL:** That story ended up hanging around for about a week, and that's why she's called a hero. Well, it turns out all of that was wrong. When Rumsfeld was asked about this the next day, he refused to comment on it, although I know he knew that she had not been shot, stabbed, and emptied her weapon on the bad guy. So it hung around.
DRAWINGS OF CLUSTER BOMBS, MISSILE STOCK PILE, STILL OF US SOLDIERS LAUNCHING MISSILE, MAIMED CHILD IN HOSPITAL BED	**V/O: DANNY SCHECHTER:** <u>INFORMATION DOMINANCE REQUIRES CENSORSHIP—LITTLE ATTENTION WAS PAID TO US WEAPONS THAT CAUSED MASS DESTRUCTION, LIKE LEGALLY PROHIBITED CLUSTER BOMBS THAT TARGET CIVILIANS.</u>

CYRON: VOICE OF RENE HORNE, SABC GRAPHICS OF CLUSTER BOMBS	**SOT: RENE HORNE, SABC** It was a cluster bomb. The bomb would multiple many bombs dropped from an aircraft on targeted areas ....
GRAPHICS OF CLUSTER BOMBS	**V/O: DANNY SCHECHTER:** SOUTH AFRICAN VIEWERS LEARNED ABOUT HOW CLUSTER BOMBS WORKED—AND WHAT DAMAGE THEY CAUSED.
CYRON: "RAINING PLANES" FILMED IN BAGHDAD, 2003 FOOTAGE FROM BAGHDAD HOSPITAL	AN UNDERREPORTED FACT: HALF OF IRAQ'S POPULATION IS UNDER THE AGE OF 15-THESE YOUNG PEOPLE BECAME A PRIMARY TARGET. THIS IS WHAT BAGHDAD"S PEDIATRIC HOSPITAL LOOKED LIKE, FLOOR AFTER FLOOR OF CLUSTER-BOMB SURVIVORS. THIS WAS FILMED NOT BY A NETWORK BUT BY INDEPENDENT FILMMAKER, PATRICK DILLON. HUMAN RIGHTS WATCH REPORTED CLUSTER WEAPONS CAUSED HUNDREDS OF CIVILIAN CASUALTIES LIKE THESE.
AIRCRAFT TAKING OFF, EXPLOSION	THERE WAS EXTENSIVE USE OF NAPALM-LIKE MARK-77 FIREBOMBS. IT WAS DENIED AT FIRST, BUT THEN ADMITTED.
ARD TV FOOTAGE OF RADIOACTIVE US TANKS	MORE ONEROUS WAS THE ALMOST TOTAL BLACKOUT ON THE USE OF RADIOACTIVE DEPLETED URANIUM, WHICH HARDENS ANTI-TANK WEAPONS—THIS IS ESPECIALLY

IRONIC IN LIGHT OF WASHINGTON'S CONSTANT CLAIMS OF AN IRAQI NUCLEAR THREAT.

THE ISSUE WAS COVERED OVER-SEAS; ARNIM STAUTH, A GERMAN JOURNALIST, DOCUMENTED THIS PROLIFERATION IN AN EMMY-WINNING REPORT FOR ARD, IN GERMANY:

FOOTAGE OF RADIOACTIVE US TANKS	**SOT: ARD GERMAN TELEVISION:** **Q: Reporter:** Are you aware that this tank is contaminated with radiation? **A: Soldier:** No, it isn't radioactive, replied the soldier. **Q: Reporter:** but we have measured it. **A:** Soldier: No it is not radioactive, not this tank. **Q: Reporter:** It was destroyed by depleted uranium ammunition. **A: Soldier:** Sorry, but I have to get back to work.
INSIDE THE COALITION MEDIA CENTER	**V/O: DANNY SCHECHTER:** THE BBC TOOK VIEWERS TO A BACKROOM AT THE COALITION MEDIA CENTER. ON THE WALL, A LIST OF SUBJECTS BRIEFERS WERE ORDERED TO AVOID. AMONG
GARDINER O/C, VARIOUS BIN LADEN SPEAKING, KNIGHT RIDDER POLL	THEM WAS DU, OR DEPLETED URANIUM.
CYRON: KNIGHT RIDDER POLL: AMERICAN REACTION: +/- 3 PERCENT WERE SOME OF THE 9-11	THERE HAS BEEN A NUMBER OF STUDIES OF MISPERCEPTIONS BY VIEWERS THAT MANY AMERICANS BELIEVE THERE WAS AN AL-QAEDA–IRAQ CONNECTION. THAT MANY AMERICANS BELIEVE THAT

HIJACKERS IRAQIS? YES: 42 % NO: 42% DON'T KNOW: 16 %	THERE WERE IRAQI HIJACKERS ATTACKING THE WORLD TRADE CENTER.
GARDINER O/C, TV RECORDING OF BUSH SPEAKING, SADDAM SITTING, BUSH SPEAKING, WTC COLLAPSING, BUSH SPEAKING, GARDINER O/C	**O/C: SAM GARDINER, FORMER AIR FORCE COLONEL:** I think that is part of the campaign—it was a very conscious effort to use terms that would have people connect in their minds Iraq and the incident of 9/11. You imply that these are the same kind of people and if they're the same kind of people they must have had something to do with it. Had they done an hour's worth of research, they could have had a paragraph in their story that said that the Pentagon says this—however—there were no however paragraphs.
PANORAMA OF PENTAGON, HOLLYWOOD SIGN, RENDON AT PANEL	**V/O: DANNY SCHECHTER:** THE NEW INFORMATION DOMINANCE STRATEGY WORKED THANKS TO ADVICE FROM MARKETING EXPERTS, HOLLYWOOD PRODUCERS AND COMMUNICATIONS SPECIALISTS LIKE JOHN RENDON, WHO WERE MONITORING THE MEDIA WORLDWIDE. THEIR JOB WAS TO KEEP THE PUBLIC WELL PROPAGANDIZED.
RENDON AT MEDIA PANEL, JOURNALISTS WRITING ON NOTE PAD	**SOT: JOHN RENDON, PENTAGON ADVISER** There were five wars in Iraq. There really was the reality of combat operations from the air, on the ground and from the sea. The second war was the war the United States saw, the third

war was the war that Europe saw. The fourth war was the war that Arab audiences saw. And the fifth war was the war the rest of the world saw. And as we monitored that in real time, we found that none of them were ever in alignment.

ELECTRONIC MAP OF IRAQ, NEWS PROMO, CIA BUILDING, RENDON AT PANEL, RUMSFELD AT THE STAKE-OUT, STAUBER O/C	**O/C: JOHN STAUBER, AUTHOR** *WEAPONS OF MASS DECEPTION:* When you look at the war in Iraq, it's at times impossible to separate media, CIA, public relations firms, government propaganda. It all came together.

9. SECTION: THE FOX NEWS EFFECT

SHOTS OF BILL O'REILLY ON MONITORS	**SOT: BILL O'REILLY, FOX:** So what is the problem here, Danny?
FOX NEWS WITH BILL O'REILLY, DANNY SCHECHTER INSIDE FOX NEWS, TV SCREEN"CONSPIRACY THEORIES," MAKE-UP B-ROLL	**O/C: DANNY SCHECHTER:** I'M AT THE FOX NEWS CHANNEL, INSIDE"FOX AND FRIENDS," A PROGRAM I MONITOR EVERY MORNING— THAT'S BEEN THE MOST EXTREME IN ITS COVERAGE OF THE WAR. I'M WAITING FOR THE MAKE-UP LADY TO COME. I'M GOING ON THE AIR TO TALK ABOUT A CONSPIRACY THAT HAPPENED FORTY YEARS AGO—THE KENNEDY ASSASSINATION. I MADE A FILM ABOUT THAT. FOX IS NOT INTERESTED REALLY IN THE CONSPIRACY THAT'S HAPPENING NOW IN TERMS OF THE MEDIA, THE MILITARY AND THE ADMINISTRATION, BUT THAT'S NOT THE SUBJECT THAT THEY HAVE ME HERE TO TALK ABOUT. THE PAST SOMEHOW CAN BE HANDLED SAFELY; THE PRESENT IS ANOTHER MATTER.

WALKING DOWN THE FOX NEWS"BUNKER," CHANGE TO FOX NEWS PRODUCTION CENTER	**O/C: DANNY SCHECHTER:** YOU KNOW WHAT THEY SAY? THAT FOX IS NOT REALLY FAIR AND BALANCED, THAT IT'S NOT EVEN NEWS. DO YOU WATCH IT?
SHOT OF DANNY GETTING MAKE-UP DONE	**O/C: MAKEUP WOMAN:** No…
MAKE-UP SESSION	**O/C: DANNY SCHECHTER:**
DANNY DRYING HIS HAIR	NO?
"FOX AND FRIENDS" GRAPHICS	**O/C: MAKEUP WOMAN:** Don't scrunch your face!
HAIRSTYLING	**O/C: DANNY SCHECHTER:** I'M SORRY …. YOU ARE THE THIRD PERSON I'M TALKING TO WHO DOESN'T WATCH IT AND YOU WORK HERE…
	O/C: DANNY SCHECHTER: YOU JUST DEAL WITH WHAT'S ON TOP OF PEOPLE'S HEADS; YOU DON'T DEAL WITH WHAT 'S IN THEIR HEADS, RIGHT?
TEASER, DANNY"FOX AND FRIENDS"	**O/C: DANNY SCHECHTER** TRUTH DOES HAVE A WAY OF COMING OUT. AND SOMETIMES IT'S SUPPRESSED FOR A LONG TIME, NEW DOCUMENTS EMERGE, HISTORIANS REVEAL THINGS THAT WEREN'T REVEALED BEFORE. I BELIEVE SO; I BELIEVE THE AMERICAN PEOPLE DESERVE THE TRUTH.
DANNY SCHECHTER INSIDE"FOX AND	**V/O: DANNY SCHECHTER:** I HAD HOPED TO CONFRONT BILL

FRIENDS,""THE O'REILLY FACTOR" PRODUCTION CENTER, 4 SCREENS WITH BILL O'REILLY, BILL O'REILLY ANCHORING, O'REILLY ANCHORING	O'REILLY BUT HE WASN'T THERE. HE IS ONE OF THE LOUD-MOUTH TALK-SHOW HOSTS THAT DEFINES FOX'S ANGRY WHITE MAN ATTITUDE—WELL-CALCULATED AS A TOOL OF POLARIZATION POLITICS—WELL-PRACTICED ON RIGHT-WING RADIO. AFTER A YEAR OF UNCRITICAL REPORTING, TO HIS CREDIT, HE ADMITTED THAT HE WAS WRONG ABOUT WMDS.
DANNY SCHECHTER SPEAK-ING FROM INSIDE FOX NEWS	**O/C: DANNY:** LADIES AND GENTLEMEN OF THE JURY I HAVE COME, NOT TO BURY RUPERT MURDOCH, BUT TO PRAISE HIM!
NEWS TEASE, INSIDE STU-DIO	**SOT: FOX JINGLE:** FAIR AND BALANCED COVERAGE, THE FOX NEWS CHANNEL!
SHOTS OF NEWSROOMS	**V/O: DANNY SCHECHTER:** FOX NEWS MAY SEEM A FUN PLACE TO ITS FANS AND A CARTOON TO ITS CRITICS—BUT ITS IDEOLOGICAL ZEAL IS SERIOUS AND CAREFULLY CALCULATED, AS LONG TIME FOR-MER PRODUCER CHARLIE REINA REVEALED ON A MEDIA WEBSITE:
CYRON: "THE ROOTS OF FOX NEWS CHANNEL'S DAY-TO-DAY ON-AIR BIAS ARE ACTUAL AND DIRECT... **CYRON:** THEY COME IN THE FORM	QUOTE;"THE ROOTS OF FOX NEWS CHANNEL'S DAY-TO-DAY ON-AIR BIAS ARE ACTUAL AND DIRECT... THEY COME IN THE FORM OF AN EXECUTIVE MEMO DISTRIBUTED ELECTRONICALLY EACH MORNING, ADDRESSING ...WHAT

OF AN EXECUTIVE MEMO DISTRIBUTED ELECTRONI-CALLY EACH MORNING, ADDRESSING …

CYRON:
WHAT STORIES WILL BE COVERED, AND OFTEN, SUGGESTING HOW THEY SHOULD BE COVERED. THE MEMO IS THE BIBLE."
—CHARLIE REINA

NEWS TEASE AND JINGLE

ANCHORS REPORTING, EMBEDDED OLIVER NORTH REPORTING, ARCHIVE FOOTAGE OF COURTROOM WITH OLIVER NORTH

STORIES WILL BE COVERED, AND OFTEN, SUGGESTING HOW THEY SHOULD BE COVERED. THE MEMO IS THE BIBLE."

FOX'S RESPONSE:"THIS CHARGE IS UNFOUNDED, PEOPLE WANT TO WORK HERE."

FOX COVERAGE INCLUDED OVERLY DRAMATIC REPORTS BY GERALDO RIVERA AND IRAN-CONTRA CON-SPIRATOR, COLONEL OLIVER NORTH.

ARCHIVE FOOTAGE OF COURTROOM WITH OLIVER NORTH

SOT: OLIVER NORTH, FORMER NATIONAL SECURITY COUNCIL STAFF:
I will tell you right now, council, and all the members here gathered, that I misled the Congress.

EMBEDDED OLIVER NORTH INTERVIEWING SOLDIER, US TANKS PATROLLING IRAQI DIRT ROADS

V/O: DANNY SCHECHTER:
COLONEL NORTH'S WAR STORIES WERE BLATANT EXERCISES IN CHEERLEADING AND DENOUNCED THE ANTI-WAR MOVEMENT.

US TANKS PATROLLING IRAQI DIRT ROADS

SOT: FOX NEWS OLIVER NORTH
UNIDENTIFIED: This is the city garbage dump
UNIDENTIFIED: I wonder why all the

	peace protesters never protest this kind of stuff … FOX: They could be planning to attack westerners.
NEWS PROMOS VARIOUS NEWS ANCHORS PROMOTING IRAQ COVERAGE.	**V/O: DANNY SCHECHTER:** WHAT WAS CALLED THE"FOX EFFECT" DROVE ALL THE TV COVERAGE TO THE RIGHT—NO NETWORK WANTED TO BE ACCUSED OF BEING UNPATRIOTIC.
TOM BROKAW ANCHORING	**SOT: TOM BROKAW, MSNBC:** Arnett gave an interview to Iraqi television in which he criticized American war planning and said his reports about civilian casualties and Iraqi resistance was encouraging to anti-war protestors in America.
PETER ARNETT ON IRAQI TELEVISION	**O/C PETER ARNETT, WAR REPORTER:** The American war planners misjudged the determination of the Iraqis …
ARNETT ON IRAQI TV	**V/O: DANNY SCHECHTER:** VETERAN CORRESPONDENT PETER ARNETT WAS TARGETED BY FOX NEWS FOR HIS DECISION TO SAY ON IRAQI TV WHAT HE WAS ALREADY SAYING ON MSNBC.
ARNETT ON IRAQI TV, ARNETT O/C	**O/C: DANNY SCHECHTER:** IF I'M WRONG, YOU DIDN'T GO ON IRAQI TV TO SAY,"I SUPPORT SADDAM HUSSEIN" DID YOU? YOU DIDN'T ENDORSE ONE SIDE OR THE OTHER?

O/C ARNETT

CARTOONS: ARNETT IN
BED WITH SADDAM

O/C: PETER ARNETT, WAR REPORTER:
Of course I didn't endorse one side. It was a part of the hysteria that developed surrounding this war. Now there is a degree of hysteria about every war that America participates in, gets involved in. This was part of a hysterical reaction and I was basically, you know, swept up in that incredible explosion of anger. There were about 157 cartoons of me in the newspaper the next morning, most of them in bed with Saddam Hussein.

ARNETT O/C

Management called up and says the pressure is too great, we've had thousands of emails and calls and it's time; we have to drop you...

INTERNET STILLS OF FREE
REPUBLIC'S HOME PAGE

FREEPER'S EMAIL REVEAL-
ING THEY"FREEPED"
ARNETT'S BOSSES AND GOT
HIM FIRED

CLIP OF AN ANCHOR IN
FRONT OF A"TROOP WALL"

PROMOTIONAL STILL OF
PHIL DONAHUE,"AMERICA
AT WAR" TEASER, NEWS
TEASE

V/O: DANNY SCHECHTER:
WHAT I'VE LEARNED AND HAS GONE UNREPORTED UNTIL NOW IS THAT THOSE EMAILS WERE NOT FROM THE PUBLIC AT LARGE BUT PART OF AN ORCHESTRATED CAMPAIGN BY FREE REPUBLIC, A RIGHT-WING ONLINE NETWORK."WE WERE FREEPED," AN OFFICIAL AT *NATIONAL GEOGRAPHIC* TOLD ME, EXPLAINING THAT 20,000 EMAILS CALLING ARNETT"A TRAITOR" BOMBARDED THEIR EXECUTIVES WHO THEN PANICKED AND DISCHARGED HIM. THE FREEPERS BOASTED OF THEIR SUCCESS.

BEFORE THE WAR, MSNBC FIRED POPULAR ANTI-WAR TALK SHOW HOST PHIL DONAHUE, REPLACING

	HIM WITH STRIDENT RIGHT- WINGERS IN A MOVE TO OUTFOX FOX. AN MSNBC EXECUTIVE CALLED FOX:"THE PATRIOTISM POLICE."
ARNETT O/C	**O/C PETER ARNETT, WAR CORRE- SPONDENT:** The rest of the world looked at my fir- ing you, know, as a, as another exam- ple of American media caving into government. SCRATCH
NEWS PROMOS PROMOT- ING IRAQ WAR COVERAGE	**SOT: FOX NEWS BITES:** What about Al Jazeera publishing those gruesome pictures of the dead soldiers? I think there was something that is culturally Arab about that. News: fair, balanced, and unafraid.
PROMO, CBS PROMO FOR"EVENING NEWS"	**V/O: DANNY SCHECHTER:** BUT ALL OF THE NETWORKS MORE OR LESS SIGNED ON TO THE OFFI- CIAL RATIONALE.
ANCHOR	**SOT: FOX NEWS CAST:** Terrorist could be planning …
SHOTS OF PIPA KNOWL- EDGE NETWORKS POLL STUDY **CYRON:** FREQUENCY OF MISPER- CEPTIONS FOX 80 % CBS 71% ABC 61 %	**V/O: DANNY SCHECHTER:** A STUDY FOUND WIDESPREAD MIS- PERCEPTIONS AMONG VIEWERS. THE PEOPLE WITH THE MOST MISINFOR- MATION WATCHED THE FOX NEWS CHANNEL, ALTHOUGH VIEWERS OF OTHER CHANNELS WERE ALSO RECEPTIVE TO INACCURACIES. PUB- LIC BROADCASTING VIEWERS AND LISTENERS WERE MISLED THE LEAST.

NBC 55%
CNN 55 %
PBS 23 %

SHOT OF PAUL RUTHER-FORD'S WEAPONS OF MASS PERSUASION	THIS CANADIAN STUDY HIGH-LIGHTS ANOTHER MISPERCEPTION ABOUT MEDIA ITSELF….
CYRON: "MOST AMERICANS WERE NOT AWARE OF HOW ONE-SIDED AND BIASED THE COVERAGE HAD BEEN. THEY BELIEVED THE NEWS MEDIA HAD SERVED THE COUNTRY WELL."	QUOTE,"MOST AMERICANS WERE NOT AWARE OF HOW ONE-SIDED AND BIASED THE COVERAGE HAD BEEN. THEY BELIEVED THE NEWS MEDIA HAD SERVED THE COUNTRY WELL."
TV SHOT OF BUSH SPEAK-ING	**SOT: PRESIDENT GEORGE W. BUSH:** Nothing like this has happened…
WAR IN IRAQ PROMO WITH VARIOUS CORRESPON-DENTS	**CNN SOT:** The war in Iraq continues, and no one takes you closer than CNN live.
WAR IN IRAQ PROMO WITH VARIOUS CORRESPON-DENTS, WAR TEASE, LIV NEWS WITH ARON BROWN	**V/O: DANNY SCHECHTER:** IN THIS WAR WHAT HAD ONCE BEEN KNOWN AS THE CNN EFFECT HAD FADED. BUT CNN WAS STILL A NEWS LEADER. I LEARNED THAT CNN MOUNTED TWO NEWS TEAMS: ONE FOR THE U.S. CHANNEL AND ONE FOR THE REST OF THE WORLD ON CNN INTERNATIONAL. WAS IT JUST DIFFERENT STROKES FOR DIF-FERENT FOLKS?
CNN'S BILL HEMMER	**O/C: DANNY SCHECHTER:** EXPLAIN TO ME WHY CNN HAD ONE TYPE OF COVERAGE FOR

	AMERICA AND ONE TYPE OF COV-ERAGE FOR THE REST OF THE WORLD.
O/C BILL HEMMER, WAR IN IRAQ PROMO FOOTAGE OF TANKS, ANCHORS WITH TANKS IN THE BACK-GROUND, CITY SHOT	**O/C: BILL HEMMER, CNN REPORTER:** Um, I'm not so sure it was different. The content was the same, the presentation sometimes is different. Um, American audiences have certain expectations of how the news is given to them.
CLIP OF RYM BRAHIMI REPORTING FROM JORDAN	**SOT: RYM BRAHIMI REPORTING, CNN.**
O/C RYM BRAHIMI	**O/C: RYM BRAHIMI, CNN CORRE-SPONDENT:** People aren't gonna hang out on the screen forever and watch your long explanations. They want to know quickly what happened because they have a job to do, too. Our job is to give them that.
O/C RIZ KHAN	**O/C: RIZ KHAN, FORMER CNN INTERNATIONAL ANCHOR:** For me it's a huge difference being able to get international news. One of the benefits I had living in Atlanta was I was there in the heart of an international newsroom. As soon as I stepped outside, domestic media never gave me that. It's a real shame, actually. Especially for the world's most powerful nation.

12. SECTION: THE POST-WAR WAR

SHOTS OF HIGHWAYS, THE	**V/O: DANNY SCHECHTER:**

APPROACH TO BAGHDAD, IRAQI KIDS AND US SOLDIERS IN CITY, BURNED OUT BUILDING, SUN RISE OVER BAGHDAD	IN JUST THREE WEEKS, THE US MILITARY SEIZED BAGHDAD WITH A SMALL ARMY OF JOURNALISTS TAGGING ALONG. ROBERT PELTON, OPERATING UNILATERALLY NOW, OBSERVED THE NETWORK NEWS OPERATIONS:;
FOOTAGE OF HOTEL LOBBY, PELTON O/C	**SOT: POBERT YOUNG PELTON, UNILATERAL JOURNALIST:** When you're a journalist in Baghdad, you live in a fancy hotel, you're hooked to the internet all the time. You've got people in New York making decisions for you, sending you story ideas that you are gonna go out and do. You get up in the morning, you got a driver, you got an air-conditioned GMC, you've got a driver, translator, a cameraman, you got a security guy, a little kind of British guy with tattoos on his arms, and off you go to shoot the story. You know you put your vest on, you get your sound bytes, you come back in time to cut it together, then the talking head does the stand-up, then boom off it goes.
FOOTAGE OF SADDAM STATUE COMING DOWN	**SOT: SOME REPORTER:** Goodbye Saddam!
CYRON: APRIL 9, 2003 FOOTAGE OF SADDAM STATUE COMING DOWN	**V/O: DANNY SCHECHTER:** THANKS TO A RECENTLY RELEASED US ARMY REPORT WE NOW KNOW, THIS MOST DRAMATIC IMAGE OF THE IRAQ WAR WAS ENGINEERED BY A PSYCHOLOGICAL OPERATIONS UNIT THAT MADE IT SEEM LIKE IT

	WAS SPONTANEOUS. MANY TV OUTLETS REPORTED THE STUNT AS EVIDENCE OF THE FREEDOM WHICH WAS NOW SAID TO BE IRAQ'S.
PHOTO MONTAGE OF BUSH'S MISSION ACCOMPLISHED STUNT	"MISSION ACCOMPLISHED" PROCLAIMED PRESIDENT BUSH IN A SCENE OUT OF THE MOVIE"TOP GUN."
PHOTO MONTAGE OF BUSH'S MISSION ACCOMPLISHED STUNT, TOM RICKS	**V/O: DANNY SCHECHTER:** *WASHINGTON POST* MILITARY REPORTER TOM RICKS DISAGREED WITH THIS ASSESSMENT:
TOM RICKS	**SOT: TOM RICKS, WASHINGTON POST:** I think the single biggest media failure was a failure that the Bush administration committed and the media committed together, which is that we tore down the goalposts at halftime. On April 9th we said game over. It turns out the game was half over.
US SOLDIERS HIDING IN GRASS, SOLDIERS SHOOTING, CARS BURNING, HEAVILY-ARMED SOLDIERS WALKING, STEET FOOTAGE BAGHDAD, IRAQIS ON LOADED TRUCK LEAVING BAGHDAD, LOOTING FOOTAGE, SOLDIERS FIRING FROM THE MARSH, CARS BURNING, LOOTING, ANGRY IRAQI CROWD, TV JOURNALISTS SHOOTING THE ANGRY STREET CROWD, US TANKS IN BAGHDAD STREETS	**V/O: DANNY SCHECHTER:** THE POST INVASION STORYLINE QUICKLY CHANGED FROM LIBERATION, TO OCCUPATION, TO RESISTANCE. THERE WAS MASSIVE LOOTING. THERE WERE PRO-SADAM PROTESTS AND DAILY ATTACKS ON US SOLDIERS; ALMOST NONE OF THE INVASION COVERAGE ANTICIPATED THIS POST-WAR CHAOS. WHILE SOME TV CREWS REMAINED,

	MOST OF THE EMBEDS WERE WITH-DRAWN, UPSETTING MILITARY COMMANDERS LIKE SCOTT RUDDER.
SCOTT RUDDER O/C	**O/C: SCOTT RUDDER, MILITARY COMMANDER:** You know, 15 April when everyone left, a new breed came over. These individuals were not part of the war, very excited about getting the information, getting it there. In the Sheraton Hotel as well as the Palestine Hotel, you can imagine huddles of reporters around high-paid taxi cab drivers to launch out, to get the story, to show up in your unit without any type of, any type of coordination or efforts. You can imagine them huddling around a bearcat scanner for the bad news.
MISSILE HEADS	**VO: DANNY SCHECHTER:** THE SEARCH FOR WMDs WAS GETTING NOWHERE FAST.
SOLDIER WITH A COKE CAN	**SOT: SOLDIER:** No one asked me to come here and fight for someone's oil .... You know what, cause half my company doesn't even own a car. You know why we came here and fought? We came here and fought for all the beautiful ladies back home and an ice-cold coke. That's why we're kicking off on somebody's butt. Thanks a lot.
WMD SPELLED, NEWS HEADLINES, CNN FOOTAGE OF BUSH, PRINT HEADLINES, IRAQI STREET FOOTAGE	**V/O: DANNY SCHECHTER:** BY YEAR'S END, WHEN NO WMDs WERE FOUND. OFFICIALS CALLED IT A MOOT POINT AND SOUGHT TO CHANGE THE SUBJECT. BY THEN

	<u>THE POST-WAR CLAIMED MORE AMERICAN LIVES THAN THE INVASION.</u> <u>STEPHEN MARSHALL OF GUERILLA NEWS NETWORK WENT TO BAGHDAD IN OCTOBER 2003.</u>
O/C MARSHALL, US SOLDIERS GUARDING HOUSES, IRAQI CHILDREN DRINKING WATER, TANK WITH MOSQUE BACKDROP	**O/C: STEPHEN MARSHALL, GUERILLA NEWS NETWORK:** Each of the major networks sort of has one crew who travel around from bombsite to bombsite. … It's all sort of guarded by the military with huge checkpoints and you know, concrete barriers; which doesn't give them the opportunity to cover what I would call the Arab street or you know, the true sort of experience of the Iraqi people.
FOOTAGE OF IRAQI STREETS	**V/O: DANNY SCHECHTER:** <u>THE REPORTING FROM IRAQ QUICKLY DEGENERATED INTO A CATALOGUE OF INCIDENTS.</u>
IRAQI STREET FOOTAGE, MARSHALL O/C, PHOTO JOURNALISTS AT WORK	**SOT: STEPHEN MARSHALL, GUERILLA NEWS NETWORK:** What's really happening now is that you have a situation where there's a bombing, a suicide bombing, say at the Baghdad Hotel, where we were at and all of a sudden everyone gets in their truck and whips over there with their security guards and everyone is on scene. Most of the people there are sort of adventure journalists. They're the guys who, you know, really they're stringers who get paid quite a lot of

money to go work in these countries, and they are simply there to get the best pictures they can. And in many ways I found it to be very cynical. We met a lot of photographers and shooters who, were really there, and only wanted to find the next disaster … get there on time, get the right footage, get back to the Palestine Hotel and start drinking beer.

You know, really in Iraq, it's the, the truism has never been more absolute that"if it bleeds, it leads." The only thing they want to get out of Iraq are bloody civilians, or, in the best-case scenario, military officials or military, or soldiers who have been hit by bombs. That's the images they want to get, which is ironic, because for the administration, those are the worse types of images.

FOOTAGE OF HOUSE, TIME MAGAZINE JESUS AND SADDAM COVER, NEWS REPORTING ON SADDAM'S CAPTURE	**V/O: DANNY SCHECHTER:** AND THEN SADDAM HUSSEIN WAS CAPTURED—TIME MAGAZINE TOOK JESUS OFF OF ITS COVER AND PUT SADDAM ON—EVERY NETWORK PLAYED IT BIG—AS IF IT WAS THE SECOND COMING.
BREMMER PRESS CONFERENCE	**SOT: AMBASSADOR L. PAUL BREMER III:** Ladies and gentlemen. We got him.
BREMMER PRESS CONFERENCE, THE CAPTURE OF SADDAM FOOTAGE, MAP OF IRAQ, FOOTAGE OF SADDAM'S HOLE	**V/O: DANNY SCHECHTER:** THE FOOTAGE WAS SUPPLIED BY THE PENTAGON. IT WAS A MAJOR PROPAGANDA COUP FOR WASHINGTON EVEN THOUGH IT WAS LATER

	REPORTED IN THE REGION THAT IT WAS THE KURDS, NOT THE US MILITARY WHO FIRST FOUND THE IRAQI LEADER IN THAT HOLE.
FOOTAGE OF HOLE	**SOT: CNN:** Inside a small wall compound ...
PROMOTION OF PROGRAM FOCUSING ON TORTURE	ON SCREEN GRAPHICS: "60 Minutes": This is a picture of an Iraqi prisoner of war.
TORTURE IMAGES	**V/O: DANNY SCHECHTER:** THE PORNOGRAPHY OF VIOLENCE TOOK AN UNEXPECTED TURN WHEN THESE PHOTOS SURFACED SHOWING ABUSES BY US SOLDIERS OF DETAINEES IN A NOTORIOUS IRAQI GULAG. CBS BROKE THE STORY IN LATE APRIL 2004. BUT ALSO HOLDING IT UP AT THE PENTAGON'S REQUEST FOR TWO WEEKS. THEIR REPORT PERMITTED A US GENERAL TO SHIFT BLAME ON TO A FEW INDIVIDUALS WITHOUT EXPLORING THE SYSTEMATIC ABUSE DOCUMENTED IN A MILITARY INVESTIGATION.
GENERAL MARK KEMMEL	**SOT: GENERAL MARK KEMMEL:** We are appalled as well, these are our fellow soldiers, these are people we work with every day—they represent us. They wear the same uniform as us. And they let their fellow soldiers down.
ANCHOR REPORTING ON WAR, TORTURE STILLS	**V/O: DANNY SCHECHTER:** CBS'S REPORT AIRED IN THE END OF APRIL.... BY EARLY JULY, THE PENTAGON HAD STILL NOT

CYRON: AMNESTY INTERNATIONAL AT ABU GHRAIB PRISON, JULY 2003 SHOTS OUTSIDE THE PRISON	RELEASED ITS FULL INVESTIGATION AND TORTURE VIDEOS…. THE PRESS WAS NO LONGER PRESSING THEM TO DO SO. WHY DID IT TAKE SO LONG FOR THIS STORY TO SURFACE? I LATER FOUND THIS VIDEO OF THE SAME PRISON SHOT BY AMNESTY INTERNATIONAL IN JULY, 2003. THEY WERE ALLEGING TORTURE THEN.
OUTSIDE THE PRISON	**SOT: AMNESTY INTERNATIONAL INVESTIGATOR:** We have documented or heard allegations of mistreatment or torture of prisoners
TORTURE STILLS	**V/O: DANNY SCHECHTER:** WHILE MIST OF THE WORLD WAS SHOCKED BT THE PICTURES, ADMINISTRATION SUPPORTERS WERE MINIMIZING THE WELL-DOCUMENTED TORTURE.
TORTURE STILL **CYRON:** PHOTO CREDIT *WASHINGTON POST* VOICE OF RADIO HOST RUSH LIMBAUGH	**SOT: RADIO HOST RUSH LIMBAUGH:** Caller: It was like a hazing fraternity prank, to stack up naked… Rush: Exactly—exactly my point.
CYRON: "WE DON'T DO BODY COUNTS." **—General Tommy Franks, US Central Command**	MUSIC: STARS AND STRIPES FOREVER "We don't do body counts." **—General Tommy Franks, US Central Command**

MEMORIAL FOOTAGE BUSH WALKS WITH HAND ON HEART **CYRON:** COALITION CASUALTIES: 1168+ SOURCE—CNN, SEPTEMBER 2004	MUSIC: STARS AND STRIPES FOREVER
MEMORIAL FOOTAGE **CYRON:** COALITION WOUNDED: 7000+ —SOURCE—DEPARTMENT OF DEFENSE, SEPTEMBER 2004	MUSIC: STARS AND STRIPES FOREVER
MEMORIAL FOOTAGE **CYRON:** OVERALL IRAQI SOLDIERS DEAD: 7,600–10,800 —SOURCE—PROJECT ON DEFENSE ALTERNATIVES, SEPTEMBER 2004	MUSIC: STARS AND STRIPES FOREVER
MEMORIAL FOOTAGE **CYRON:** IRAQI CIVILIAN CASUAL-TIES: 100,000 —SOURCE, THE LANCET, BRITISH MEDICAL SOCIETY, NOVEMBER 2004	MUSIC: STARS AND STRIPES FOREVER
CYRON: MEMORIAL FOOTAGE COST OF CONQUEST: $136,069,989,152 —SOURCE WWW.COSTOFWAR.COM, SEPTEMBER 20, 2004	MUSIC: STARS AND STRIPES FOREVER

CYRON: MEMORIAL FOOTAGE <u>COST OF TV COVERAGE:</u> <u>$35,000,000+</u> <u>—SOURCE BROADCASTING</u> <u>& CABLE, JULY 2004</u>	MUSIC: STARS AND STRIPES FOREVER
CYRON: MEMORIAL FOOTAGE <u>PROFITS MADE ON WAR</u> <u>COVERAGE: UNKNOWN</u>	MUSIC: STARS AND STRIPES FOREVER
CYRON: MEMORIAL FOOTAGE <u>NUMBERS OF WMD FOUND:</u> <u>0</u>	MUSIC: STARS AND STRIPES FOREVER
MEMORIAL FOOTAGE THOMAS RICKS AT MUSE- UM PANEL	**O/C: THOMAS RICKS, MILITARY REPORTER, *WASHINGTON POST*:** The war is still going on. Its outcome is still undetermined. The United States has not won this war.

13. SECTION: VIEWS IN THE ARAB WORLD

VARIOUS ARAB NEWSCASTS REPORTING ON THE WAR, US COVERAGE OF WAR IN IRAQ	**V/O: DANNY SCHECHTER:** <u>THE WAR YOU SAW DEPENDED ON</u> <u>WHERE YOU LIVED. THE ARAB</u> <u>WORLD SAW A DIFFERENT WAR</u> <u>THAN THE ONE WE DID.</u> <u>IRONICALLY, MANY US NETWORKS</u> <u>RELIED ON ARAB OUTLETS: AL</u> <u>JAZEERA, ABU-DHABI TV AND</u> <u>OTHER NETWORKS, FOR FOOTAGE</u> <u>OF THE BOMBINGS. THEY SHOWED</u> <u>THEIR COVERAGE STRIPPED OF</u> <u>THEIR NARRATIVE. AL JAZEEERA</u> <u>FINANCED ITS COVERAGE WITH</u> <u>FEES PAID BY US NETWORKS.</u>

FOOTAGE OF MOTHER WITH MAIMED CHILD IN HOSPITAL, EMILY BELL O/C	**O/C: EMILY BELL, EDITOR, *THE GUARDIAN*:** The addition of Al Jazeera this time around was as important as the addition of CNN to the rest of the world in 1991.
FOOTAGE OF LIT CITY, COLLAGE OF AL-JAZEERA REPORTERS, NEWSROOM AND ON-AIR PROMO, VARIOUS OF ARAB WAR PROMO COVERAGE AND REPORTERS	**V/O: DANNY SCHECHTER:** AL JAZEERA WAS FORMED BY FORMER BBC JOURNALISTS AS A COMMERCIAL SATELLITE CHANNEL. IT PROMOTES ITSELF DRAMATICALLY AND WAS FIERCELY COMMITTED TO OFFERING DIVERSE PERSPECTIVES, ALTHOUGH IN THE US AND BRITAIN, IT WAS FALSELY DENOUNCED AS A ONE-SIDED PROPAGANDA ORGAN. ITS CORRESPONDENTS WERE OFTEN BRAVE AND TOOK RISKS. THEY SAW THEMSELVES AS INDEPENDENT AND BALANCED, ALTHOUGH THEIR STYLE WAS MUCH HOTTER AND MORE AUDACIOUS THAN THEIR WESTERN COUNTERPARTS.
NEWS PROMOS FADING HAFEZ AT NEW SCHOOL UNIVERSITY PANEL ON MEDIA AT WAR	**SOT: HAFEZ AL-MIRAZI, AL JAZEERA WASHINGTON BUREAU CHIEF:** Before 9/11, many government-controlled networks or newspapers used to call Al Jazeera the Israeli-CIA-backed network, because we put Israeli officials on the air, we invite Americans, we put Bush more than any other leader in the Arab world. So we were suspected to being the Israeli people trying to divide the Arab world, the opposition against the government.

And the media was so positive about us before 9/11 here. But immediately after, we put the"bad guys" for America, as for the balance, they behaved the same way that other government-controlled media in the Arab world did to us.

AIRCRAFT FLYING, DANNY ARRIVING IN DUBAI FOR THE ARAB MEDIA SUMMIT, FOOTAGE FROM INSIDE THE SUMMIT	**V/O: DANNY SCHECHTER:** <u>THE ARAB MEDIA ALSO WAS DEBATING THE COVERAGE. FOR A DEEPER UNDERSTANDING OF? THEIR PERSPECTIVES, I WENT TO DUBAI IN THE GULF REGION.</u> <u>WELCOME TO THE ARAB MEDIA SUMMIT. HUNDREDS OF JOURNALISTS FROM AROUND THE REGION DEBATED COVERAGE ISSUES, OFTEN DISAGREEING WITH EACH OTHER AND THEIR WESTERN COLLEAGUES.</u> IT WAS THERE I MET TV ANCHOR, NEMA ABU WARDA. SHE ROSE TO CHALLENGE CNN CORRESPONDENT NIC ROBERTSON:
NIMA ABU WARDA GRILLING CNN REPORTER NIC ROBINSON	**SOT: NIMA ABU WARDA, DUBAI TV:** Now my second comment is to you, CNN, regarding Amanpour's comments. Amanpour said that CNN was muzzled. She talks of an atmosphere of fear of reporting with what's going on uh, of collusion perhaps, is what she's insinuating between the Bush government and CNN.
NIC ROBERTSON, NIMA ABU WARDA	**SOT: NIC ROBERTSON, CNN REPORTER** That is absolutely not what she said.

These were private comments she made outside of CNN.

SOT: NIMA ABU WARDA, DUBAI TV:
These were comments made on a TV program, I understand...

SOT: NIC ROBERTSON, CNN REPORTER:
Outside, outside of CNN...

SOT: NIMA ABU WARDA, DUBAI TV
But it's not private when it's on television, live television.

SOT: NIC ROBINSON, CNN REPORTER
Thank you very much. Let me answer your first question.

MEDIA SUMMIT, DANNY TALKING TO NIMA	**O/C: DANNY SCHECHTER:** DO YOU THINK HE WAS UNCOMFORTABLE TALKING ABOUT IT?
O/C NIMA, FOOTAGE OF ANDERSON AT MEDIA SUMMIT	**O/C: NIMA ABU WARDA, DUBAI TV** Oh, extremely uncomfortable. He turned away. I was going to say, are you gagging me? Because that's exactly what he did. He dismissed me. I was dismissed. Swat. Swatted like a fly on the wall.
NIMA TALKING TO DANNY IN THE GARDEN	**V/O: DANNY SCHECHTER:** NIMA TOLD ME ABOUT THE TV COVERAGE OF THE WAR SHE WATCHED:
NIMA TALKING SPLICED IN WITH TV COVERAGE EXAMPLES: US WAR IN IRAQ	SOT: NIMA ABU WARDA, DUBAI TV I would flick English-Arabic and Arabic-English and you would be com-

PROMO, IRAQI TV, SCRATCH, NIMA O/C	paring/contrasting stories and just seeing the angles and what was being said because ultimately you get different stories from the different perspectives. SCRATCH
VARIOUS ARAB NETWORK WAR COVERAGE	**SOT: NIMA ABU WARDA, DUBAI TV** On the Arabic TV stations, I would see what war is really like, the blood and gore, the mess that really happens when a bomb hits a building.
CNN WAR COVERAGE	**SOT: CNN:** Ten percent are the so-called dumb bombs.
NIMA O/C, US BREAKING NEWS REPORT ON THE WAR	**SOT: NIMA ABU WARDA, DUBAI TV** On CNN you would see more of the strategic stuff.
O/C KHALED AL MAEENA	**O/C: KHALED AL MAEENA, SAUDI EDITOR:** So the viewer in this part of the world thought only one side, or a lopsided version of the war was being given.
FOOTAGE OF DISPLACED MOTHER WITH YOUNG CHILDREN	**SOT: ABU DHABI TV OF REFUGEE FAMILY:** We are refugees going from one place to the other, and we can't reach our homes. We came from Umar Q'ulsar, and G-d knows what has happened in Umar Q'ulsar. Look what is happening to us, look at my children.
ARAB JOURNALIST INTERVIEWS MEN SMOKING, HOUSE BURNED DOWN,	**O/C: LENA JAFUSI:** Well, one of the things that's missing is indigenous voices to freely and openly

OLD WOMAN CRYING, O/C LENA JAFUSI	be shown, be allowed to appear. You don't get people from the area really given proper hearing.
O/C NIMA	**O/C: NIMA ABU WARDA, DUBAI TV** People have to take responsibility. There is a moral responsibility. I think journalists have to take on more of that burden, more of that responsibility. It is your profession, your chosen profession, after all.

14. SECTION: JOURNALISTS TARGETED?

BOMB GOING OFF IN BAGHDAD HEADLINES ABOUT JOURNALISTS, TANK FIRING, HEADLINES JOURNALISTS KILLED, TANK FIRING, MORE HEADLINES, SHOTS AT BUILDING, TANK, MORE HEADLINES, HELICOPTER SHOOTING, EXPLOSION, NIGHT SHOTS, MORE HEADLINES, SOLDIERS AT ROADSIDE, CAR BLOWS UP, HEADLINES, COLLAGE OF STILLS OF KILLED JOURNALISTS	V/O: DANNY SCHECHTER: JOURNALISTS AND MEDIA WORKERS WERE TARGETED IN IRAQ. WAS IT DELIBERATE, TO KEEP THE STORY ON MESSAGE BY INTIMIDATING NON-EMBEDDED JOURNALISTS? HOW DID THE MEDIA INDUSTRY CHALLENGE THESE KILLINGS? SOME WERE KILLED BY SO-CALLED "FRIENDLY FIRE"—OTHERS, VICTIMS OF CALCULATED ATTACKS, MISSILES, TANK SHELLS AND BOMBS DROPPED ON OR NEAR JOURNALISTS.
INJURED PEOPLE CARRIED AWAY STILLS OF KATE ADIE, FOOTAGE OF CRYING MAN AND VIEW OF CITY	SOME MEDIA CRITICS CONCLUDED IT WAS INTENTIONAL, ALTHOUGH THE PENTAGON DENIED IT. BEFORE THE WAR, THE BBC'S KATE ADIE REPORTED SHE WAS TOLD BY THE PENTAGON THAT INDEPENDENT JOURNALISTS COULD BE TARGETED.
FOOTAGE OF AL JAZEERA'S TARIQ SITTING ON THE	THE ARAB MEDIA CENTER IN BAGHDAD, WHOSE COORDINATE HAS BEEN GIVEN TO THE PENTAGON,

ROOFTOP, PLANE CLOSING IN, TARIQ CARRIED OUT IN CARPET, FOOTAGE OF THE PALESTINE HOTEL	WAS BOMBED. AL JAZEERA'S TARIQ AYOUB SEEN HERE SITTING ON A ROOF WATCHING THE PLANE THAT WOULD SOON KILL HIM COME CLOSER AND CLOSER.
ABU DHABI TV ANCHOR	**SOT: ABU DHABI TV ANCHOR:** Welcome. A US tank shelled the Palestine Hotel, which is crowded with the journalists, killing two cameramen: one of them works for a Spanish network, and the other one works for Reuters.
SHOT OF AN AMERICAN TANK ON THE BRIDGE ACROSS FROM THE PALESTINE HOTEL IN BAGHDAD	**V/O: DANNY SCHECHTER:** NOW, ANOTHER INCIDENT-LOOK AT THIS: AN AMERICAN TANK ON THE BRIDGE ACROSS FROM THE PALESTINE HOTEL IN BAGHDAD. A SOLDIER WOULD LATER CLAIM HIS TANK WAS FIRED ON. LISTEN CAREFULLY. THERE ARE NO SOUNDS:
TANK ON THE BRIDGE O/C SAMIA NAKHOUL SHOT OF BAGHDAD	**O/C: SAMIA NAKHOUL, REUTERS:** We moved to the Palestine Hotel because the Pentagon asked our organizations to let us leave Al-Rashid Hotel because it was a target, and when we moved to the Palestine Hotel our organization told the Pentagon that we were at the Palestine Hotel so that every news organization knew.
SHOT OF FIRING AMERICAN TANK ON THE BRIDGE ACROSS FROM THE PALESTINE HOTEL IN BAGHDAD— FRAME SHAKES	**V/O: DANNY SCHECHTER:** AGAIN, MINUTES LATER, NO SOUNDS WERE HEARD, NO ONE FIRING AT US SOLDIERS. SUDDENLY, WITHOUT PROVOCATION...

THE SHOT COMES DIRECT-LY IN THE CAMERA ANGLE–THE SHOT THAT KILLED SAMIA O/C	**O/C: SAMIA NAKHOUL, REUTERS:** Suddenly we saw an orange glow and this is basically the tank shell that hit our office…
CAMERA SHOTS FROM INSIDE THE HOTEL AFTER THE TANK ROUND HIT. PANIC, REPORTERS YELLING, BLOOD, CONFU-SION	**SOT: HOTEL RECORDINGS:** Come on, come on, come on guys…
CAMERA SHOTS FROM INSIDE THE HOTEL O/C SAMIA	**O/C: SAMIA NAKHOUL, REUTERS:** You know you can imagine the panic–we were wounded. It was me and another photographer.
INSIDE THE HOTEL FOOTAGE, JOURNALISTS WOUNDED AND ONE KILLED. CHAOS, COL-LEAGUES ASKING OTHERS TO LEAVE. FOOTAGE OF THE DEAD AND WOUNDED CARRIED OUT	**SOT: HOTEL RECORDINGS:** Ahhh … My G-d. Are you okay? Get the fuck out of here ….
CRYING JOURNALISTS SHOT OF BAGHDAD PANORAMA	**O/C: SAMIA NAKHOUL, REUTERS:** I can't imagine that they would target journalists, you know. I couldn't believe why they would target us. What have we done to them?
INTERNATIONAL FEDERA-TION OF JOURNALISTS PUB-LICATION COVER	**V/O: DANNY SCHECHTER:** AFTER THE WAR PRESS FREEDOM GROUPS WERE STILL DEMANDING A REAL INVESTIGATION. THE PENTA-GON'S VICTORIA CLARKE TOLD ME THERE WAS A REPORT THAT SHOWED THAT THE SOLDIERS WERE ACTING IN SELF-DEFENSE.

SHOT OF TANK ON THE BRIDGE ACROSS FROM THE PALESTINE HOTEL, SAMIA O/C	**O/C: DANNY SCHECHTER:** <u>WAS THERE ANY ATTEMPT TO FIND OUT THE FACTS INDEPENDENTLY OR A THOROUGH INVESTIGATION?</u>
SAMIA O/C	**O/C: SAMIA NAKHOUL, REUTERS:** No, the Pentagon never interviewed me personally, or anyone. I don't think any foreign colleague was interviewed by the Pentagon.
SAMIA O/C PANORAMA VIEW IRAQ	**V/O: DANNY SCHECHTER:** <u>SAMIA'S COMPANY, REUTERS, DEMANDED AN INDEPENDENT INVESTIGATION, BUT MOST MEDIA COMPANIES DID NOT EVEN PRESS ON THIS ISSUE. NO ONE WAS HELD ACCOUNTABLE. IT WAS ALL PASSED OFF AS AN ACCIDENT; THE FOG OF WAR, AND ALL THAT.</u>
PANORAMA VIEW IRAQ	**SOT: DANNY SCHECHTER** SO WHAT ABOUT DAMAGE TO YOU PERSONALLY?
SAMIA O/C, SCENES FROM INSIDE THE HOTEL WHERE THE BLAST TOOK PLACE	**O/C: SAMIA NAKHOUL, REUTERS:** I was hit in the brain. I had a brain operation. It took me a long time to recover, but you know I was blessed. I survived. But it gave emotional damage and physical damage. But you know, mostly emotionally. I lost a colleague—we covered a war together. He was next to me and he died.
FOOTAGE FROM ARAB JOURNALISM PRIZE CEREMONY IN UNITED ARAB EMIRATE	**V/O: DANNY SCHECHTER:** <u>THE DEBATE ABOUT KILLING OF JOURNALISTS CONTINUES. THE RESPECTED MEDIA HISTORIAN PHILLIP KNIGHTLY CONCLUDED,"I</u>

BELIEVE THAT THE OCCASIONAL
SHOTS FIRED AT MEDIA SITES ARE
NOT ACCIDENTAL AND THAT WAR
CORRESPONDENTS MAY NOW BE
TARGETS."

THE MEDIA WAR HAD DRAWN
BLOOD.

15. SECTION: GOVERNMENT POWER AND CORPORATE CONTROL

O/C DANNY SCHECHTER STAND-UP TIMES SQUARE	**O/C: DANNY SCHECHTER:** IF YOU WANT TO KNOW WHY THE WAR WAS PACKAGED AND REPORTED THE WAY IT WAS, YOU HAVE TO KNOW SOMETHING ABOUT OUR AMERICAN MEDIA SYSTEM. IT'S A SYSTEM DOMINATED BY JUST A HANDFUL OF COMPANIES, AND THEY'RE ALL AROUND ME HERE IN THE CHAOS OF TIMES SQUARE. ALL THE BIG BRANDS: MTV, VIACOM, BERTELSMANN, ABC, NBC, REUTERS. THEY SURROUND ME PHYSICALLY. WHAT THEY REPRESENT IS THE POWER OF MEDIA—POWER TO PROMOTE ECONOMIC AND POLITICAL AGENDAS. WHAT THEY REPRESENT TODAY IS A MERGER OF NEWS BIZ AND SHOW BIZ. WHAT THEY REPRESENT IS A CONSUMER CULTURE. TO THEM, THE WAR WAS A PRODUCT. THEY SOLD IT, AND WE BOUGHT IT.
SHOT OF GENERAL ELECTRIC BUILDING, NEW YORK CITY—NBC PARTY FOOTAGE OCTOBER 16, 2003	**V/O: DANNY SCHECHTER:** MOST NETWORKS REMAIN UNCRITICAL OF THEIR COVERAGE. NBC WON THE US MEDIA WAR AS THE HIGHEST RATED NETWORK.

NEIL SHAPIRO'S SPEECH TO THE NBC EMPLOYEES AT THEIR CELEBRATORY PARTY. CROWD CLAPPING	**SOT: NEIL SHAPIRO, PRESIDENT NBC NEWS:** NBC's coverage on broadcast, on cable, was simply first rate.
NBC PARTY FOOTAGE **CHRYON:** GENERAL ELECTRIC WON CONTRACTS FOR IRAQI RECONSTRUCTION WORTH $600.000 —*HARPER'S MAGAZINE*	V/O: DANNY SCHECHTER: THE NETWORK CELEBRATED ITS VICTORY IN IRAQ WITH A PARTY IN THE POSH RAINBOW ROOM IN A BUILDING NAMED AFTER A GENERAL: GENERAL ELECTRIC, THEIR PARENT COMPANY. THEY RELEASED A BOOK AND DVD ON THE WAR FOR IRAQI FREEDOM. ANCHOR TOM BROKOW PAID TRIBUTE TO A POPULAR CORRESPONDENT, DAVID BLOOM, WHO DIED IN IRAQ.
NBC PARTY FOOTAGE, TOM BROKAW SPEAKING	**SOT: TOM BROKAW, NBC:** I'm so proud of the men and women of NBC news, who had the common bond of courage and determination to go into the heart of darkness …
MUSEUM OF RADIO AND TELEVISION	**V/O: DANNY SCHECHTER:** I CAUGHT UP WITH TOM BROKAW AT THE MUSEUM OF RADIO AND TELEVISION. I ASKED A QUESTION FROM THE FLOOR.
MUSEUM OF RADIO AND TELEVISION	**SOT: TOM BROKAW, NBC:** I want to go to the audience now if we can . . . **SOT: OTHER VOICE** Please raise your hands… **SOT: TOM BROKAW, NBC:** … Danny Schechter I know has a question right down here, we might as well get it out of the way ….

MUSEUM OF RADIO AND TELEVISION	**SOT: DANNY SCHECHTER:** <u>HOW COULD THE MEDIA, YOUR INSTITUTION PARTICULARLY, HAVE DONE A BETTER JOB OF BEING A LITTLE BIT MORE SKEPTICAL AND A LITTLE MORE CRITICAL?</u> APPLAUSE
MUSEUM OF RADIO AND TELEVISION, SOT: TOM BROKAW	**SOT: TOM BROKAW, NBC:** I think your suggestion is that we took the pipe. And if you go back and review the coverage on network television, newspapers, the Wall Street Journal, the New York Times, certainly, and any other publication in this country .... during that very vigorous time of the UN debate for example, there were lots of other voices that were heard, great skeptical voices. But many times people hear what they're inclined to hear ...
O/C JEFF SCHNEIDER	**O/C: JEFF SCHNEIDER, ABC NEWS EXECUTIVE:** And the idea that somehow it's packaged and spun back at corporate headquarters to fit some sort of greater agenda, I personally find outrageous and ridiculous.
O/C JEFF SCHNEIDER	**SOT: DANNY SCHECHTER:** <u>BUT LISTEN I'M NOT BEING CONSPIRATORIAL CAUSE I WORKED AT ABC NEWS FOR 8 YEARS. SO I'VE BEEN IN THE CONTROL ROOMS, I'VE BEEN INVOLVED, I WORKED AT CNN BEFORE THAT ... I'M NOT MAKING</u>

	THIS UP. I'M NOT INVENTING IT. THERE WAS CLEARLY AN APPROACH. THERE WAS AN IDENTI-FICATION BY MUCH OF THE AMERI-CAN MEDIA WITH THE AMERICAN MILITARY. I THINK THAT'S SORT OF UNDENIABLE. HOW CAN YOU EVEN DENY THAT? IF YOU LOOK AT THE CRITICS AND HOW MANY CRITICS THERE WERE ...
O/C JEFF SCHNEIDER	**O/C: JEFF SCHNEIDER, ABC NEWS EXECUTIVE:** I can't speak to the critics ... All I can say is, I can't speak for the entire American media.
O/C JEFF SCHNEIDER	**O/C: DANNY SCHECHTER:** OK, TALK FOR ABC ...
O/C JEFF SCHNEIDER	**O/C: JEFF SCHNEIDER, ABC NEWS EXECUTIVE:** TALKING FOR ABC, I THINK THAT WE TOLD IT STRAIGHT AHEAD.
NEWS PROMO FOOTAGE	**SOT: ABC PROMO:** More Americans get their news from ABC News.
O/C: SANDY SOCOLOW	**O/C: DANNY SCHECHTER:** THERE WAS A SUIT HERE WHO I SPOKE TO, A VICE PRESIDENT OF ABC NEWS.
O/C: SANDY SOCOLOW	**O/C: SANDY SOCOLOW, EXECUTIVE PRODUCER,"CBS NEWS WITH WAL-TER CRONKITE":** Oh really?

O/C: SANDY SOCOLOW	**O/C: DANNY SCHECHTER:** AND, YOU KNOW, HE WAS, YOU ... THEY CRITICIZE US ON THE LEFT, THEY CRITICIZE US ON THE RIGHT, SO THEREFORE WE MUST BE DOING IT THE RIGHT WAY. IN OTHER WORDS, YOU KNOW, IT'S A KIND OF A CONVENTIONAL KNEE-JERK RESPONSE.
O/C: SANDY SOCOLOW	**O/C: SANDY SOCOLOW, EXECUTIVE PRODUCER,"CBS NEWS WITH WALTER CRONKITE":** I've used that line myself, I can't tell you how many times.
O/C: SANDY SOCOLOW	**O/C: DANNY SCHECHTER:** BUT WHAT'S MISSING FROM IT? IS IT TRUE?
O/C: SANDY SOCOLOW	**O/C: SANDY SOCOLOW, EXECUTIVE PRODUCER, "CBS NEWS WITH WALTER CRONKITE":** Well, dead bodies are missing from it.
IRAQ WAR PROMO FOOTAGE	**SOT: ABC NEWS:** ABC News: unique, brave, provocative, unmatched
IRAQ WAR PROMO FOOTAGE WITH VARIOUS ANCHORS, O/C MICHAEL WOLFF	**SOT: MICHAEL WOLFF, *VANITY FAIR* MAGAZINE** Remember, Disney does not want ABC to be in the news business. There's so much pressure on these news organizations to be something, not rock the boat, not be a problem ...
BLURRED SCREEN, EYES WATCHING	**SOT: ABC NEWS:** "... Pentagon is following the planning

"and has the latest on a possible time-
line."
"... Jessica Lynch is no longer a prisoner of war ..."
"The efforts to keep the supply lines
running north of Baghdad."

EYES, VARIOUS NETWORK WAR PROMOTIONS, O/C SHELDON RAMPTON, SCREEN.	**O/C: SHELDON RAMPTON, CO-AUTHOR *WEAPONS OF MASS DECEPTION*:** One of the reasons I think why the media fell so easily into this pattern of selling the war, is that really is what the American media is designed to do is to sell things. It's a commercial media; it's a propaganda system and everyone knows it.
FCC HEAD QUARTERS BUILDING NEWSPAPER DRAWING STATING THAT THE FCC JEOPARDIZES MEDIA DIVER-SITY	**V/O: DANNY SCHECHTER:** OUR SYSTEM OF BROADCAST MEDIA IS REGULATED BY THE FCC—A GOV-ERNMENT AGENCY ORIGINALLY SET UP TO PROTECT THE PUBLIC INTER-EST. TODAY THAT REGULATORY BODY PROMOTES DEREGULATION-MORE POWER TO MEDIA MOGULS. THE HEAD OF THE FCC JUSTIFIES MEDIA CONCENTRATION ON THE GROUNDS THAT ONLY BIG COMPA-NIES CAN COVER A WAR LIKE THE ONE IN IRAQ.
DANNY STAND-UP OUTSIDE FCC HEADQUARTERS	**O/C: DANNY SCHECHTER:** JUST BEFORE THE WAR IN IRAQ BEGAN, AMERICAN MEDIA COMPA-NIES BEGAN LOBBYING THE FCC FOR RULE CHANGES THAT WOULD BENEFIT THEIR BOTTOM LINES. THERE WAS A QUESTION RAISED:

	DID THE FCC AGREE TO WAIVE THE RULES IF THE MEDIA COMPANIES AGREED TO WAVE THE FLAG?
O/C: JEFF CHESTER	**O/C: JEFF CHESTER, DIRECTOR, CENTER FOR DIGITAL DEMOCRACY:** You don't go in and report critically on an administration that you hope will give you billions and billions of dollars in new policies.
O/C KHAZEN, MURDOCH NEXT TO UN SECRETARY GENERAL KOFI ANNAN, CHINESE FLAG ON SCREEN	**O/C: JIHAD AL KHAZEN, FORMER REUTERS:** We have been in this business long enough to be very careful. But I am sure working in, and hoping that support of the war would get them that deal. Remember what Rupert Murdoch did when he was in China. He was the only one defending China despite all their abuses of human rights, because he was working for a TV deal, which eventually got in China.
O/C JEFF CHESTER	**O/C: JEFF CHESTER, DIRECTOR, CENTER FOR DIGITAL DEMOCRACY:** The reason the coverage, in part was so tepid, was so timid was because these same media companies like news corp. Fox, GE, NBC, Viacom, CBS, were trying to curry favor to win the support of the Bush Administration for this huge giveaway on media ownership.
MEDIA COLLAGE, NEWS PROMOS VARIOUS NEWS ANCHORS PROMOTING IRAQ COVERAGE, *WASH-*	**O/C: CONGRESSMAN MAURICE D. HINCHEY:** This is not something that happened yesterday. It didn't happen overnight.

INGTON POST BUILDING, NBC BUILDING, NEW YORK TIMES HEADLINE, AND NEWS PROMOS. O/C HINCHEY, RONALD REAGAN SWORN IN, GEORGE HERBERT WALKER BUSH, GEORGE W. BUSH ADDRESSING THE NATION	It has been going on here in the United States for about two decades, at least. And it's been processed; it's been an organized, concerted, thought-out, well-planned, and well-executed process. Going back to the Reagan Administration, flowing through the first Bush Administration, and now being picked up successfully so far by the second Bush Administration.
O/C NICHOLAS JOHNSON	**O/C: NICHOLAS JOHNSON, FORMER FCC COMMISSIONER:** Power generally, not just media power; power tends to go with power. Primarily they want to support whoever is in the White House, they want to support government, they want to support large, other large, corporate interests. They don't want to rock the boat, generally.
O/C HINCHEY	**O/C: CONGRESSMAN MAURICE D. HINCHEY:** This is a plan, it's a plan, it's not serendipitous, it doesn't happen accidentally. It's what they want. They want to be able to control the political discussion.
O/C STAUBER STILL OF MICHAEL POWELL	**SOT: JOHN STAUBER, CO-AUTHOR *WEAPONS OF MASS DECEPTION*:** Who was the FCC commissioner with whom they were trying to curry favor? Who was acting on their behalf during this period? It was Michael Powell, the son of Colin Powell.
MARK FIORE ANIMATION	**ON-SCREEN ANIMATION:** Satirical sound with animation, making fun of Michael Powell:

"The evils of media consolidation will never get past our fortifications."

STILL OF MICHAEL POWELL & MICHAEL WOLFF O/C MICHAEL WOLFF	**O/C: MICHAEL WOLFF, *VANITY FAIR* MAGAZINE:** I think it's very clear that the major media companies in this country had business before the government. Boom, it's a conflict of interest.
SOCOLOW O/C	**O/C: SANDY SOCOLOW, EXECUTIVE PRODUCER"CBS NEWS WITH WALTER CRONKITE":** In my day, there was no, there was really a wall between news and the rest of the organization.
O/C JOHN STAUBER	**O/C: JOHN STAUBER, CO-AUTHOR *WEAPONS OF MASS DECEPTION:*** It becomes sort of a, you scratch my back, I scratch your back.
SOCOLOW O/C	**O/C: SANDY SOCOLOW, EXECUTIVE PRODUCER"CBS NEWS WITH WALTER CRONKITE":** Did you see any coverage on television about the whole controversy? About the FCC and the new rules? I mean there was hardly any to speak of. There must have been some somewhere that I missed. But it was so minor, and so ineffectual in terms of informing the public of what's going on.
O/C ADELSTEIN	**O/C: JOHNATHAN ADELSTEIN, FCC COMMISSIONER:** The people need to try to take back the airwaves; they need to try to restore the democracy to the airwaves.

16. SECTION: LESSONS LEARNED AND WHAT TO DO?

DANNY SCHECHTER'S DESK WITH NEWSPAPER SPREADS, FAN, BLACK AND WHITE FOOTAGE FROM VIETNAM OF YOUNG CAPTURED VIETNAMESE BOYS BEING BLINDFOLDED BY US TROOPS, STILLS OF US TROOPER SITTING ON A PRISONER IN IRAQ, OTHER TORTURE IMAGES FROM IRAQ, STENCILS FROM BARCELONA, REMOTE CONTROL, DANNY SCHECHTER IN HIS LIVING ROOM WATCHING NEWS, NEWS PROMOS VARIOUS NEWS ANCHORS PROMOTING IRAQ COVERAGE, BEST OF THE BOMBS FOOTAGE, BOY IN HOSPITAL IN IRAQ, MORE BEST OF THE BOMBS, HEADLINE FROM PAPER SLAMMING CIA INTELLIGENCE ON IRAQ, ARTICLE MENTIONING PRESS"GROUP THINK"

V/O: DANNY SCHECHTER:
IRAQ QUICKLY BECAME THE APOCALYPSE I FEARED, AS GHOSTS OF THE CRIMES OF VIETNAM SEEMED TO BE COMING BACK TO HAUNT US.

ALL OVER THE WORLD, PEOPLE CAME TO SEE THE UNITED STATES NOT AS HEROIC LIBERATORS BUT BRUTAL OCCUPIERS.

I FOUND THESE GRAPHICS STENCILED ON THE WALLS OF BARCELONA:

I SAW HOW MEDIA OUTLETS SUPPRESS SCRUTINY OF POLICIES, PREFERRING TO SHOW IMAGES RATHER THAN EXPOSE INTERESTS. MAJOR MEDIA COVERS THE WORLD THROUGH THE EYES OF THOSE IN POWER—DOWNPLAYING THE BRUTAL IMPACT OF WAR AND ITS OWN ROLE IN PROMOTING IT.

IN JULY 2004, A SENATE COMMITTEE BLASTED THE CIA FOR MISREPORTING ON WMDs IN IRAQ. IT CRITICIZED WHAT IT CALLED"GROUP THINK." COULDN'T THE SAME PHRASE BE APPLIED TO OTHER WMDS? MEDIA WEAPONS OF MASS DECEPTION.

O/C STAUBER

O/C: JOHN STAUBER, CO-AUTHOR *WEAPONS OF MASS DECEPTION:*
The lesson is don't trust the mainstream media; if you want to really

find out what's really happening, you can't be a news consumer, you have to be a critical thinker.

O/C PELTON	**O/C: ROBERT YOUNG FELTON, REPORTER:** TV is not the same medium it was ten years ago, or twenty years ago. You don't really have the luxury of providing detailed analytical coverage of the war. You basically get an eyeball shot, and that's it.
O/C GARDINER	**O/C: SAM GARDINER, FORMER AIR FORCE COLONEL:** It's one thing to talk about this war, but as you look to the future, if you didn't like this, you're really not gonna like what's gonna come down the road the next time.
O/C GARDINER	**O/C: SAM GARDINER, FORMER AIR FORCE COLONEL:** It's one thing to talk about this war, but as you look to the future, if you didn't like this, you're really not gonna like what's gonna come down the road the next time.
O/C CHESTER	**O/C: JEFF CHESTER, CENTER FOR DIGITAL MEDIA:** Just as there is an investigation out now as to the failure of the intelligence community, we need an investigation into our journalistic community.
O/C NIMA	**SOT: NIMA ABU WARDA, DUBAI TV:** Media hasn't really been taken to task at all. There is no global watchdog that's saying you didn't do you job

well. Media people seem to be more comfortable repeating the words of politicians, repeating statements that come out in press, etc., than actually probing and trying to find out what it really means–"Is it true? Is it true?"

	O/C: DANNY SCHECHTER: CAN WE FIGHT BACK AGAINST DECEPTIVE NEWS AND MASSIVE MEDIA CONCENTRATION? CAN WE FIGHT BACK AGAINST JINGOISM POSING AS JOURNALISM? CAN WE AFFORD NOT TO FIGHT BACK?
MILITAINMENT NEWS COVERAGE	**MEDIA COLLAGE:** Fox: Should they–you know–use the MOAB–the Mother Of All Bombs? SCRATCH
MILITAINMENT AND WAR PROMOTIONS NEWS SHOWS, ANIMATION, NEWS PROMOS, VARIOUS NEWS ANCHORS PROMOTING IRAQ NEWS SHOWS, DANNY SCHECHTER O/C	**O/C DANNY SCHECHTER** <u>I JOINED THE MEDIA TO SPOTLIGHT THE PROBLEMS OF THE WORLD AND CAME TO SEE THAT THE MEDIA IS ONE OF THOSE PROBLEMS. I BELIEVE IN FREEDOM OF THE PRESS BUT NOT JUST FREEDOM FOR THOSE WHO OWN THE PRESS. WHAT CAN WE DO TO HOLD THE MEDIA MORE ACCOUNTABLE? THINK ABOUT IT. NOW I'VE HAD MY SAY .... IT'S YOUR TURN.</u>
FOOTAGE OF BUSH PLANE WITH CREDITS	Music out/reprise:"MEDIA WAR," POLARITY1

CREDITS

PRODUCED AND DIRECTED BY:

Danny Schechter

PRODUCER

Anna Pizarro

CAMERA

David Chai
Bob Coen
Dan Devivo
Justin Elliot
Shilpi Gupta
Simon Kim
Michael Lee
John Miglietta
King Molapo
Kozo Okumura
Nick Pannacciulli
Anna Pizarro
Craig Secker
Stan Staniski

PRODUCTION ASSISTANCE

Danielle Gibson
Shannon Johnsen
Andy Kamons
Angelica Locin
Nathalie Rothschild
Jillian Selsky
Thomas Shomaker

PRODUCTION SUPPORT

Maria Garagorri
Esti Marpet
John Parman

POST PRODUCTION SUPERVISOR

Kristine Sorensen Cardoso

ADDITIONAL EDITORS

Lenny Charles
Bill Davis

PRODUCTION ADMINISTRATIVE DIRECTOR

Glenn Beatty

CHIEF OF STAFF & STUFF

Eileen O'Brien

OUTREACH

Steve Baldwin
David DeGraw
Emily Hackel
Jennie Jeddry
Nikki Oldaker
Mimi Roberson

ACCOUNTING

Pat Horstman
Bernstein and Drucker

LEGAL

Coudert Brothers
Sam Israel
Steven Schechter

MUSIC
Nenad Bach

"The End"
Written and performed by
The Doors
Published by Doors Music
Company
Courtesy of Elktra Entertainment
Group
By arrangement with Warner
Strategic Music

Jun Shiina & Eric Miller
Freeplay Music
Speechwerks
Polarity1 ©2004
Sine Language Music / BMI

"O.I.L."
Written and performed by David
Rovics
Licensed courtesy of Daemon
Records

"I Need To Know"
Performed and written by Stephan
Smith
Published by Stephan Smith
Publishing
Licensed courtesy of Rounder
Records

Vortex

SPECIAL THANKS

Abu-Dhabi TV

Amnesty International

Anyscreen Productions

Arab Media Summit

ARD TV

BBC Correspondent Series

BBC Radio and Four Corner's Amber Dawson

Ben Cashdan, Sipone Productions, Johannesburg

Camera Planet

CBC and the "Deadline Iraq" team

Center for Defense Information

Democracy Now!

Dubai Press Club

FAIR

Mark Fiore, cartoonist

France 3 Television

George Washington University School of Journalism

The Guardian

Guerilla News Network

Gwendolen Cates

Jane Power

Kino and Cape Talk Radio, Capetown South Africa

Mosaic Program, Worldlink TV

Mark Achbar

MediaWatch Australia

NBC

New York Magazine

Patrick Dillon

Renee Horne & South African Broadcasting (SABC)

Robert Young Pelton

Seton Hall University

Steven Whitehouse

The Guardian

The New School University, New York

United Nations Visual Materials Library

Vivien Demuth

War Cry International Cinema

World Electronic Forum

UN World Electronic Forum

INVESTORS AND DONORS

Anonymous
Stanley Buchthal
Abe Eisner
Randy Fertel
Wendy Gordon
Adelaide Gomer
Steve Green
Janet Rogozinski

Arthur Segel
Martha Older
Anant Singh
Andrew Stone
Lelani Wood
Shelly Drobney
Gail Furman

FRIENDS AND ADVISORS

Ben Cashdan
Mary Ellen Churchill
Richard Cooperstein
Jeff Dowd
Jack Garrity
Tim Karr
David Kleiler
Mark Kusnetz

Mediachannel.org
Chuck O'Brien
Noah Kimerling
Ray Gaspard
Tim Robbins
Tony Sutton
Oliver Sutton
Jack Garrity

EXECUTIVE PRODUCERS

Anant Singh
Barbara Kopple
Rory O'Connor
Steve Green

WMD–GLOBALVISION L.P.

Glossary

Animation: Animated elements

B-Roll: News footage used to illustrate points made in the film

Close-up: Title shots

Collage: A series of fast-paced images used in the film

Credits: Lists of production personnel, special thanks, and sources of footage

Chyron: Graphic animation such as titles on screen. Chryron is actually the name of a machine, but the term has become generic in the same way that Xerox is often used interchangeably with photocopying.

Graphic: Use of graphic information

O/C (On Camera): Comments by the narrator when on camera

Tease: Visual material that often precedes the opening titles

Title sequences: The name of the production entity, the film title and the director, placed at the start of the film.

Section: *WMD* is segmented into sections, each with separate titles

SOT (Sound on Tape): Interview clips or sound bites

Still: Use of still images or photos

V/O: Voice over narration

Who's Who in *WMD*

The Interviews

Nima Abu-Warda, anchor, Dubai Television

Johnathan Adelstein, FCC commissioner

Kate Adie, veteran BBC correspondent

Mohammad Al Douhri, Iraq's pre-War ambassador to the United Nations; interviewed at the Arab Media Summit in Dubai (2004)

Jihad Al Khazen, editor, Al Hayat; former correspondent, Reuters

Khaled Al Maeena, Saudi Arabian editor, *Arab News*

Hafez Al-Mirazi, Washington bureau chief, Al Jazeera

Kofi Annan, UN Secretary-General

Jon Alpert, filmmaker and former contributor to NBC News

Mohammad Al Sahaf, former minister of information for Saddam Hussein

Eric Alterman, columnist, *The Nation;* author of several books on media and politics

Christiane Amanpour, veteran CNN international correspondent for

William Arkin, news analyst, NBC News; writer on national security affairs

Peter Arnett, Pulitzer-Prize-winning war correspondent, hired by *National Geographic* to cover Baghdad during the Iraq War and used by NBC as an on-air reporter.

Tariq Ayoub, Al Jazeera bureau chief, killed by US bombing in Iraq

Ashleigh Banfield, former up-and-coming news star for MSNBC, reporting from hot spots around the world

Emily Bell, editor *MediaGuardian* and *The Guardian* (UK) media section

David Bloom, NBC correspondent; died while covering the Iraq War

Rym Brahimi, former CNN Baghdad correspondent

L. Paul Bremer, III, former head of Washington's Coalition Provisional Authority

Tom Brokaw, anchor, NBC News, reporter for the *New York Times,* based in Baghdad

George W. Bush, President and Commander-in-Chief

Leslie Cagan, veteran anti-war organizer and strategist; director, United for Peace and Justice

Gwendolen Cates, photojournalist embed on assignment for *People* magazine

Jeff Chester, director, Center for Digital Media

Victoria Clarke, media advisor for the Pentagon; oversaw the embed program

Janine di Giovanni, reporter, based in Baghdad for the *London Times*

Patrick Dillen, independent filmmaker

Phil Donahue, former talk show host, fired by MSNBC on the eve of the Iraq War

John Donovan, correspondent, ABC's "Nightline"; covered both wars in Iraq

Greg Dyke, former director general, BBC; forced to resign over BBC coverage of British weapons scientist David Kelly, although the substance of the coverage was later verified.

Michael Eliott, an editor at *Time* magazine

Curtis Ellis, radio journalist

Matthew Fisher, **Patrick Graham** and **Patrick Brown**, Canadian journalists interviewed for CBC's "Deadline Iraq" program

Tommy Franks, commander of US Forces during the invasion of Iraq

Sam Gardiner, retired US air force colonel

Amy Goodman, host of "Democracy Now," a radio and TV program

David Halberstam, former Vietnam correspondent, removed from Vietnam by the *New York Times* for coverage deemed critical but later won Pulitzer Prize for the coverage

Bill Hemmer, host, CNN "American Morning" program

Seymour Hersh, Pulitzer-Prize winning investigative reporter; exposed the My-Lai massacre and later the prison torture at Abu Ghraib prison in Iraq.

Maurice Hinchey, member of Congress, New York (22nd district)

Rene Horne, South African Broadcasting (voice only)

Yousef Ibrahim, retired veteran Middle East correspondent, the *New York Times* and the *Wall Street Journal*

Lena Jafusi, professor of media studies, United Arab Emirates

Nicholas Johnson, former FCC commissioner

Riz Kahn, former CNN International anchor

John Kampfner, producer, BBC News; contributor, *New Statesman*

Greg Kelly, embed with Fox News. (His boss, John Moody, refused to be interviewed for *WMD.*)

Phillip Knightly, media historian, author, *The First Casualty*

Ted Koppel, anchor, ABC "Nightline"; embedded during the "war for Iraqi freedom"

Marc Levin, documentary and motion picture director whose dramatic feature film, *Slam,* won the Grand Jury Prize at the Sundance Film Festival and the Camera D'Or at Cannes, 1998

Rush Limbaugh, conservative talk show host

Jake Lynch, reporter for BBC, UK; editor, Reportingtheworld.org; holds seminars for journalists as part of "peace journalism," whose mission is to promote conflict resolution.

Jessica Lynch, US soldier captured in Iraq, celebrated as a military hero in the media

John (Rick) MacArthur, publisher, *Harper's* magazine; author *The Second Front,* the definitive study of the role of the media in Gulf War I

David Marr, anchor, "Media Watch Australia," a feisty media criticism program shown on Australian TV

Stephen Marshall, filmmaker, Guerilla News Network

Clive Myrie, embed with BBC News

Samia Nakhoul, Reuters bureau chief in the Gulf; anchor for Abu Dhabi TV; wounded in attack on Palestine Hotel, Baghdad (April 2004)

Oliver North, former military colonel who figured in the Iran-contra scandal; admitted lying to Congress; filed special reports from Iraq for Fox News.

Bill O'Reilly, controversial anchor of "The O'Reilly Factor" on Fox News Channel

Robert Young Pelton, independent journalist, filmmaker and author

Sheldon Rampton, co-author with John Stauber of *Weapons of Mass Deception* (to be distinguished from Danny Schechter's book, *Embedded: Weapons of Mass Deception*)

Charlie Reina, former Fox News Producer, exposed political control of Fox stories

John Rendon, PR guru and Pentagon media strategist. He refused to be interviewed.

Harvey Rice, reporter, *Houston Chronicle*

Tom Ricks, military reporter, the *Washington Post*

Geraldo Rivera, correspondent, Fox News

Max Robbins, editor, *Broadcasting & Cable*

Nic Robertson, chief international correspondent, CNN

Donald Rumsfeld, US Secretary of Defense

Scott Rutter, highly-decorated military commander in the Iraq War

Jeremy Scahill, reported from Iraq for "Democracy Now"

Jeff Schneider, vice president, ABC News

Neil Shapiro, president, NBC News

Sandy Socolow, former executive producer, CBS "Evening News" with Walter Cronkite

John Stauber, co-author with Sheldon Rampton of *Weapons of Mass Deception* on the selling of the Iraq War (to be distinguished from Danny Schechter's book, *Embedded: Weapons of Mass Deception*)

Arnim Stauth, reporter, ARD Germany

Jon Stewart, host of "The Daily Show," Comedy Central Channel

Archbishop Desmond Tutu, Nobel-Prize winning South African leader of the fight against apartheid. He considered the Iraq War "evil" even as President Bush labeled Saddam Hussein an "evildoer."

Dominique de Villepin, Interior Minister and former Foreign Minister of France; led the opposition to the US preemptive war strategy at the UN Security Council.

"War Cry," name used by the peace activist shown in a protest at Ground Zero in New York.

General William Westmoreland, US General during the Vietnam War

Jim Wilkenson, White House political operative; helped run Coalition Media Center in Doha

Ian Williams, UN-based international journalist; author of *Deserter: George Bush's War on Military Families, Veterans, and His Past,* in which he confronts President Bush's military service.

Michael Wolff, media columnist, *Vanity Fair*

Gary Younge, correspondent the *Guardian*

Comments/Reviews of Film

NEW HAVEN ADVOCATE

Schechter's film doesn't try to do the Eric Alterman shtick of trying to prove that the "mainstream" media is right-oriented. That's a chowderhead analysis in any event. The mainstream media is eager to give the people what they want. It is eager to make money. It is eager for validation and desperate to continue proving its valence and worth, which of late has meant an undue reliance on technological-wonders reportage, generally presented with a dose of superpower smugness. Superpower smugness is neither a right nor a left issue.

AL JAZEERA

Are you influenced by Noam Chomsky and his theory of manufacturing consent?

Noam Chomsky doesn't watch television; he is more of an analyst of the *New York Times* and elite journalism so I didn't go to him for an interview.

I was more interested in journalists who covered the war and how they were debating it. So I feel that Chomsky had a brilliant analysis of media, but more of it is oriented toward print. It doesn't always take into account the techniques of the media.

What do you think of Chomsky's critics who accuse him of overestimating the sophistication of media control, and that—in reality—it is more to do with day-to-day decisions and market forces?

I don't buy the conspiracy theories of media. I remember a group of Syrians came to our office and they said: 'We agree with you because we really know the Jews run everything.' This was their analysis. I said, excuse me, Rupert Murdoch is not Jewish the last time I looked.

You know the problem is corporate media and corporate-controlled media and how they operate within their framework." —Interview with *Al Jazeera*

BuzzFlash.com Review

If BuzzFlash handed out our own Oscars, hands down we'd give Danny Schechter the best film expose' of the media for his gripping new documentary *Weapons of Mass Deception*. *WMD* is a scathing indictment of how the media colluded with the Bush administration to sell an unjust and unnecessary war in Iraq to the American people like it was nothing more than rolling out a new product for better ratings.

Rather then being watchdogs, Schechter reveals with stunning clarity how the media became lapdogs and he tells his story using the media's very own techniques such as rapid editing, music, graphics, gripping footage, and animation on top of his stellar work as an investigative reporter. Schechter says he is fighting fire with fire through *Weapons of Mass Deception* and the result is a political tour de force that is an entertaining and disturbing portrait of how the American media utterly failed in its job to tell the truth about the buildup to the war. A failure measured by the somber toll on American soldiers, 1,420 killed and 10,622 wounded in Iraq and counting in addition to the scores of Iraqi people who have been killed.

TV GUIDE

The bottom line of such films as Schechter's—muckraking documentaries like the thematically linked *OUTFOXED* and *UNCOVERED: THE WAR ON IRAQ* (both 2004) also distributed by Cinema Libre Studios—is the quality of ammunition lobbed at their targets. Schechter has the goods and by framing his argument with a history of independent war coverage past and present (the international press doesn't toe the Pentagon line) highlights how far we've fallen.

BUFFALO NEWS

WMD will be an important historical record of a media failure that helped lead the country to war. But it's also a call to action.

Schechter wants people to reclaim the public airwaves by demanding media reform.

"I've had my say," Schechter concludes. "It's your turn."

NEW YORK TIMES

(Schechter's) notoriety and creativity led to jobs in the mainstream media, first at CNN, where he worked briefly, and then as a producer at the ABC news program "20/20," where he worked for eight years. Not surprisingly, it was a difficult marriage, one he said that ended when "news was replaced by infotainment."

He left in 1988 to help start Globalvision, an independent media company. *The Daily News* described him as "a hero of downward mobility."

"I want to produce the counter narrative," he said, "but there is less and less room for this in our media system. My film will be broadcast on television stations in Australia, Spain, the Middle East and Japan. I am waiting for a station here with the guts to broadcast it." (WMD was later aired on the Independent Film Channel)

INTER PRESS SERVICE

An incisive new documentary is taking aim at the U.S. media's one-sided coverage of the war in Iraq, arguing that its collective complicity deceived the populace and made the war possible.

ST. LOUIS POST DISPATCH

Do you remember, lo those many weeks ago, when it was still permissible to ask why our soldiers were dying in Iraq, and to count the civilian casualties, and to follow the money trail? No? If the mainstream press continues down the path that's charted in this late-arriving documentary, the debate that recently galvanized the electorate will become as hard to remember as the tradition of investigative journalism.

Danny Schechter is a former ABC news producer who knows, literally and figuratively, where the bodies are buried. Now working as a "self-embedded" media critic, Schechter turns his lens on the industry itself, specifically how it covered the invasion of Iraq. .... it's still vitally important.

RIVERFRONT TIMES (ST. LOUIS)

Danny Schechter. (unrated) This movie, from writer-director Danny Schechter, would play well on a bill alongside *Fahrenheit 9/11* and *Control Room;* the self-proclaimed "Media Dissector" and former ABC, CNN and MTV News producer damns not only the Bush administration's reasons for going to war in Iraq but also the media for being cheerily complicit by swallowing the party line without gagging. If nothing else, you will walk out of the movie thinking you can believe nothing and trust no one.

SILVER CHIPS ONLINE (WASHINGTON D.C. AREA)

Who would believe that American media networks would lie to their viewers? Although many liberals and conservatives alike would scoff at the presumption that the media is unbiased, director and narrator Danny Schechter explains why the most powerful networks in America manipulated the truth and the footage Americans saw before, during and after the war in Iraq in his ground-breaking documentary *WMD: Weapons of Mass Deception.*

Schechter creates one of the more level documentaries this year. Starting with a short narrative wherein Schechter questions the honesty of the large TV networks and newspapers such as NBC, Fox, ABC, CBS, *The Washington Post* and *The New York Times,* the movie has a Michael Moore feel.

Contrary to most of the anti-war, biased documentaries bombarding the silver screen, *WMD: Weapons of Mass Deception* actually does what a documentary is meant to do: present information and allow the viewer to form his or her own opinion. Schechter even forewarns the audience during the first sequence in the film that, after looking at the evidence, this is "his say," encouraging the viewer to go out and develop his or her own conclusions. Despite the lengthy run time, *WMD: Weapons of Mass Deception* is sheer brilliance.

SAN FRANCISCO CHRONICLE

WMD: Weapons of Mass Deception is a documentary about the failure of the news media to do its job in the run-up to the Iraq war. It makes a persuasive case that the media, instead of asking probing questions, too often took at face value the Bush administration's assertions about the dangers posed by the Saddam Hussein regime and its alleged "weapons of mass destruction." According to filmmaker and narrator Danny Schechter, media professionals—especially those in TV news—didn't respond like journalists in these critical months but like shills and cheerleaders.

AUSTIN AMERICAN-STATESMAN

He brings his case against the mainstream media to this documentary. And it's a powerful one: The points he makes were addressed in *Fahrenheit 9/11,* and it's gratifying to see them expanded upon. Schechter paints an administration that expertly "marketed" the war. While he's clearly appalled by the White House, Schechter expresses even deeper ire for his old colleagues in TV news, who he argues got swept up in the administration's "story line" for war and abdicated their duty to question those in power.

BOSTON GLOBE

Deception follows the company's other films, *Outfoxed: Rupert Murdoch's War on Journalism* and *Uncovered: The War on Iraq,* which covered similar thematic terrain. And like those movies, *Deception* is engrossing and provocative, maybe more so—eventually, the ideas and suspicions come to the movie's forefront, and over the 98-minute runtime, Schechter settles for being the messenger, not the star, doing a serviceable job in laying out a quick history of modern war coverage and letting other people make points, too.

BOSTON PHOENIX

Those who have been fans of Danny Schechter, *The News Dissector,* since his days at WBCN FM, long before that became another Clear Channel fiefdom (and there's a topic for dissection), will welcome this documentary about the Orwellian state of the American "news" media. Schechter is everything journalism today is not—skeptical, unslick, and investigative. As for what we can do, his advice is as provocative as it is terse: "Think about it."

ROCKY MOUNTAIN NEWS

The film won the Maysles Brothers Award for Best Documentary at the recently concluded 27th Starz Denver International Film Festival.

Daniel Schechter's pointed documentary—made by someone who views journalism as more calling than job—includes an impressive array of interviews with American and foreign journalists.

Schechter, who has worked for both the mainstream and alternative media, holds the feet of the media to the fire in this well-researched documentary about the largely uncritical attitude adopted by major TV and press outlets in the months prior to the Iraq war.

VANITY FAIR

Danny Schechter, perhaps the nation's longest-practicing media critic ("Danny Schechter the news dissector" was his moniker back at WBCN, in Boston, in the 1970s), has a documentary film (Schechter in his shambling unyuppifiedness out—Michael Moore's Michael Moore) about the media and the war, *WMD: Weapons of Mass Deception,* now in previews. It is something of a comic masterpiece. It shows, vividly, the media pretense, all dead certainty and farcical pomposity, against the now evident confection and put-up job and balderdash and mess of sentiment and bromides and unexamined blah-blah which constituted almost everybody's tale of the war.

CHICAGO READER

Veteran independent media analyst Danny Schechter presents a comprehensive and devastating critique of the TV news networks' complacency and complicity in the war on Iraq. The video begins with a parody of *Apocalypse Now* that's as funny as anything by Michael Moore, but Schechter means business, and this quickly turns to a rigorous dissection of economic and political factors that have turned our major media outlets into conduits for Pentagon "mili-tainment."

But most of this is brilliantly argued and scrupulously documented, proving beyond a doubt that the Bush administration's retailing of its "master narrative" was a carefully orchestrated element of the war. A must-see.

SACRAMENTO BEE

A self-described "network refugee"—Schechter is a former "20/20" producer—the filmmaker studied 720 hours of live war coverage and found the news misshaped and misreported. He takes us from the days of Vietnam, when a reporter "did not get on the team" (Peter Arnett), to today's "handcuffed, managed news reporting" (Christiane Amanpour). Patriotic fervor followed, notes Schechter, who adds, "The Bush administration used 9/11 as a pretext to implement secret plans to invade Iraq.

... Patriotic correctness swept through the news business. There was more debate in the streets than on TV, which relayed the government's spin without much question. Without their cheerleading, there would have been no consensus for war."

Schechter opens his powerful film with a quote from Marshall McLuhan: "If there were no coverage, there would be no war."

REVIEWS OF DANNY SCHECHTER'S EARLIER BOOK: *EMBEDDED: WEAPONS OF MASS DECEPTION* (Prometheus Books 2003)

"In this compelling inquiry, Danny Schechter vividly captures two wars: the one observed by embedded journalists and some who chose not to follow that path.It was a war that was scarcely covered, he reminds us. That crucial failure is addressed with great skill and insight in this careful and comprehensive study which teaches lessons we ignore at our peril."   —Noam Chomsky

"Schechter tells the tawdry tale of the affair between officialdom and the news boys—who, instead of covering the war, covered it up."

—Greg Palast, author and BBC journalist

"This is the best book to date about how the media covered the second Gulf War or maybe miscovered the second war. Mr. Schechter on a day to day basis analysed media coverage. He found the most arresting, interesting, controversial, stupid reports and has got them all in this book for an excellent assessment of the media performance of this war. He is very negative about the media coverage and when you read this book you will see why he is so negative about it. I recommend it."   —Peter Arnett

"I'm your biggest fan in Iraq. Your book is amazing. Amazing. I started reading it last night and I haven't been able to ... stop reading. I spent the night sitting up in front of the computer, reading page after page. I only stopped when the electricity went off and then I tried sleeping—but sleep wouldn't come because I kept thinking of some of the things you had written-especially about the embedded journalists. ... I hope it sells 3 million copies and that it becomes required reading everywhere. Not for your sake, for our sake and the sake of all the ignorant people out there. I don't know how many fans you have—or how many you will eventually have but I mean every single word. I lived through that incredible lie."

—Riverbend, Iraqi Blogger, Author of *Baghdad Burning*